The McGraw-Hill
36-Hour
Cash
Management
Course

Other Books in The McGraw-Hill 36-Hour Course Series

The McGraw-Hill
36-Hour
Cash
Management
Course

William L. Sartoris
Associate Professor of Finance
Indiana University

Ned C. Hill
Joel C. Peterson Professor
of Business Administration
Brigham Young University

McGraw-Hill, Inc.
New York   San Francisco   Washington, D.C.   Auckland   Bogotá
Caracas   Lisbon   London   Madrid   Mexico City   Milan
Montreal   New Delhi   San Juan   Singapore
Sydney   Tokyo   Toronto

Library of Congress Cataloging-in-Publication Data

92-47075

1 2 3 4 5 6 7 8 9 0   DOC/DOC   9 9 8 7 6 5 4 3

ISBN 0-07-054935-4 {HC}
ISBN 0-07-054936-2 {PBK}

The sponsoring editor for this book was Caroline Carney, the editing supervisor was Marion B. Castellucci, and the production supervisor was Donald Schmidt. This book was set in Baskerville by North Market Street Graphics.

Printed and bound by R. R. Donnelley & Sons Company.

This book is printed on recycled, acid-free paper containing a minimum of 50% recycled de-inked fiber.

To Karen and Claralyn and our families

Contents

Preface

The subject of cash management has rapidly evolved over the past two decades. Modern cash management started in 1947 with RCA's request to its banks to provide a service for collecting and processing checks more quickly. This was the first lockbox. For many years cash management was a topic of concern only to very large corporations. This was in part due to ignorance of what constitutes cash management and what it can do for an organization. Perhaps this ignorance was epitomized by the reaction of a CEO a few years ago to the question of what cash management practices his firm employed. His response was, "We don't really deal with cash management. We are too busy borrowing money to stay alive to have to worry about cash management." Today it is recognized that all organizations, large or small, for-profit or not-for-profit, public or private, must be concerned with cash management. Effective cash management reduces the pressure on the organization. It also reduces costs. This cost reduction results from processing payments or receipts more cheaply. It may result from decreasing idle balances in bank accounts. It may result from decreasing required short-term borrowing. It may result from more accurate and longer-range forecasts of cash flow needs or availability. And it may result from a move to more efficient electronic payments or electronic data interchange.

At the same time cash management has expanded its penetration, it has also expanded its scope. It has moved from a narrow focus of collecting and disbursing cash to encompass the whole range of treasury activities. Its systems provide the primary interface between customers and the credit function or between suppliers and accounts payable.

At the same time organizations became more sophisticated in their cash management practices, banks discovered the revenue potential of providing cash management products and services. Cash management products are no longer confined to money centers or superregional banks. Most banks of almost any size provide a range of cash management services to their business clients.

Accountants have become more heavily involved in cash management activities in two ways. First, they are responsible for auditing the systems for proper controls. Second, they serve as a financial sounding board for some of their smaller clients.

This book is an attempt to bring together the institutional factors important in good cash management practices and the modern tools and techniques used to evaluate alternative practices. The focus is on achieving a level of cash management understanding that is sufficient to be conversant with users and providers of cash management services, to identify areas for potential improvement, and to possess the analytical structure and techniques to evaluate alternative practices.

We would like to thank our colleagues in the academic, banking, and corporate finance communities for their insights and information. We are indebted to the challenging questions asked by students of cash management with whom we have had contact.

We particularly thank our families for their understanding and patience for the late nights and early mornings at the word processor. We also thank Caroline Carney, our editor, and the production staff at McGraw-Hill for their support during the writing, editing, and production process.

WILLIAM L. SARTORIS
Bloomington, Indiana

NED C. HILL
Provo, Utah

Instructions
and Study Plan

This is a concentrated, self-study course that can be completed at your own pace in short time segments. It is designed for a variety of students of finance: an *executive* who must deal with treasurers and cash managers; an *accountant* whose clients need advice on designing, controlling, or managing their cash management systems; a *financial manager or controller* for a small to medium-size firm whose job has been expanded to encompass handling and planning for cash flows and dealing with the credit function; a *banker* whose customers are asking for cash management services; or *anyone* who needs a quick overview of some of the latest developments in the move from cash management to treasury management. The course assumes a basic understanding of financial terminology and the structure of an income statement and balance sheet for an organization. Consisting of only 36 hours of assignments, the course provides an overview and the basic concepts in the key areas of cash management. The course provides a structure to study the issues in cash management, discusses the institutional arrangements that have a primary influence on what can be done, outlines the factors to consider in addressing the issues, and provides the financial tools to resolve these issues. Although the course focuses on an analytical process for addressing the issues, it does not become enmeshed in sophisticated quantitative techniques. Refinements and increased depth in the application of statistical techniques are left to a more advanced course.

Plan for Your Study Sessions

The serious student of this course will want to adhere to the following guidelines:

1. Develop a schedule for your study sessions. The schedule should be realistic in terms of the time that you can steal from your other activities. Significant gaps in time between sessions may result in a lack of continuity, may require extra time to review prior concepts and tie the topics together, and may lead to a sense of frustration with your progress and a lagging willingness to complete the study.

2. Set a definite time for your study sessions. Best results are obtained if a definite time period on specific days is set aside, say, 7:30 to 9 p.m. on Tuesday and Thursday evenings.

3. Study in a place where you can concentrate. This is particularly important if it has been some time since you have been "enrolled" in a course.

4. Read with a pencil, paper, and calculator. Most financial topics can be mastered only by working through numerical problems. Work through the numerical examples in the chapters both to understand them and to satisfy yourself that they are correct. Work the Self-Test problems at the end of each chapter. Attempt to work the problems completely without reference to the answers at the back of the book until you are certain you have the right answer or have exhausted your mental resources in trying.

Program of Study Sessions— Average of 1½ Hours Each

Lesson 1.   Read Chap. 1. A straight reading of the chapter will likely not take the full time period. Spend some time thinking about the structure of the accounting statements for your business, or a business with which you are familiar. Concentrate on the differences between accounting income and cash flows and how the income statement provides a link between the balance sheet at two different points in time.

Lesson 2.   Read Chap. 2 to the end of the section titled "Cost and Benefit of Float" and answer Probs. 1 and 2. Be sure you are comfortable with the different types of balances and how they are affected by the various payment alternatives. Make sure you understand how to calculate both the amount and the opportunity cost of float. We will use this concept throughout many of the following chapters.

Lesson 3.   Read the remainder of Chap. 2 and answer Prob. 3. If possible, obtain an actual account analysis statement from a company or a bank and determine how you could use the information to decide on how to compensate the bank.

Lesson 4.   Read Chap. 3 and answer the Self-Test questions. Look at the back of one of your canceled checks that was mailed to a distant payee and see if you can determine how it was cleared. Look at the MICR line on your check and identify the elements in your bank's transit routing number.

Lesson 5.   Read Chap. 4 and answer the test questions. Do you make or receive any value transfers by ACH? Which ones would you be willing to do?

Lesson 6.   Read Chap. 5 and answer the Self-Test questions. Think about the EDI transactions done by companies with which you are associated. If they aren't doing any, in which areas should they consider the use of EDI?

Lesson 7.   Read Chap. 6 through the end of the section titled "Improving the Collection System," under "Collecting Mailed Checks," and answer Prob. 1. If you have trouble with the calculation of float or the cost of float, review the concepts in Chap. 2.

Lesson 8.   Read the remainder of Chap. 6 and answer Prob. 2. Does your company use a lockbox for collection? See if you can determine which of your creditors have you send your checks to a lockbox. Think about how the banking regulations in your state affect the concentration problem for retailers with multiple locations.

Lesson 9.   Read Chap. 7 to the end of the section titled "Release of the Check" and answer Prob. 1.

Lesson 10.   Read the remainder of Chap. 7 and answer Prob. 2. Examine a sample of the checks you, or your company, receive to see if you can determine if any of your payors are using controlled disbursing or are disbursing from remote sites.

Lesson 11.   Read Chap. 8 to the end of the section titled "Portfolio Composition." Be sure you understand the distinction between asset and firm liquidity. How liquid are companies with which you are associated? What means do they use to provide backup liquidity?

Lesson 12.   Read the remainder of Chap. 8 and answer the questions. Select two or three short-term securities from the financial pages of a newspaper and determine the price and the effective yield if held to maturity. Call a bank and ask for the stated rate and the effective annualized rate on a CD. See if you can determine the compounding period and the number of days in the year for the interest quote.

Lesson 13. Read Chap. 9 to the end of the section titled "Personal Guarantees" and answer Probs. 1 and 2.

Lesson 14. Read the remainder of Chap. 9 and answer Prob. 3. This problem involves a fairly substantial amount of calculation. The use of spreadsheet software on a PC would be beneficial, but not necessary. It is easiest to lay out the answer in columns, with the month in the first column, the loan outstanding in the second column, the interest to be paid in the third, the unused credit line in the fourth, and the commitment fee to be paid in the last column.

Lesson 15. Read Chap. 10 to the end of the section titled "Leases" and answer Probs. 1 and 2.

Lesson 16. Read the remainder of Chap. 10 and answer Prob. 3.

Lesson 17. Read Chap. 11 to the end of the section titled "Relating Variables to Timing." Carefully work through the numerical examples in the chapter.

Lesson 18. Answer Probs. 1 and 2 at the end of Chap. 11. For Prob. 1, first work through the forecast assuming the interest is based on the loan outstanding at the end of December. After determining the forecasted new loan at the end of the year, go back through one more iteration using the average loan for the year to determine the amount of the interest. Spreadsheet software is particularly useful for Prob. 2. For simplicity in Prob. 2, assume the interest on the loan for any one month is due the following month.

Lesson 19. Read the remainder of Chap. 11 and answer Prob. 3. What other types of cash flows are readily amenable to a distribution forecasting approach?

Lesson 20. Read Chap. 12 to the end of the section titled "Other Considerations." Carefully work through the numerical example in the chapter.

Lesson 21. Read the remainder of Chap. 12 and work out the problem in the Self-Test. Think about the credit policy and its implementation in companies with which you are associated.

Lesson 22. Read Chap. 13. Determine the monitoring procedures that are used for companies with which you are associated.

Lesson 23. Answer the problem at the end of Chap. 13. Again, spreadsheet software will be helpful, but it is not necessary. How could you use the information gained from credit monitoring to improve the cash forecasting?

Lesson 24. Read Chap. 14 and answer the problems. How is your business affected by international transactions and exchange rate fluctuations?

Lesson 25. Take the final examination. You should allow up to two hours. See the instructions on the first page of the examination to send the examination in for grading and to receive a certificate of achievement.

1
Introduction to Cash Flows

Introduction

Cash management as a focus of financial activity is relatively new. In the 1950s banks were the only financial institutions that processed payments, few short-term investment opportunities were available, information system response time was measured in weeks rather than seconds, and interest rates were very low. In fact, some economists even argued whether cash balances were sensitive to interest rates. By the late 1970s all that had changed. The National Corporate Cash Management Association was chartered and was holding annual meetings with attendance in the thousands. By the 1980s cash management had become a recognized specialty, requiring those wishing to become a certified cash manager to undergo an examination process and meet specific experience requirements. In the 1990s the focus of cash management broadened to treasury management. The National Corporate Cash Management Association changed its name to the Treasury Management Association. The changes were more than just in the name. As cash management was expanding from its narrow beginnings into a much broader concept of treasury management, the corporate finance function was also undergoing an evolution. The old controllership and auditor focus of finance was shifting to a decision-making function. New technology was eliminating the need for a large cadre of "bean counters" to record transactions and make sure the columns were added correctly. The transactions business of the finance function was being automated or reengineered out of existence. Cash managers led the way in the use of personal computers to gather, process, and transfer information. As they automated the routine part of the job, they naturally evolved into treasury decision makers. As the 1990s continue, the cash (treasury) manager will become a more important force in the application of financial and analytical decision making to all the areas dealing with the operating decisions of the firm.

Evolution is not costless. Those caught in the middle of evolutionary changes either adapt and lead or get stuck in the tar pits. The only way to maintain adaptability is through continued education. We believe it is not just coincidence that the move toward continuing education and lifetime learning in business is accompanying this evolution. The purpose of this book is to encapsulate the environment, functions, and analytical tools that are important for cash management. Cash management specialists will gain from a review and broadening of their horizons. However, the primary beneficiaries of this book are likely to be controllers who are now asked to perform broader finance functions, accountants whose clients are asking cash management advice, chief executive officers (CEOs) whose boards are asking cash management questions, and bankers who find their clients more interested in corporate services than in loans.

Focus on Cash Flows

What Is a Cash Flow?

Cash is the medium an economic society uses for storing and exchanging value. It is how we pay our bills. It is how we get paid for our labor or other services. It is the mechanism we use to measure relative value. For example, our economic society values a $200 tape player twice as much as a $100 tape player. If it didn't, the $200 tape player would not sell and either production would cease or the price would be lowered.

However, cash, or money, has little, if any, intrinsic value. It is simply what we as a society agree it is worth. The South Pacific Yap tribe used gigantic carved stones as money. Native Americans used wampum, strands of beads, as money. The English used sterling silver as money. Today we use electrons on silicon chips as money. In essence, cash, or money, is anything that an economic society agrees will serve for exchange of value. The critical factor is that it is accepted by all players as the medium of exchange.

Cash Flows Versus Accounting Income

It is unfortunate that accounting income is denominated in the same terms as is cash: in the United States it is in dollars. This sometimes gives the illusion that accounting income, or profits, is like cash flow. It is not. Try spending the accounting income to pay your supplier. Try using your share of the accounting income in the stocks you own to buy groceries. An economic pundit once said, "There is only one thing that you can do with accounting income: report it."

This is not to imply that accounting income is useless. It is carefully constructed to match revenues with expenses required to produce the goods. It is designed to recognize the gradual deterioration of the income-generating capabilities of a piece of machinery. What it does not do is capture what has been used to transfer value or can be used to transfer value. For example, accounting income recognizes revenues when the product is sold. It doesn't matter whether the product is sold for cash, on 30 days' credit, or on terms of 90 days same as cash. Value is not transferred from the customer to the seller until the bill is paid (with money of some sort). Similarly, accounting recognizes the purchase of an asset, say, a forklift truck, as a change in the form of an asset. No expense has occurred.

Accounting income and cash flow differ for several reasons. Accounting income recognizes revenues when the sale takes place, not when collection occurs. It recognizes expenses when the product is sold, not when the expenditures to suppliers and employees occur. It does not recognize making a purchase as an expense or selling an asset as income. It does not recognize incurring or retiring a debt. Note, these last two transactions are recognized by the accounting *system* and will affect the balance sheet, but they do not directly affect accounting *income*. In looking at the financial impact of decisions, cash managers identify the cash flows connected with the decision and determine if the change in cash flows adds value for the firm.

Trade-Off between Transactions and Time Value Costs

Most activities involve at least two types of costs: transactions costs and time value costs. *Transactions costs* are the costs to initiate and complete an activity. Bank fees to initiate a wire transfer, a brokerage fee to sell a security, the salary of the assistant treasurer responsible for maintaining banking relations are all examples of transactions costs. *Time value costs* are the costs incurred because of a delay in the transfer of value. They are the interest-type costs of having to wait to receive value. Of course, if you can make others wait for value, the time value costs are actually benefits to you. We will frequently use the term *opportunity cost rate* to describe the percentage rate at which time value costs are assessed. It is the rate that is either paid for or could be earned on funds while waiting to receive value. Almost all cash management decisions involve both transactions costs and time value costs. Cash managers can make costly mistakes by focusing exclusively on one and ignoring the other. Unfortunately, that is exactly what many people, particularly those not directly connected with cash management, have done. We frequently hear people say that cash management is only an issue when interest rates are high. They are missing a major part of the reason for cash management activities if they ignore transactions costs.

The 1980s: Time Value Costs

The 1980s started with U.S. interest rates at the highest level they had been in the memory of all living business people. This was also the time that banks were unbundling and assessing explicit charges for their services. Many banks did not have an accurate assessment of the cost of their services, so they tended to undercharge their customers. In this environment, time value costs were much more critical than transactions costs. Models developed to assist in decision making, such as lockbox location models, focused on time value costs and totally ignored transactions costs. The high opportunity cost rate provided treasurers with a large incentive to capture the time value costs both by advancing cash inflows and delaying cash outflows. In many cases these time value costs swamped the transactions costs; thus few mistakes were made by ignoring transactions costs.

The 1990s: Transactions Costs

As the 1980s ended and the 1990s began, interest rates had fallen. Time value costs fell relative to transactions costs. At the same time, advances in communication and computer technology made it possible to gather information and conduct transactions with a speed that one would have marveled at a decade earlier. The focus shifted to minimizing transactions costs. A key way to reduce transactions costs is to get rid of manual processes. Manual processing costs are variable costs: they increase as volume increases. Most costs for automated, electronic processes are primarily fixed: the costs do not change for a wide range of volumes. In addition, manual processes have high error rates. If properly planned and instituted, electronic processes have a much lower error rate. The danger in the 1990s is that the errors of the 1980s will be repeated, only in the opposite direction: transactions costs will be minimized without regard to time value costs.

The Future: Which Costs?

Good cash management focuses on the balance of transactions costs and time value costs. As the relative importance of these costs shift—because of changes in labor, productivity, or interest rates—cash management practices should change. If advances in technology continue to shorten succeeding generations of products and services, cash managers will have to review their activities constantly to avoid the fate of dinosaurs. Cash managers who focus on the total costs of their systems are more likely to be flexible in responding to changing conditions because they simply must shift the emphasis, rather than develop a new way of thinking.

Business Cash Flows: Inflows, Internal Flows, and Outflows

There are three major types of cash flows for organizations: inflows, internal flows, and outflows. Inflows come primarily from customers paying for products and services. These are permanent transfers of value from customers to the selling firm. Outflows primarily consist of payment for factors of production, such as labor, materials, or taxes. These are also permanent transfers of value. Internal flows consist of cash flows that move around within the firm, say, from a divisional bank account to the headquarters account, or funds that *temporarily* move into or out of the firm, say, investment in marketable securities or the use of a short-term bank credit line. Although this latter cash flow involves parties external to the firm, the cash flows are temporary, or at least planned that way. The expectation is they will be reversed at some time in the future. Figure 1-1 presents a diagram of these cash flows. The cash inflows and outflows are directly related to the operating activities of the firm. The timing and the amount of cash inflows from customers are a function of the level of sales and the credit policy of the seller. The timing and amount of cash outflows are a function of the level of sales, the suppliers' credit policies, and the seller's payables and

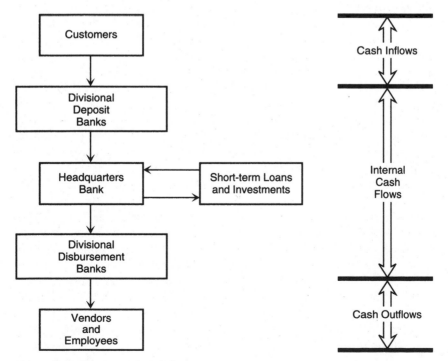

Figure 1-1. A company's cash flows.

wage and salary policy. Changes in cash inflows and outflows are directly affected by changes in the level of operating activities or operating policies. Changes in internal cash flows may be influenced by changes in the level of operating activities, but not directly. For example, an increase in sales may increase the size of the materials inventory. If the balance of cash inflows and outflows is sufficient to fund this additional inventory, no action may be needed. If not, the treasury manager may decide to sell some marketable securities or to use some available bank financing. Thus, the amount of funds in securities or in loans is affected by the change in operating activities, but only after a positive action by management.

Remainder of the Book

The next three chapters contain the background for understanding the environment in which cash management takes place. Chapter 2 covers the different types of balances in the banking system, and describes how different payment forms affect the float in these balances and how balances can be used to compensate banks for their services. Chapters 3 and 4 discuss how value is transferred through paper and electronic payments. Chapter 5 deals with electronic data interchange, which is a system for electronically communicating with trading partners as well as transferring value. Chapters 6 and 7 discuss the design and operation of collection, concentration, and disbursement systems in cash management. Chapters 8 through 11 are concerned with liquidity management, that is, supplying the funds required to meet obligations. Chapter 8 details the measurement of liquidity and the use of short-term investments to provide liquidity. Chapters 9 and 10 cover the use of bank and nonbank credit arrangements. Chapter 11 develops the use of cash forecasting as a way both of estimating and of managing cash flows. Chapters 12 and 13 examine the credit policy and procedures of the firm, with a focus on the interface and interaction of the cash manager with the credit function of the company. Finally, Chapter 14 covers the additional issues involved in cash management when a company deals on an international basis.

Throughout the book we focus on an analytical approach to decision making. Note, however, that *analytical* does not necessarily mean *quantitative*. While we deal with numbers (it couldn't be called finance without numbers), the analytical process focuses on identifying the problem, determining the information available, specifying the objectives, and structuring a solution that helps to achieve the objectives. We assume a basic understanding of accounting and financial statements. However, our primary focus is on the cash flows involved in the decisions. In many cases we ignore taxes. This is not because taxes are unimportant, but rather because they tend to affect all the cash flows for a particular decision in the same way.

Including taxes would unduly complicate the analysis without affecting the conclusions.

Each chapter, except this one, terminates with a Self-Test. The problems in the test illustrate the key concepts in the chapter. Solutions to the problems are given at the end of the book. We also include a glossary of key terms at the end of the book. These terms are all defined in the text; however, the glossary provides a ready reference.

2
Understanding and Analyzing Bank Balances

Introduction

April Jackson, a fifth grade student and the daughter of Sue Jackson, the treasurer of Acme Industries, has recently started a job as a newspaper carrier. April is trying to understand how much cash she has in her business. April asked Sue, "Is the cash balance the total of the coins and dollar bills in my collection bag, or is it the amount of money that I have in my newspaper account at the bank?" The question started Sue thinking about the different ways the term *cash* is used, and how different people measure Acme's "cash." When the office manager refers to cash, he means petty cash in the office safe. The controller's reference to cash is the balance listed in the cash account on Acme's books. The teller at the company's bank uses the term *cash balance* to refer to the ledger balance currently reported by the bank's information system. The account officer's reference to the cash balance is likely to be Acme's end-of-day collected balance available to earn credits to pay for the loan commitment and other bank services. In this chapter we examine these different definitions of cash balance and analyze how and when they are affected by receipts and disbursements. In addition, we explore how bank account analysis information can be used to identify the differences between these balances, and determine whether cash balances should be used to compensate banks for services provided.

Types of Cash Balances

Company Book Balances

A company's accounting system is set up to record and classify all identifiable transactions that have an impact on the financial position of the business. The *company cash book balance* (usually called the *company book balance* or just the *book balance*) reflects the net impact on the cash position of accounting entries. Inflows include items such as over-the-counter cash receipts from customers, checks mailed to the company for payment of invoices, and electronic transfers credited to the company's account at the bank. Outflows include currency payments for incidental purchases, checks written to pay for goods and services, and wire transfers to purchase securities. These transactions are recorded on the company's books in accordance with the prevailing accounting conventions and as soon as they can be objectively identified.

The debits and credits to cash on the company's books are done both to provide an audit trail for specific transactions and to follow standard accounting procedures consistent with the general ledger system. As we discussed in Chap. 1, recognition of an accounting transaction frequently is not the same as a cash flow or a transfer of value. Thus, the cash balance on the company's book represents the net result of the company's accounting entries, and not value that is actually available to the firm.

Bank Balances

Ledger Balances. Bank *ledger balances* in an account reflect a *bank's* accounting entries to record all activities that affect the account. The ledger balance might be considered the "normal" bank balance, that is, the balance that would be reported by most banks' systems if you call and ask for a report on the balance in your account. Ledger balances are credited (increased) for any deposits made to the account on the day the deposits are recognized, and are debited (decreased) for any withdrawals from the account on the day the withdrawal is made. Again, we emphasize the ledger balance, like the company book balance, is an accounting balance and may not represent value to the company.

If a transaction results in a negative ledger balance, the account is considered to be in an *overdraft* position. The U.S. banking system does not currently provide for automatic overdraft banking. Thus, the holder of an overdrawn account must take some explicit action to bring the balance up to or above zero. If the ledger balance is less than the amount of an instrument presented for payment, the account is said to be in a nonsufficient funds (NSF) condition. A notification of such is usually returned with the unpaid check to the depositor of the check.

Available Balances.   Bank *available balances,* also called *collected balances,* reflect the monetary value in the account at the bank. The available balance represents the real economic value available to the account holder. The available balance is increased or decreased when *value* is transferred into or out of an account. Items such as coin and currency or wire transfers, which result in an immediate transfer of value, increase the available balances at the time the deposit is made. Checks and other delayed availability transfers, such as some Automated Clearing House (ACH) payments, increase available balances only after some delay. The available balance represents value that can be transferred to other economic entities. The available balance also represents the balance that can earn credits to pay for certain services. From the bank's standpoint, the available balances in demand deposit accounts determine the amount of reserves the bank must maintain.

Since available balances represent value in an account, it would seem that a bank should use this definition of balances to determine whether a presentation for a payment should be honored or returned because of insufficient funds. For some banks this is true. However, some banks may allow payment when the available balance is negative as long as the ledger balance is positive. Whether a bank will allow an available balance to go below zero depends upon bank policy and the arrangement with the particular account holder. Some banks are willing to allow a limited number of negative available balances during a month, as long as the average available balance is positive. Other banks require a firm to have a credit line in force to be implemented whenever the available balance goes negative. The only way to be certain is to discuss this issue with your bank and make sure that you both understand when the bank considers the account in an overdraft position.

The Effect of Receipts and Payments on Balances

Company Book Balances

The impact of different receipts and payments on the three different types of balances can most easily be explained by analyzing a numerical example. Let's start by examining the effect of receipts and disbursements on the company book balance for Acme Industries, located in Anderson, Indiana. Acme starts Monday morning with a company book balance of $25,000. The morning mail contains a $5000 check from a customer, drawn on the Second National Bank of Quincy, Illinois. The check is received in the mail room, where the receiving clerk notes the amount of the check on the invoice, initials it, and stamps the check with the Acme Industries "For

Deposit Only" stamp. Next, the clerk keys the receipt of $5000 into the accounting system. This receipts file will later be reconciled with the deposit file for audit and control purposes. The clerk then forwards the invoice to accounts receivable to update the customer's record and sends the check to the cash manager's office to be processed and deposited. The clerk in the cash manager's office fills out a deposit slip for Acme's account at the First National Bank of Anderson (FNA) and keys the deposit of $5000 into the accounting system. Acme's books reflect the addition of $5000, and the cash balance increases to $30,000. The deposit is scheduled to be taken to the local branch of FNA by 3:30 p.m.

If this were the only activity affecting the cash balance for the rest of the week, Acme's book balance would appear as shown in Table 2-1. The average balance for the week would be $30,000. Note, for simplicity, we are only calculating the average balance for the week. More typically the average balance would be calculated for the month.

We now add a second transaction. A check in the amount of $8000 is written on Monday to pay a supplier in Wheeling, West Virginia. The $8000 is subtracted from the cash balance on Monday, resulting in an ending balance of $22,000. If these two activities are the only ones affecting the cash balance, the average cash balance for the week will be $22,000. The net impact of these two activities is reflected in the numbers in Table 2-2.

Table 2-1. Acme Company Book Balance with One Deposit
(000 Omitted)

Activity	Mon.	Tues.	Wed.	Thurs.	Fri.	Sat.	Sun.
Beginning balance	$25	$30	$30	$30	$30	$30	$30
Deposits	+5						
Withdrawals							
Ending balance	$30	$30	$30	$30	$30	$30	$30

Average ending balance = $30.

Table 2-2. Acme Company Book Balance with One Deposit and One Check Written
(000 Omitted)

Activity	Mon.	Tues.	Wed.	Thurs.	Fri.	Sat.	Sun.
Beginning balance	$25	$22	$22	$22	$22	$22	$22
Deposits	+5						
Withdrawals	−8						
Ending balance	$22	$22	$22	$22	$22	$22	$22

Average ending balance = $22.

Bank Balances

Ledger Balances. Acme's deposit of $5000 is made at the Ninth Street Branch of FNA, which has a cutoff time of 2 p.m. Checks received at the branches are sent to the main office of FNA for processing and entry into the check clearing system. The 2 p.m. cutoff time at the branch allows FNA time to transport checks from the branches to the check processing area for processing before the bank closes its books for the day, perhaps 4 p.m. Since the deposit is received by the branch at 3:30 p.m.—past the 2 p.m. cutoff time—FNA recognizes the deposit as having occurred on the next *business* day, Tuesday, and adds it to Acme's ledger account balance as of Tuesday. (Most banks use a batch update on their information system, which is run overnight when other system requirements are low. Thus, the balance reporting system might not actually *record* the check as a deposit until late Tuesday night or early Wednesday morning, but it is credited as a deposit as of Tuesday and included in Tuesday's ending balance.) If Monday's beginning ledger balance for Acme was $25,000, the bank will report an ending balance of $25,000 on Monday and $30,000 on Tuesday. The average balance for the week will be $29,286 (see Table 2-3). Delays in conveying a deposit to the bank result in the bank ledger balance being lower than the company book balance.

Most banks do not have their accounts open on Saturday and Sunday, even though they might maintain some activities on these days. Consequently, a transaction missing the cutoff time on Friday will not be recorded until Monday, the next business day. A delay in a deposit on Friday affects three days' ending balances. This means that activities on Friday can have three times the impact as those on other days.

Returning to our second scenario, we can see how the combination of making a deposit of $5000 and writing a check for $8000 on Monday affects the bank ledger balance. The check is received by the supplier, processed, and deposited late on Wednesday afternoon. The check enters the check clearing system and is presented to FNA for payment on Friday. Upon presentation, the bank deducts the amount of the check and transfers value out of Acme's account. The average ledger balance in Acme's account is $25,857, as shown in Table 2-4. There is usually a time lag

Table 2-3. Acme Bank Ledger Balance with One Deposit
(000 Omitted)

Activity	Mon.	Tues.	Wed.	Thurs.	Fri.	Sat.	Sun.
Beginning balance	$25	$25	$30	$30	$30	$30	$30
Deposits		+5					
Withdrawals							
Ending balance	$25	$30	$30	$30	$30	$30	$30

Average ending balance = $29.286.

Table 2-4. Acme Bank Ledger Balance with One Deposit and One Presentment
(000 Omitted)

Activity	Mon.	Tues.	Wed.	Thurs.	Fri.	Sat.	Sun.
Beginning balance	$25	$25	$30	$30	$30	$22	$22
Deposits		+5					
Withdrawals					−8		
Ending balance	$25	$30	$30	$30	$22	$22	$22

Average ending balance = $25.857.

between the day a check is written and recorded on the company's books and the day the check is presented for payment at the bank. This delay results in the company's book balance being lower than the bank ledger balance during this time.

For most companies the total dollar amount of checks written during a month is close to the total amount of deposits made during the month. The time between recording deposits on the company's books and receiving ledger balance credit is usually shorter than the time between a check being written and presented for payment. This means the impact on the difference between book and ledger balance is greater for checks written than for deposits made. Consequently, the bank ledger balance will generally be higher than the company book balance.

Available Balances.   The check deposited by Acme drawn on the bank in Quincy, Illinois, will be sent by FNA to the Federal Reserve Bank branch in Indianapolis and then to the Federal Reserve Bank in Chicago, and finally it will be presented to the Quincy bank for payment. If everything works according to the schedule, value is transferred from the Quincy bank to FNA when the check is presented. Assuming the clearing takes one day, there is a one-day delay in receipt of value (one-day availability) for the deposited check. This is one day *after* the bank has recognized the deposit for ledger credit. Thus, the available balance is increased by $5000 on Wednesday (see Table 2-5).

Items that transfer value immediately, such as coin and currency, *on-us* items (items involving a bank's own branches and affiliates), or wire transfers, are credited to the available balance at the same time the ledger balance is credited. There should be no difference between the ledger balance and the available balance for deposits of these types of items. However, if the deposit is made after the cutoff time, there may still be a difference between the company's books and the bank balance.

On Friday the $8000 check is presented for payment. Since there are sufficient funds in the account, FNA honors the check and transfers value to the bank in which the check was deposited. At the same time, the bank

Table 2-5. Acme Bank Available Balance with One Deposit
and One Presentment
(000 Omitted)

Activity	Mon.	Tues.	Wed.	Thurs.	Fri.	Sat.	Sun.
Beginning balance	$25	$25	$35	$30	$30	$22	$22
Deposits			+5				
Withdrawals					−8		
Ending balance	$25	$25	$30	$30	$22	$22	$22

Average ending balance = $25.143.

transfers value out of Acme's account. This transfer of value results in a reduction of $8000 in the available balance. As we can see from Table 2-5, the average available balance in the account for the week is $25,143.

We have seen that deposits increase the available balance either at the same time the ledger balance is increased or only after a delay. Withdrawals from an account affect the ledger balance and the available balance at the same time. Therefore, the available balance should always be less than or equal to the ledger balance.

Payment System Float

The term *float* generally refers to any delay in the movement of funds. However, a reference to a specific type of float may depend upon the context of the analysis. The above example included two types of float in the deposit activities: *processing float* due to the delay in getting the deposit to the bank and *availability float* due to the delay in value transfer (crediting the available balance) for the deposited check. The latter is frequently referred to as *bank float,* both because it is caused by banking system check clearing delays and because it is the only portion of float that the bank can measure directly. The total processing and bank float are frequently referred to as *deposit float.* The float connected with the outgoing payment is *disbursement float.* Disbursement float is composed of *mail float* (from Acme to the supplier), supplier processing float (the time for the supplier to get the check to the deposit bank), and *clearing float* (the time it takes for the check to be presented for payment). Figure 2-1 contains a schematic representation of the elements in these two major float categories. *Net float* is defined as

Net float = disbursement float − deposit float

Although float can be measured as the number of days' delay, it is usually more meaningful to measure float in dollars or dollar days. This captures both the time of the delay and the amount of the funds being delayed. The dollar days of float are calculated by multiplying the time delay by the

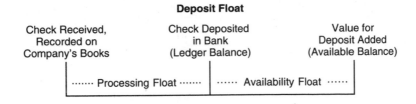

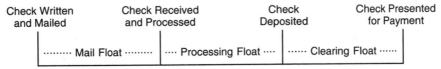

Figure 2-1. Deposit float and disbursement float.

amount of the payment involved. For example, the processing for Acme is 1 day × $5000 = 5000 dollar days. If this is averaged over the week, we have an average of $714 in processing float for the week. The average float is important because, as we will discuss below, banks use average balances and average float in monthly statements. We can see in the first scenario, where the only activity is the deposit of the $5000 check, that the average processing float is equal to the difference between the average book balance and the average ledger balance, $30,000 − $29,286 = $714. The bank float on the one deposit item is 5000 dollar days, which results in an average bank float for the week of $714. This is also the difference between the ledger and the available balances at the bank, $25,857 − $25,143 = $714.

The treasurer has direct access to the company's books, and, therefore, the company book balance. Unfortunately, the treasurer should be managing the available balance, since the available balance represents the real monetary value of the cash in the business. The difference between the book balance and the available balance is equal to the difference between deposit and disbursement float. Above we defined this difference as net float. The net float for Acme is

$$\text{Net float} = (4 \text{ days} \times \$8000) - (2 \text{ days} \times \$5000) = \$22,000$$

If we divide this by 7, we get the average net float:

$$\text{Average net float} = \$22,000/7 = \$3143$$

The difference between the average company book balance and the average available balance for Acme is $25,143 − $22,000 = $3143. Thus, we can use net float to go between book and available balances as follows:

Company book balance = bank available balance − net float

For Acme this is $22,000 = $25,143 − $3143.

This concept is useful if the treasurer is trying to manage the available balance at the bank by working from the company book balance figures. Assume that the following pattern holds for Acme: On an average day it receives nine checks of an average size of $5000, and on an average day it pays out five checks of an average size of $8000. The average net float for Acme is

Deposit float = 9 checks/day × $5000/check × 2-day delay = $90,000

Disbursement float = 5 checks/day × $8000/check × 4-day delay = $160,000

Net float = $160,000 − $90,000 = $70,000

The average bank available balance will be $70,000 larger than the company book balance.

The treasurer can use this net float amount to manage the available balances while monitoring the company book balances. If the treasurer of Acme carries an average cash balance of $10,000 on the company's books, the average value that is actually available at the bank is $80,000. Alternatively, assume that the treasurer has decided that it is necessary to carry only an average available balance of $40,000 to maintain adequate liquidity and to compensate the bank for services provided. What should be the average level of company book balances? We can use the net float relationship to solve for the desired company book balances as follows:

Company book balance = bank available balance − net float

Company book balance = $40,000 − $70,000 = −$30,000

Thus, the treasurer should manage the cash balance on the company's books to maintain an average of −$30,000. Is this illegal or unethical? No. The company book balance is only an accounting entry. The real value in the cash account is the available balance at the bank. This has a positive value of $40,000. Is this unusual? Again, the answer is no. Disbursement float is larger than deposit float for most companies. If they are managing their balances to eliminate excess value tied up in the cash account, they likely have negative book balances. We now examine when this might be perceived as a problem and how to address it.

Red Book Balances

A negative book balance is sometimes called a *red book balance*. If the company is privately held and the top management and the owners (or direc-

tors) understand why the cash balance is negative, this presents no problem. However, many managers of publicly traded firms are reluctant to
issue a financial statement with a negative cash balance. They fear that
some people may think either that the firm is in poor financial condition or
that it is practicing unethical cash management. Of course, neither is true.
Several actions can be taken to "window-dress" the balance sheet to avoid
showing the red book balances. For example, to avoid having to report the
negative book balance of $30,000, Acme might choose one of three alter-
natives: borrow money, combine cash and marketable securities, or create a
net drafts payable account.

Borrow Money.   A partial balance sheet for Acme Industries is shown in
Panel A of Table 2-6. One way to avoid showing the red book balance is for
Acme to borrow $31,000 from its bank on the balance sheet date. Acme
would show a cash balance of $1000 (see Panel B of Table 2-6). While this
gets rid of the red book balance, it is costly because Acme borrows and pays
interest on funds it didn't need. Note that it also changed the total amount

Table 2-6. A Partial Balance Sheet for Acme Industries
(All Numbers in $1000)

Panel A: Show Red Book Balance			
Cash	(30)		
Marketable Securities	35	Trade Accounts Payable	140
Accounts Receivable	200	Accrued Expenses	70
Inventories	150		
Total Current Assets	355	Total Current Liabilities	210
Panel B: Borrow Funds			
Cash	1		
Marketable Securities	35	Trade Accounts Payable	140
Accounts Receivable	200	Accrued Expenses	70
Inventories	150	Bank Loan	31
Total Current Assets	386	Total Current Liabilities	241
Panel C: Combine Cash and Marketable Securities			
Cash and			
Marketable Securities	35	Trade Accounts Payable	140
Accounts Receivable	200	Accrued Expenses	70
Inventories	150		
Total Current Assets	355	Total Current Liabilities	210
Panel D: Create a Net Drafts Payable Account			
Cash	40	Net Drafts Payable	70
Marketable Securities	35	Trade Accounts Payable	140
Accounts Receivable	200	Accrued Expenses	70
Inventories	150		
Total Current Assets	425	Total Current Liabilities	280

of current assets and current liabilities. This will change some of the balance sheet ratios, such as current ratio or quick ratio, that creditors may be watching.

Combine Cash and Marketable Securities.   If Acme holds marketable securities in an amount greater than the negative cash balance, it can simply combine these two accounts on the balance sheet. Acme's balance sheet now shows a total of $35,000 in the cash and securities account (see Panel C in Table 2-6). Notice that there was no change in the total current assets or liabilities; thus, none of the ratios change. Of course a firm must have sufficient marketable securities to be able to use this procedure.

Create a Net Drafts Payable Account.   A third alternative is to list the cash account as the amount of the available balance at the bank, $40,000. This, after all, does represent the real value of the cash position of the company. A current liability equal to the amount of the net float, $70,000 in Acme's case, is created (see Panel D in Table 2-6). This represents the net difference between the deposits that are not credited as an available balance and the checks that have been written but not yet paid. Some financial people feel this is the fairest way to represent the cash position of the company. However, some accountants are reluctant to use this procedure, and it may not be allowed for some highly regulated companies, such as insurance companies.

Cost and Benefit of Float

Float represents a delay in the transfer of value. The delay is a cost if it is in a transfer to the firm and a benefit if it is in a transfer from the firm. The amount of the cost or the benefit depends upon the opportunity cost of funds to the firm as well as upon the amount of float. In our initial example, Acme's processing and availability delayed the receipt of value for two days from the time the check was received by the company. Assume the treasurer could invest funds at a rate of 8 percent per annum. The cost of this delay is calculated as

$$\text{Cost of delay} = \$5000 \times 2 \text{ days} \times (0.08/365) = \$2.19$$

On the other hand, the delay in the clearing of the check written to the supplier gave Acme a benefit:

$$\text{Benefit of delay} = \$8000 \times 4 \text{ days} \times (0.08/365) = \$7.01$$

This type of calculation determines the float cost or benefit for an individual payment item. While this is useful for large individual payments, it is usually more meaningful to identify the cost or benefit for average float. In the above example, Acme had an average net float of $70,000. This means $70,000 more is available in the bank than is reflected on the company's books. What was the cost or benefit to the treasurer of this float? For an average day at a rate of 8 percent per annum, this float is worth the following:

$$\text{Value of float} = \$70,000 \times (0.08/365) = \$15.34$$

Over a 30-day month this float is worth $30 \times \$15.34 = \$460.27$. For a year it is worth $365 \times \$15.34 = \$5600$.

Thus, to calculate the value of float for an individual item, multiply the dollar amount of the item by the number of days of delay and by the daily opportunity cost rate. To calculate the value of the average float for one day, multiply the average float by the daily opportunity cost rate. To obtain the value for a longer time period, simply multiply the daily value times the number of days in the longer time period.

How Banks Determine Availability

We now know why banks give delayed availability and the impact that it has on float and the several definitions of balances. How do banks determine the number of days' delay in granting availability? Can you determine the availability that will be assigned to a deposit before the deposit is made? How do you know if the bank is granting you the availability that you should get on your deposits?

Methods Used to Calculate Availability

Most banks use one of three methods of assigning availability to checks deposited: average bank availability, average availability for a test period, and actual item availability. We discuss each of these and the advantages and disadvantages of each for the bank's customers.

Average Bank Availability.   Some small banks do not have a very sophisticated information system. The system may be designed to capture only accounting information, and may not be able to track when value is actually received for deposited checks. In this case, the bank may be able to measure only the ledger balances of its account holders. In fact, some small banks may actually use a larger correspondent bank to process and clear "foreign" check deposits. The correspondent bank will give the small bank an availability delay on the checks processed. This may be reported to the small bank as a difference between the ledger and the available balances held at the correspondent bank. The small bank then applies the *average bank* *availability,* as a percentage of ledger balances, to all accounts to determine the difference between ledger and available balances.

While this a simple process, it results in some depositors subsidizing other depositors' float. Assume that a bank has an average availability float from its deposits with a correspondent bank of 20 percent of its ledger balances kept in the correspondent account. Let's compare how this method of assigning availability affects two hypothetical companies: firm A receives customers' checks drawn mostly on local banks, and firm B receives customers' checks drawn on banks from all across the country.

Firm A makes an average deposit of $10,000 per day of checks that should receive one-day availability. Thus, the float generated should be an average of $10,000 dollar days. (To keep the example simple, ignore the impact of Saturday and Sunday.) Firm A maintains an average ledger balance of $100,000. The availability float assessed to firm A is 20 percent of the average ledger balance, or $20,000. Thus, the average available balance recorded for firm A is $80,000. In essence, firm A is being penalized by being credited with $10,000 less value than actually is in the account.

Firm B makes an average deposit of $12,000 per day of checks that should receive two-day availability. The float generated should be an average of $24,000. The treasurer for firm B closely controls the balances and maintains an average ledger balance of $35,000, and so its available balance should be $11,000. The bank assesses firm B the same average figure of 20 percent, or an availability float of $7000. Firm B is credited with an average available balance of $28,000, or $19,000 more than the real value in the account.

The situation may be even worse for some companies. Firm C is a fast-food restaurant accepting only cash and currency. All of its deposits should be immediately available (that is, have the same-day ledger and available balance credit). However, if the bank uniformly applies the average float factor to *all* accounts, firm C's account will be assigned an availability float.

Average Availability during a Test Period. Some banks may have an information system that is capable of capturing the availability float generated by individual accounts, but it is not a regular part of their processing. These banks will do a study of each account periodically—usually for one month each year. They track the deposit activities into the account during the test period and determine the average amount of bank float generated. This average float may be measured either as an absolute dollar amount or as a percentage of the ledger balance held during the test period. This float figure is applied to the ledger balances for the other months during the year. As long as the deposits into the account and the average ledger balances are reasonably steady throughout the year, this may be a reasonable approximation of the real value in the account.

Actual Item Availability.   The most accurate measure of the float generated by deposits into an account is *actual item availability*. The bank automatically measures the float associated with each item deposited into an account and charges that account with the delayed availability. This essentially is the process described earlier in this chapter for the deposit of $8000 by Acme. The bank has a table in its information system for the availability of each transit routing number. As the magnetic ink character recognition (MICR) line on the check is scanned by the reader/sorter, availability is assigned, based on the value from this table. The amount and the availability delay are recorded for the account into which the check was deposited. This procedure allows the bank to determine, and to report to the account holder if desired, the amount that is available today, that will become available the next business day, and so on. The bank float, or the difference between the ledger balance and the available balance, is determined each day. The average bank float for the reporting period (usually a month) is determined by averaging the daily float figures.

How to Read
an Availability Schedule

The table of availability delays based on transit routing numbers is called an *availability schedule*. This schedule is published and provided to the bank's customers. An example of an availability schedule for a bank in Pittsburgh is given in Table 2-7.

A key time on an availability schedule is the cutoff time for ledger credit. Any item not processed by this time is treated as a next-business-day item, and it is necessary to add one business day to the availability. The cutoff time may be explicitly stated—as it is in this example—or it may have to be found by looking at the time for an on-us item.

The first segment of the availability schedule specifies the time a deposit item must be processed to receive immediate availability. For example, a check drawn on a Birmingham City bank [i.e., a bank receiving a direct delivery of checks from the Fed rather than one whose checks are first sent to the Birmingham regional check processing center (RCPC)] has a transit routing number of 0620-xxxx. The first two digits of the transit routing number designate the Federal Reserve district, and the next two numbers designate the routing within the district. The last four digits are the unique bank identification numbers within the Fed district. For a check drawn on a bank with a 0620 transit routing number the depositor will receive same-day availability as long as the item is processed by 1:30 a.m. The first issue is how in the world do you make a deposit before 1:30 a.m.? Clearly, an over-the-counter deposit must be made the previous day. However, the availability schedule also applies to lockbox deposits. (We will discuss

Table 2-7. Fourteenth National Bank of Pittsburgh Availability Schedule (6 p.m. Ledger Cutoff)

Immediate Availability

	Transit route	Receipt deadline	Fractional availability
Alabama			
Birmingham City	0620-xxxx	1:30 a.m.	98
Birmingham RCPC	0621,0622-xxxx	8:30 p.m.	95
Florida			
Jacksonville City	0630-xxxx	1:30 a.m.	100
Jacksonville RCPC	0631,0632-xxxx	8:30 p.m.	100
Miami City	0660-xxxx	1:30 a.m.	96
Miami RCPC	0670-xxxx	8:30 p.m.	100
Indiana			
Chicago RCPC	0712,0719-xxxx	8:30 p.m.	95
Indianapolis			
Indianapolis City	0740-xxxx	1:30 a.m.	100
Indianapolis RCPC	0749-xxxx	10:30 p.m.	95
Bank One	0740-0001	5:30 a.m.	98
INB	0740-0005	5:30 a.m.	98
Merchant National	0740-0006	5:30 a.m.	98
Louisville RCPC	0813,0839		
	0863-xxxx	8:30 p.m.	100
One-Day Availability			
Alabama			
New Orleans RCPC	0651-xxxx	1:30 p.m.	97
Idaho			
Portland RCPC	1231-xxxx	1:30 p.m.	90
Salt Lake City RCPC	1241-xxxx	1:30 p.m.	85

the functioning of a lockbox in Chap. 6.) Banks process most of the lockbox deposits at night. Say a check in the amount of $10,000 is processed at 1 a.m. on Tuesday. Since it is before 6 p.m., it receives ledger credit on Tuesday, and since it is before 1:30 a.m., it also receives availability credit on Tuesday. If the check had not been processed until 3 a.m., it would still have received ledger credit, but it would not be available until Wednesday.

Note that the last column in Table 2-7, headed "Fractional Availability," has a value of 98 for these checks. The fractional availability of 98 means that the bank will grant immediate availability (Tuesday) for 98 percent of the amount of the check, $9800, and one-day availability for the remaining 2 percent, $200. The rationale is that 98 percent of the time the bank will be successful in presenting the check for payment on the same day, whereas 2 percent of the time value will not be received until the next business day. The bank is passing on the average availability and absorbing any deviations from the average.

Some banks use whole-day availability rather than fractional availability. These banks make an adjustment after the fact for those situations in which they are not able to receive value on the day promised. This adjustment affects the average available balances on which earnings credits are paid, but not the ability of the firm to withdraw funds. With the use of whole-day availability a bank may appear to be more aggressive with its availability schedule, but it is forcing the depositor to absorb any variation in the actual transfer of value.

Look at the checks drawn on a bank whose checks clear through the Birmingham RCPC. From Table 2-7, these checks have a cutoff time of 8:30 p.m. At first glance, it appears that virtually all checks with this transit routing number would be granted immediate availability. This is not the case. A bank counts days differently than we normally count days. To see how this actually works, look at Fig. 2-2. To the bank the day ends at 6 p.m., the ledger cutoff time. Anything occurring after this time is considered to be as of the next day. Suppose a check drawn on the Birmingham RCPC is processed on Wednesday at 9 a.m. Is this prior to 8:30 p.m. Wednesday? Not if we count bank days. The bank's Wednesday started at 6 p.m. Tuesday for "normal time." Thus, 9 a.m. Wednesday is after 8:30 p.m. bank time. The deposit missed the cutoff time for immediate availability. Ninety-eight percent will be credited as becoming available on Thursday, and the other two percent will be credited as of Friday.

A cautionary note is necessary when using an availability schedule. The availability times apply to when the items are processed by the reader/sorter. The most common use of an availability schedule is for lockbox customers, where the bank moves the items from the lockbox processing area directly to the check processing area. If checks are deposited over-the-counter at the teller window, time must be allowed for the teller to process the deposit and to transport the checks to the check processing area. This is particularly time-consuming if the deposit is being made at a location, such as a branch office, which is remote from the check processing area. This is the reason many banks post signs stating that deposits after a speci-

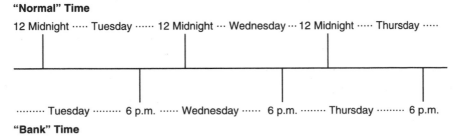

Figure 2-2. Availability schedule time line.

fied time, say, 2 p.m., will be credited as of the next business day. If this cut-off time is missed, add one business day to the availability schedule.

Bank Account Analysis

Banks are profit-making organizations (or at least they try to be) and as such want each account to be profitable. Most banks are willing to convey most of the information that they use in analyzing the profitability of an account to the account holder. They do this in the form of an account analysis statement. This statement is usually provided each month, although other reporting periods may be arranged depending upon the needs of the customer or the practices of the bank.

Basic Account Analysis Information

Although the format varies widely across banks, account analysis statements usually contain the following basic information: the service activities used during the period, the charges for those activities, and the average balances held during the period. The information contained in a typical account analysis statement is shown in Table 2-8.

Service Charges. The first segment of the account analysis statement in Table 2-8 contains information on the bank services used, the activities in

Table 2-8. Account Analysis for Acme Industries

Summary of Activities for June 1993			
Activity description	Quantity	Price per unit	Total charge
Monthly account maintenance fee	1	12.00	12.00
Deposits made	20	1.00	20.00
Checks deposited	2140	0.07	149.80
Deposit items encoded	2140	0.02	42.80
Checks paid	545	0.12	65.40
Wire transfers	3	15.00	45.00
Coin and currency counting	20	2.00	40.00
	Total service charges		$375.00

Summary of Balances for June 1993	
Average ledger balance	$180,000.00
Float	20,000.00
Average available balances	$160,000.00
Earnings credit rate after reserve requirements	5.40%
Earnings credits on balances	$710.14
Cash fees due (excess credits)	($335.14)

the account for the month, and the charges. Most of the service charges are volume-sensitive; that is, the charge is based on the number of units of the service used. For example, Acme deposited 2140 checks during the month. The dollar amount of the checks had to be encoded by the bank. The charge is $0.07 per check deposited and an additional $0.02 per check encoded, or a charge of $149.80 + $42.80 = $191.60. The total charge for all services used during the month is $375.

Average Balances. The treasurer of Acme maintained an average balance of $180,000 during the month of June. The average float from the deposited checks was $20,000 during the month. (Recall that bank float comes from delayed availability on checks deposited.) The average available balance was $160,000. This is the balance on which the earnings credits are earned.

The bank specifies an earnings credit rate, in this case 6 percent. This credit rate is earned on the balances after reserves. Since reserves are 10 percent of the available balances, the bank credits the account at a rate of 0.90×6 percent = 5.4 percent. This annual rate has to be adjusted to the monthly time period. Most banks make this adjustment by dividing by 365 (366 in a leap year) and multiplying by the number of days in the month. This results in total credits earned of $710.14.

Alternatively, the bank could adjust for the reserve requirements by determining the balances after reserve requirements and then applying the full 6 percent (adjusted to the 30-day monthly rate). The balances after reserve requirements would be $0.90 \times \$160,000 = \$144,000$. Applying the earnings credit rate of $0.06 \times (30/365) \times \$144,000$ will yield $710.14. This is the same amount obtained in the above calculation.

Bank Compensation. Acme received $710.14 in earnings credits on the balances carried during the month, but only had service charges of $375. Since balance credits are at least equal to the service charges, Acme does not have to pay any cash fees for the services used. Since banks cannot legally pay interest on corporate demand deposit accounts in the United States, the bank cannot pay Acme the $335.14 in excess credits. Whether the excess credits are of any value to Acme depends upon the bank's policy with regard to carrying credits over to the next period. If the bank allows a carryover, and if Acme can reduce its balances sufficiently, the $335.14 can be applied to next month's service charges. If the bank does not allow carryover (an increasing trend), Acme loses the excess credits.

What if Acme had generated less earnings credits than service charges for the month? Say the ledger balances averaged only $80,000. With the same float, this would be an average available balance of $60,000. Applying the 5.4 percent rate would generate $266.30 in earnings credits. Acme would have $375.00 − $266.30 = $108.70 in charges not covered by credits.

The bank would bill Acme for the difference of $108.70, to be paid either by Acme writing a check or by the bank debiting the account.

The compensation arrangement is not symmetrical. If earnings credits are insufficient to cover service charges, the company has to pay cash fees to make up the difference. If excess earnings credits are generated, the bank says "Thank you."

Compensation by Balance Credits. What level of balances would allow Acme to cover all service charges, without generating any excess credits? We can use the information from the account analysis statement to determine this balance level. To cover the service charges exactly, Acme would have to generate earnings credits of $375. We can divide the service charges by the earnings credit rate to obtain $375.00/(5.4 percent × 30/365) = $84,490.74. This represents the average amount of available balances that Acme would need to cover all service charges with balance credits. Adding the bank float of $20,000 results in average ledger balances of $104,490.74. If the treasurer could reduce the balances to this level, she could invest the remaining $75,509.26 in securities to generate interest income. If these funds were invested for 30 days at an annual rate of 6 percent, Acme would have earned $372.37.

Can Acme benefit by having the treasurer reduce the balances below the $104,490.74 required to cover the service charges? The answer to this is yes. But how far can the balances be reduced? Assume the treasurer has determined that Acme needs $60,000 in available balances ($80,000 in ledger balances) to provide the desired level of liquidity. If June's available balance had averaged $60,000 instead of $160,000, the treasurer could have invested $100,000 to earn $493.15. Acme would have generated earnings credits of $266.30 on available balances of $60,000 and would have to pay cash fees of $375.00 – $266.30 = $108.70. The cash fees of $108.70 must be subtracted from the interest earnings to obtain the net benefit of $384.45. We know that $372.37 of this came from reducing the balances to the point where there were no excess credits. The remainder, $12.08, came from being able to invest funds at the full 6 percent while losing balance credits at a rate of 5.4 percent. This represents the deadweight loss generated by the reserve requirements.

How to Compensate the Bank

Although banks prefer to have their clients compensate for services by balance credits, they generally allow clients to choose any mix of balance credits and cash fees. What factors favor compensation by balance credits, and what factors favor compensation by cash fees?

Factors Favoring Balance Compensation. First, bank compensation by balance credits is easy. Just leave balances in the account and the service charges are covered. Second, bank charges become "soft" costs. This may be an issue with some public agencies in times of budget stringency. If compensation is with balance credits, bank fees can be reduced, even if it does cost the organization in terms of lost interest. Frequently, the person who is responsible for banking relations is not responsible for investments. In addition, it may be difficult to identify the interest that was lost due to carrying balances to compensate the bank. Third, since banks seem to favor compensation by cash fees, some treasurers are of the opinion that banks will be more willing to make concessions to customers who compensate by balance credits.

Factors Favoring Cash Fees.   First, payment by cash fees may be cheaper due to the reserve requirements on deposit balances. This represents a deadweight loss, because the client earns less on the balances (by ten percent under the current conditions). Second, it is easier to control the payment for services by cash fees. Because the earnings credit rate changes with interest rates, the amount of balances required for compensation will change from month to month. This may present problems in monitoring and controlling the level of balances. Third, payment by cash fees causes an explicit recognition of the cost of bank services and may be an incentive to control banking costs more closely.

Mixed Compensation.   The optimal compensation for most firms will be to use a combination of balance credits and cash fees. The treasurer will maintain available balances at the level necessary to provide the desired liquidity for normal payments. These balances will generate cash fees. If earnings credits from these transactions balances are not sufficient to cover all service charges, the treasurer will pay for the remainder with cash fees.

Summary

We have discussed three types of balances: company book balances, bank ledger balances, and bank available balances. The difference between ledger balances and available balances, called bank float, is due to delayed availability on deposit items. The amount of bank float can be controlled by knowing and meeting a bank's availability cutoff times. Company book balances differ from the bank balances because of both deposit float and disbursement float. Net float, disbursement float minus deposit float, is equal to the difference between the company book balance and the bank available balance. The value of float, a cost for deposit float and a benefit for disbursement float, is determined by the product of the amount of the item, the number of days' delay, and the daily interest rate. A bank account analysis reports the service charges and average balances for a month. Information from an account analysis can be used to determine how the bank should be compensated for services provided. The best compensation method for most firms is to hold balances at the minimum required for transactions or liquidity purposes and pay cash fees for any charges not covered by earnings credits from the transactions balances.

Self-Test

1. Stinson's Supply Company begins Monday morning with $10,000 recorded on its book, bank ledger, and available balances. It receives and writes checks in the amount shown below. Checks received are processed internally for one day before being deposited in the bank. One-half of the checks have a one-day availability delay, and the other half have a two-day availability. Checks written by Stinson are in the mail and clearing system for an average of three days before being presented for payment.

   Required: Determine the company book, ledger, and available balance for each day. Determine the average balances for the week and the average value of the bank float, deposit float, and disbursement float.

Day	Checks written	Checks received
Mon.	$10,000	$16,000
Tues.	$15,000	$ 2,000
Wed.	$ 7,000	$ 6,000
Thurs.	$ 8,000	$ 8,000
Fri.	$18,000	$20,000
Sat.	—	—
Sun.	—	—

2. Tony's Trattoria has an average net float of $55,000. Tony believes that he should maintain an average available balance of $20,000 to cover transactions demands. Tony has the opportunity to earn 9 percent per annum on invested funds.

   Required: Determine the average balance that Tony should keep on the company books to maintain the desired transactions balance. How much would Tony be losing if he tried to maintain the $20,000 as an average book balance instead of an available balance? (Assume a 360-day year and a 30-day month for convenience in calculation.)

3. Kores, Inc., has service charges of $500 per month at its bank. The bank offers an earnings credit rate of 6 percent per annum. Kores has bank float of $10,000. Determine the level of ledger and available balances that Kores should maintain to compensate the bank with earnings credits and not generate any excess credits. (Assume a 360-day year and a 30-day month for convenience in calculation.)

3

Paper Payment Systems

Introduction

High Test Steel receives regular checks denominated in Mexican pesos from a large customer in Monterrey. High Test deposits these checks in a local bank and considers its cash "collected." When checks are written on the local bank account, they sometimes bounce even though company books appear to show a positive cash balance. What High Test's cash manager fails to realize is that a check does not really represent cash value but only the order to transfer cash value from one bank account to another. The actual transfer of value usually takes place with some time delay to permit banks to move the check from one place to another. In the case of a Mexican check the bank does not give credit until that check is returned to Mexico, exchanged for a dollar-denominated check at the prevailing exchange rate, sent back to the deposit bank, and then passed through clearing channels. This process may take several weeks before High Test actually receives cash value it can use to pay employees or invest. A better understanding of how the payment system actually works would have helped the cash manager make better use of High Test's cash resources.

Types of Payment Systems

A payment system refers to how cash value is transferred from one party to another. It includes (1) policies and procedures for crediting and debiting balances, (2) a medium (or media) for storing and transmitting payment information, and (3) financial institutions that process the information flow. An effective cash manager possesses a firm understanding of how payment systems work. In the United States we have several types of payment systems. Some are based on physical media such as paper or metal, and some are based on electronic communications. In this chapter we discuss the physical payment systems: coin and currency, paper check, and credit cards. In the next chapter we discuss wire payments and ACH payments. Before we can understand payment systems, however, we have to discuss the role banks and the Federal Reserve play in the payment system.

Commercial Banks

A commercial bank is defined as a depository institution that takes deposits and makes business loans. There are other depository institutions besides commercial banks. Savings and loan associations and mutual savings banks also take deposits, but they have not been heavily involved in making commercial loans or servicing corporate customers. They were organized primarily to fund residential housing. Credit unions take deposits and make loans but are limited to doing business with credit union members. A small-business proprietor may be a credit union member and obtain credit union services. On the whole, corporations deal primarily with commercial banks for credit and other banking services.

Deposits at Commercial Banks

Banks provide cash management services to firms in several areas: (1) they store the firm's cash in deposit accounts, (2) they help firms collect and disburse cash, (3) they provide short-term loans, (4) they provide several short-term investment opportunities, (5) they serve as a fiduciary for the firm's retirement funds, and (6) they provide consulting services in cash management and other fields. In this chapter we focus primarily on the first two roles, storing and moving cash value. Later chapters discuss banks' additional roles in cash management.

Time Deposits.   There are two main types of deposit accounts at a commercial bank: time deposits and demand deposits. For a time deposit, the cash must be held in a bank for a specified time period. A savings account is a type of time deposit, and a certificate of deposit (CD) is another type of time deposit. Because the interest rate paid on a savings account is relatively low, most corporations do not hold such accounts. Banks publish schedules of rates they are willing to pay on CDs, basing the rates on the amount of time the cash is left in the CD. A two-year CD, for example, may pay a 4.5 percent annual rate, while a five-year CD may pay a 5.2 percent annual rate. Longer-term CDs almost always give higher interest rates than shorter-term

CDs. Once the CD is purchased, the holder must keep the CD for the time specified in order to be paid the quoted interest. If the CD is cashed in early, some or all of the interest may be lost. Regular CDs are not sold to other parties before maturity. On the other hand, large-denomination CDs offered by larger commercial banks are called *negotiable CDs* and may be bought and sold before maturity.

Demand Deposits.   Demand deposits, as the name implies, may be withdrawn at any time by the presentation of a check or other valid transfer instruction. Demand deposits are checking account balances. Current bank regulations prohibit corporations from receiving interest on demand deposits. On the other hand, individuals, partnerships, and not-for-profit corporations can receive interest on demand deposits.

A related type of account available to corporations is a money-market deposit account (MMDA). While these accounts do pay interest, a corporation is limited in the number of withdrawals it can make from the account each month. Because of this limitation, corporations generally do not use MMDAs.

Another type of account that is available to proprietorships and nonprofit corporations is the so-called super NOW account. *NOW* stands for *negotiable order of withdrawal,* meaning that the piece of paper used to withdraw funds from the account is not technically a check even though it looks and is processed like one. In earlier days when laws forbade that interest be paid on any demand deposit accounts, the NOW was used to withdraw funds from a savings account, and so it escaped the provision of the law. A NOW account is essentially a checking account that pays a variable interest rate depending on the average or minimum balance in the account during the month. Usually the rate is fairly low, but there are no restrictions on the number of checks that may be written against the account. Proprietorships and non-profits should use super NOW accounts rather than regular checking accounts. Banks differ in how they compute interest on these accounts, and so it is advisable to shop around for a good rate and a bank that will base the interest on the average balance and not the minimum balance. Also be aware that some banks levy heavy charges if the minimum balance in the account falls below a certain level.

Reasons for Demand Deposits.   Why do corporations keep money in demand deposits earning no interest? Such an account is highly liquid, meaning that cash may be transferred out on a moment's notice. The task of the cash manager is to keep just enough in demand deposits to provide the firm with needed liquidity while at the same time not keeping too much cash in a nonearning account. Some observers think that Congress may eventually permit corporations to earn interest on demand deposit accounts. Until that happens, one of the cash manager's primary tasks will remain balancing between demand deposits and interest-bearing investments.

Compensating Balances.   Firms may also keep cash in demand deposits to compensate the bank for its services. When a demand deposit is used in this way, it is called a *compensating balance.* A bank may require that credit lines, check processing charges, and other services to the firm be compensated by holding demand deposit balances. While a bank may not pay explicit interest on demand deposits, it may nevertheless give "earnings credits" based on the level of balances held. Chapter 2 discusses this topic in more detail.

Eurodollar Deposits.   Large banks can help a firm put its money in another type of deposit account called *Eurodollar deposits.* Cash placed in a Eurodollar deposit actually goes into the account outside the United States. U.S. dollars held offshore are called Eurodollars even though they may not all be in Europe. A firm may want to put some cash in Eurodollar deposits because these accounts often give a higher rate of interest than that paid by commercial banks in the United States. There are two types of Eurodollar deposits. Eurodollar time deposits (TDs) are held in the bank until they mature. Such deposits cannot be sold before maturity. Eurodollar CDs are sold by London banks and may be bought and sold in the secondary market before maturity.

The Federal Reserve System

The Federal Reserve Act of 1913 created the Federal Reserve System ("the Fed") in an effort to improve bank supervision, to develop a nationwide clearing system for checks, to serve as the U.S. Treasury's banker, and to provide liquidity by making emergency loans available to banks. One of the Fed's other major roles is to manage the country's money supply and therefore attempt to manage economic growth.

Organization of the Fed.   The Federal Reserve is headed by a group of seven board members (one of whom is chair) appointed by the President of the United States to 14-year terms. The long term supposedly insulates the members from political influence. There are 12 semiautonomous district banks located in:

1	Boston	7	Chicago
2	New York	8	St. Louis
3	Philadelphia	9	Minneapolis
4	Cleveland	10	Kansas City
5	Richmond	11	Dallas
6	Atlanta	12	San Francisco

In addition there are 25 branches of the Fed in other major cities and 11 additional regional check processing centers. In each of these 48 cities, check processing occurs. Each commercial bank in the country is assigned to one of the twelve district banks. The Fed also processes checks for other financial institutions besides banks.

Federal Reserve Regulations.   The Fed regulates banks through a series of regulations that enforce acts of Congress relating to banks. While the details are generally not of interest to cash managers, it is crucial to note that these regulations influence the kinds of services banks can provide to corporations. Therefore, to some extent, Fed regulations define the tasks cash managers must accomplish. For example, since banks are generally forbidden from taking deposits across state lines (there are many exceptions), if a corporation receives out-of-state deposits, the cash manager must devise methods of collecting deposits at multiple banks. One bank usually cannot provide that service.

Federal Reserve Deposits.   The Fed can be thought of as a banker's bank. Whereas a firm keeps some of its cash in bank deposits, commercial banks keep some of their cash in Fed deposits. These deposits are called Federal Reserve balances or deposits. Currently a bank must keep on average 10 percent of its demand deposits with the Fed. The rate may change from time to time as the Fed tries to stimulate or slow the economy. The Fed does not pay interest to banks for these deposits.

Reserve deposits are very important in the movement of cash. In fact, cash moves between bank A and bank B when the Fed reduces bank A's reserve balance and increases bank B's reserve balance. Payment instructions passing through the Fed cause the reserve account balances to go up and down. The instructions may take one of several different forms: a piece of paper called a check or an electronic message called a wire transfer.

It may be a little unsettling to realize that about 80 percent of what we call liquid "cash" is actually in the form of magnetic information residing in bank and Fed computers. Only 20 percent of the most liquid measure of the money supply exists as coin and currency. If one includes time deposits and other short-term investments, then coin and currency represents only a tiny fraction of the money supply.

Payment Systems

There are five basic types of value transfer in the United States. The first three are primarily paper-based and rely heavily on manual processing: coin and currency, check, and credit/debit cards. The last two are primarily electronic-based and rely more on automated processing: wire transfer and automated clearinghouse transfers. This chapter discusses paper-based payments, and the following chapter treats electronic-based transfers.

Coin and Currency

For coin and currency, cash value information is stored on the medium of metal or paper. Value transfer is simple: the payor just hands the medium to the payee and value is transferred. No intermediary is needed since value is represented by the medium itself and whichever party holds the medium holds the value. Coin and currency transactions are simple, but this simplicity has its drawbacks. The most serious drawback is lack of security and control. Any party that can get possession of the coin or currency holds the value. No record need be maintained that would allow an auditor to reconstruct the path of the cash flow. This makes currency the payment of choice for drug dealers, thieves, tax evaders, and others who do not want to leave any transaction record. Money laundering means taking cash flows through several unrecorded currency transactions before finally leading the cash flow through one of the other more useful but recordable payment mechanisms.

The coin and currency payment system is also used by firms that sell products and services directly to consumers over the counter. Transit authorities, fast-food chains, petroleum retailers, vending machine servicers, and other retailers, for example, receive a large percentage of their revenues in the form of coin and currency.

Security.   Since coin and currency represent value to the bearer, security problems are a prime attribute of this type of payment. The cash could be lost or stolen at the collection point or in transit to the deposit bank.

To cope with security problems at the collection point, two approaches are used. The first involves physical security. Safes, locked cabinets, thick-glass partitions, alarm systems, police guards, and armored cars are among the devices used to physically protect coin and currency. There is, of course, a cost-benefit trade-off for any type of security measure. Armored car service to pick up cash deposits may be expensive but may be cost-justified in some high-risk areas.

The second security measure, often used in conjunction with physical security measures, is creating a flow of information that is independent of the flow of cash. A cash register is a device that helps create an independent information flow. When cash is received from a customer at the grocery store checkout line, the salesperson tallies up the bill on the cash register and receives a cash payment. The cash register thereby creates a source of information about how much cash should have been received that is independent of the cash being deposited into the register drawer. At the end of the day the amount in the till should correspond to the amount totaled by the register. The customer is involved as an independent third party verifying the register receipt. The salesperson cannot charge the customer $30, deposit $20 in the till, and pocket the extra $10. Either the customer would notice that the register tape was only for $20, or the register tape and the till amount would not agree.

The need to create an independent information flow is one reason firms insist that employees strictly follow cash register procedures, especially when it comes to changing information from previous transactions. To void a previous transaction, a cashier must often receive approval from a third party and/or receive a signature from a customer that money was given back.

With cash, there is some risk that the depositing firm's employees or bank employees may steal the firm's deposited coin and currency. For example, when the firm's night manager deposits cash in a night depository, there is a risk that either the manager or a bank employee could remove cash from the bag and claim that the bank must have lost some of the deposited cash. To protect itself and the firm, the bank or firm may insist that a locked deposit bag be used and that a representative of the firm be present when, the next day, the bag is unlocked. Most firms and banks, however, consider the inconvenience to be more troublesome than the risk of loss.

Counting Coin and Currency. Counting coin and currency is another drawback to this payment mechanism. Although some banks and firms have automated optical scanning equipment to count currency, most currency is manually counted. On the other hand, coins are most often counted by mechanical devices. Coin counters sift coins by size into slots and count each coin. A less expensive process is to separate coins into denominations and weigh them. Though less accurate, the cost saved is often more than the value of added accuracy. Banks, of course, charge fees for counting and packaging coin and currency. Sometimes the firm can do the job less expensively itself.

How Banks Treat Coin and Currency. If a coin and currency deposit is made before the time the bank specifies as its cutoff time (often around 3 or 4 p.m.), the deposit is credited to the depositor's available balance that day. It simply means that the firm can use the balance to cover clearing checks or invest in securities on the same day it makes a coin and currency deposit. However, sometimes the bank will require that the coin and currency be counted before they are considered deposited. This may mean that a 3:30 p.m. deposit (if the cutoff time is 4 p.m.) may not receive availability until the following business day if the bank takes 45 minutes to do the counting. Night deposits are almost always credited the following business day. Keep in mind that the Fed allows banks to count all coin and currency deposits as part of their Federal Reserve balance requirement. The bank gets credit for a counted coin and currency deposit, and, therefore, the depositor should be able to have use of those funds, too.

The Role of the Fed in Coin and Currency. The Fed acts as an intermediary by transporting coin and currency from banks that have a surplus to banks that are net users of coin and currency. Banks try to schedule deliveries of coin and currency to and from the Fed to coincide with projected needs of their depositors. Although banks generally have a buffer of coin and currency in bank vaults, they may require advance notice if a firm is going to remove a significant amount at any one time. Banks and the Fed carefully monitor the coin and currency flowing through their operations and sort out defects. Worn coins are melted down, and old bills are shredded. Government mints produce new coins and print new bills continually to replace old ones and meet the demands of the banks.

Checks

In the United States, approximately 53 billion paper checks were processed in 1992. Checks are the most popular payment system for smaller corporate-to-corporate and consumer-to-corporate transactions. In contrast to coin and currency, checks do not contain value themselves. A check is an order written on a piece of paper to transfer cash value from one bank account to either another bank account or to the payee in some other form (such as currency). A commercial bank or other depository institution and sometimes the Fed are needed to process the check and make the value transfer. Checks may be written for any size and are relatively inexpensive to process.

Since the check passes through at least one bank, it provides an auditable third-party record of a transaction. A check is somewhat limited in the amount of information it may contain to explain the transaction. Therefore, a check transaction is typically accompanied by additional information that explains the transaction to the payee. For example, the payor may want to include a remittance advice with a check. The remittance advice explains which invoices are being paid with the check and notes any discounts or other deductions applied. This information enables the payee to credit the appropriate account.

How Checks Transfer Value. Figure 3-1 illustrates how a $1000 check transfers value from a payor in Boston to a payee in San Diego.

Check Preparation. The payor in Boston writes, types, or prints the amount both in numbers ("$1000") and, to lessen the chance of error, in words ("One thousand dollars and 00/100 cents"). The check is then signed by hand or stamped by a signature facsimile plate. Some companies have recently started using computerized "signatures" that include a few special print characters that can only be printed with a specialized printer. One or more signatures may be required by the payor for control purposes. With the exception of very large dollar checks, banks usually do not exam-

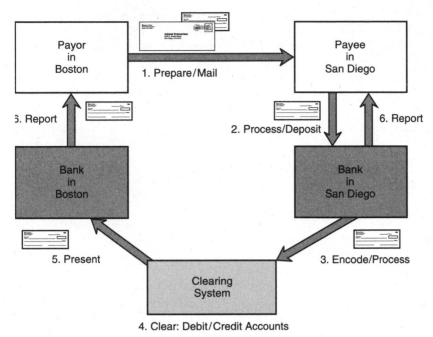

Figure 3-1. The check clearing process.

ine check signatures. They may, however, reject a check if only one signature is present but there are two signature lines.

Most checks are preprinted with the payor's bank account information contained in magnetically readable characters along the bottom of the check. Larger-volume check writers, however, may want to use check stock and print not only the payee and the amount but also the bank account information at the time the check is prepared. Chapter 7 explains why that may be desirable.

Check Delivery. A great majority of checks are sent through the mail although some are sent by courier or are hand-delivered.

Payee Processing. Upon receipt of the check, the payee or its designated service provider processes the check by recording the amount on the payee's cash ledger and applying $1000 to the payor's account receivable.

Deposit. The payee endorses the check and deposits it in a demand deposit account in its San Diego bank. Assuming the check is deposited before the bank's cutoff time, the payee receives a $1000 ledger (accounting) credit for that business day. The payee, however, may not be able to use the funds until one or more business days' delay. This availability delay was discussed in Chap. 2.

Bank Processing. The San Diego bank records information about the check, credits the payee's account, and physically transports the check to whichever clearing system it decides to use to move the check back to the Boston bank. We discuss clearing alternatives later in this chapter.

Check Clearing.   Clearing means giving credit to the San Diego bank, transporting the check to the Boston bank, and deducting $1000 from the Boston bank's account with the clearing system. Actual value transfer is nothing more than a computer entry. The clearing system may be the Federal Reserve System, or it may be another bank. Since the check must be physically transported through the clearing system, a time delay is necessary to ensure that the payee does not receive credit for the check before the payor receives a debit.

Check Presentment.   The check is physically presented by the clearing system to the Boston bank, which subtracts $1000 from the payor's demand deposit account.

Reporting.   Both banks provide reports to their respective parties in the form of monthly bank statements and, sometimes, daily deposit reports.

Information Contained on a Check

MICR Line.   Checks are processed by automated equipment that magnetically or optically reads essential information from the check. This information is stored along the bottom of the check and includes the payor's bank number, the payor's account number, the sequence number of the check, and the amount of the check. Figure 3-2 shows where this information is located. The line of information is called the MICR (Magnetic Ink Character Recognition) line.

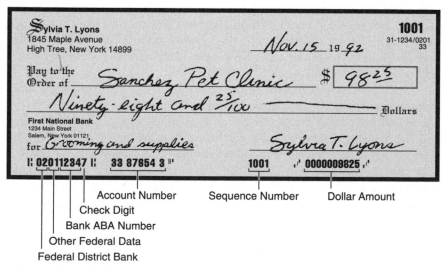

Figure 3-2. Sample check.

The first two digits of the bank number block indicate in which Federal Reserve district the payor's (sometimes called the drawee) bank is located. For example, "01" in the first two places would indicate the first Fed district, or the Boston Fed. Numbers greater than 12 indicate the drawee is a savings and loan or a credit union. The next two digits are used by the Fed to specify branches or regional check processing centers within a district. The next four digits refer to the identification number of the payee's bank. Each bank (or other depository institution) has a unique number within a particular Fed district. These eight digits are called the bank's transit routing number. The ninth digit is a check digit for preventing misreads.

Alternative Check Clearing Procedures. There are several different types of clearing procedures whereby a check can find its way from the payee's deposit bank back to the payor's disbursement bank.

On-Us Checks. If the payee deposits the check in the same bank on which it is drawn, the check is termed an *on-us* check. Clearing the check involves just one bank. Accounting entries are made to decrease the payor's account and increase the payee's account. Assuming the cutoff time is met, the payee receives value and the payor loses value at the end of that business day.

Local Clearinghouse. Financial institutions in the same metropolitan area often operate a local clearinghouse. Each institution has an account with the other, and clearing then involves a daily exchange of checks between all parties. Bank 7 presents checks to bank 8, and bank 8 presents checks to bank 7. The net difference in the two presentments is handled by the accounts the banks have with each other or is reported to the Federal Reserve for settlement.

Correspondent Banks. Banks often use correspondent banks (banks that have accounts with each other) to collect their checks. A suburban bank, for example, may have an account with a larger bank that is a member of a large metropolitan clearinghouse. The smaller bank would deposit into its account with the large bank all checks drawn on clearinghouse members. This gives the small bank access to the clearinghouse without meeting the volume criteria often imposed on members.

Federal Reserve Banks. The Fed also acts as a check clearing agent. As discussed above, each depository institution has a reserve account with the Fed. Checks deposited at the Fed are reflected by an increase in the bank's reserve account. The bank, however, may not receive credit for the check on the day it is deposited. The Fed also has an availability schedule based on where the check is drawn. This delay is necessary so that the Fed can transport the check back to the drawee bank. The Fed operates an extensive transportation system for moving checks from one check processing point to another.

Direct Send to a Correspondent Bank. A deposit bank may choose to bypass the Federal Reserve clearing system and send a check directly to a correspondent bank in a distant city. This is called a *direct send*. The bank may choose to do this because it can receive available credit for the deposit faster than if the bank were to go through the Fed. Large banks use direct sends to get faster availability for their customers and compete with other banks.

Why Should a Cash Manager Care about Check Clearing?   The faster the bank can process and clear a check back to the drawee bank, the faster the depositor can get access to cash. If your firm is using a small local bank to process your checks, you may have to wait several days before you can use your deposited cash. This is especially a problem if a significant portion of your checks are drawn on distant banks. The small bank is probably not a member of a local clearinghouse and probably uses the Fed or correspondent bank to process out-of-area checks. If you were to switch to a larger bank that was a member of a local clearinghouse and that had an aggressive direct-send program, you may be able to use your funds one or two days earlier. Suppose you have check revenues of $5 million per year, and suppose a more aggressive bank could make funds available to you two days earlier than your present bank. The value of this at 10 percent opportunity cost is

$$(\$5,000,000 \ / \ 365) \times 0.10 \times 2 = \$2740/\text{year}$$

If the cost of using the more aggressive bank is $500 per year, then the savings would be $2240 per year.

The decision to go with a more aggressive bank depends on the type of checks the firm receives. If a firm has a large volume of checks that are drawn on out-of-area banks, it may pay to find a bank that has an aggressive direct-send program. If the vast majority of a firm's checks are drawn on local banks, then direct sends (which, by the way, cost more) may not be cost-justified.

Returned Checks.   What happens when a check bounces? A check may be returned for several reasons. The account may be closed or nonexistent. Or there could be insufficient funds (account balance smaller than the amount of the check). The check must then be processed back through the same channels. Routing a check backward is often a tedious task, taking several business days. For this reason, banks often impose a hold period on accounts. This means that the account holder may not remove the deposited amount from the account even if the funds have been declared available. The bank must allow sufficient time to make sure the check doesn't come back as a return item. The law now limits the number of business days in the holding period. The timing may change but is currently one business day for local checks; two for nonlocal, in-state checks; and five for out-of-state checks. After a check has become available but before the hold period elapses, the bank may pay the firm earning credits for the amount of the deposit. Many banks waive the hold period for established corporate customers. In addition, depositors who normally keep several days' worth of deposits in the bank anyway will not even notice the effect of the hold period.

Payment Instruments Related to Checks.   Other payment instruments are similar to checks in the way they clear but different from checks in several features.

Payable through Draft (PTD).   A check is drawn against a bank, but a payable through draft is drawn against the payor and is not automatically paid by the bank even if there are funds in the account. When a PTD is presented to the drawee bank, the payor has 24 hours in which to honor or to refuse payment. Insurance firms may allow field agents to issue PTDs for claim settlements. Before the PTD reaches the bank, the insurer can make sure the claimant has a valid insurance policy and all else is in order. If not, the insurer simply declines to cover the check. A PTD is therefore like a check with an automatic stop payment built in.

Preauthorized Check (PAC).   Checks are drawn by the payor and sent to the payee. A preauthorized check is a check drawn by the *payee* against the account of the *payor.* The MICR line of the check contains the payor's account number and bank number. The payor must, of course, authorize the payee to draw such a check against its account. PACs are most commonly used when the payor makes regular payments of the same amount. They are, therefore, useful for mortgage, insurance, budget utility, and other similar repeat payments. As we see in the next chapter, an automated clearinghouse payment turns out to be simpler and cheaper than a paper PAC.

Money Order.   The risk in accepting a check is that the payor may not have sufficient cash in the disbursement account to cover the check when presented. A money order greatly reduces this risk because the payor simply has a more creditworthy third party (such as the post office, bank, drug chain, etc.) write the check. The money order is then drawn against a more creditworthy payor. The post office or bank that issues the money order assumes payment responsibility because the payor has already paid in coin and currency before the money order is produced.

Depository Transfer Check (DTC).   A DTC is simply a preprinted check with the payee's name already filled in. No signature is needed. The amount is entered when the transfer amount is determined. Therefore a DTC is valid only for prespecified payments and may not be directed to other parties. One of the most popular uses for DTCs is in the area of cash concentration, which means the movement of cash from distant depository banks into the firm's concentration bank.

Traveler's Checks.   Traveler's checks are prepaid drafts similar to money orders. The risk of insufficient funds is transferred to the bank or other party that issues the traveler's checks. For protection of the holder, traveler's checks require the holder to sign the check a second time when the check is used.

Government Warrants.   Warrants are like checks, but they may not be paid until certain requirements are fulfilled and/or until a specified date. The state of California issued warrants to employees during the summer of 1992 because the state had no authority to spend cash. The warrants were not cashable until a later date.

Sight Draft.   Very similar to a warrant, a sight draft must generally be accompanied by other documents showing that the terms of a transaction have been met. Sight drafts are often used in foreign trade transactions.

Time Draft.   Like a sight draft, a time draft is payable subject to documentation but, in addition, is subject to specified time delays. Time drafts are also used in foreign trade transactions and are sometimes tied to letters of credit.

Check Availability Schedules and Actual Time Delays.   As discussed in Chap. 2, banks assign availability based on where a check is drawn. However, the actual delay depends on whether the availability posted time is met and on what day of the week the deposit is made. Availability schedules are always stated in terms of business days, but the cash manager is concerned about calendar days. Table 3-1 shows the relationship between scheduled availability and actual time delay.

For example, suppose the availability schedule designates that a check drawn on any bank in Chicago receives one-day availability if deposited by 11 a.m. You take a check to the bank by 9 a.m. Tuesday morning, and the

Table 3-1. The Relationship between Scheduled Availability and Actual Time Delays

| | Business-Day Availability Delay | | |
| | | Actual business delay in receiving availability | |
Scheduled availability delay	Weekday deposit made	Before posted availability time	After posted availability time
0	Mon., Tues., Wed., Thurs.	0	1
	Fri.	0	3
1	Mon., Tues., Wed.	1	2
	Thurs., Fri.	1	4
2	Mon., Tues.	2	3
	Wed., Thurs., Fri.	2	5

Note: An intervening holiday adds one day to all nonzero time delays.

Example: If a deposit were made Monday before the posted availability cutoff time and the availability delay is two days according to the schedule, the check becomes available two business days later (Wednesday). If the same type of check were deposited after the posted time on Monday, it would become available three days later (Thursday). If the same check were deposited after the posted time on Wednesday, the check would be available five days later (Monday). If that Monday were a holiday, the delay would be six days (Tuesday).

bank processes it by 10:45 a.m. Therefore, the check makes the posted time. You would be able to use the cash in that account one business day later, or Wednesday morning. If you deposited the check at 11:30 a.m. Tuesday, you have missed the posted time and would not be able to use the funds until Thursday.

Now suppose you deposited the same Chicago check on Friday at 11:30 a.m. Since you missed the posted time for one-day availability, your check would not become available until two *business days* later. Saturday and Sunday are not counted, so that means your check would not be available until the following Tuesday. Very few banks have availabilities greater than two days, and many large banks do not have availabilities longer than one.

If a bank holiday falls on one of the days between the deposit day and availability day, an extra day is added. For example, if the following Monday were a holiday, the Friday 11:30 deposit mentioned above would not become available until *Wednesday.*

Reducing Losses from Check Payments. While checks are harder to misappropriate than cash, firms face the risk that unauthorized employees or outsiders may use checks to steal cash from the firm. There is also a risk that the firm may be paid by check and then find the check is returned after services or goods are already provided to the customer.

Example 1: Employee Embezzlement. One firm in the Chicago area discovered that an employee was writing unauthorized checks to himself and then falsifying payment records to hide the embezzlement. This process went on for 18 months and resulted in several hundred thousand dollars in losses. By the time the auditors discovered the crime, the employee had disappeared. The firm sought compensation from the bank because the employee's signature was not one authorized according to the signature card on file with the bank. As mentioned above, banks do not generally verify signatures of checks against authorized signature cards. The court ruled that the firm itself could have examined its own paid checks and thereby discovered the problem itself in a timely way. The court decided that common banking practice did not require the bank to examine all signatures. This case serves to illustrate some of the principles of secure check payment system design:

1. Check stock should be physically secure and inaccessible to unauthorized employees.

2. The employee writing checks should not have access to the system that authorizes payments and the system that reconciles paid checks. These three functions must be separated so that embezzlement would require at least three people to conspire together.

3. Audits should be made on a timely basis and include examination of signatures and payees.

4. Reconcilement should examine check sequence numbers. Those who misuse checks often remove checks from the backs of checkbooks where their absence is not as noticeable.

Example 2: Bad Checks.   A local grocery store used to accept customers' personal checks for purchases. A study revealed that bad checks accounted for nearly 2 percent of revenues for one year. That amount was sufficiently large to completely outweigh potential profit that year. Something had to be done to reduce the number of bad checks and yet not alienate regular customers. Among steps taken were the following:

1. Only local (same county) checks were accepted unless the customer had a check guarantee card. A check guarantee card uses the credit card system to verify that the customer has adequate credit to cover the check. If the check is returned, the store can send through a credit card voucher and be assured of payment.

2. Computer software was installed to accompany the store's scanning system. The software kept a file on the bank account numbers of past customers. When a store clerk entered the account number into the computer, the number was searched to make sure that account had a history of valid checks. If the account had no record or had been responsible for past bad checks, a message would come up on the register and the clerk would require a check guarantee card. Hence, regular customers were able to have their checks honored quickly.

3. A sign announcing a large bad-check fee was posted near each register.

4. Cashiers received training in spotting fraudulent checks and IDs.

5. The store employed the services of a check collection agency. Any remaining bad checks were turned over to this agency for collection. If such checks could be collected, the agency charged about 50 percent of the value of the check.

The result was that the store now receives very few bad checks and, at the same time, has not inconvenienced its regular customers.

Credit Cards

Many retail businesses accept credit cards for consumer payments. A credit card voucher is similar to a check in some ways but very different in others. Like a check, a credit card voucher represents the promise of the customer to pay the receivable at a later time. With a check, the time delay is only a few days, but with a credit card voucher the delay is at least a month; and if the card holder chooses, payments may extend out years. To avoid uncertain time delays, the payee almost always discounts the credit card voucher at a bank and accepts less than the face value of the voucher. Checks in the United States, by banking regulation, are not discounted.

The amount of the discount is subject to negotiation between the merchant and the bank and depends on prevailing market interest rates. For example, a small retailer may receive a 3 percent discount on credit card vouchers, while a large nationwide chain may negotiate a 0.7 percent discount. When a credit card voucher is presented to the bank, the firm's account is usually credited with the discounted amount the same business day.

The credit card voucher or an electronic equivalent of the voucher is then sent through the credit card system back to the customer's credit card bank. That bank then bills the customer, who pays at a later time. As long as the merchant performs the appropriate verification steps, the voucher passes from the merchant to the credit card processing system *without recourse*. This means that if the customer doesn't pay the bill, the merchant does not have to refund the money already paid to the merchant.

There are currently large communication networks that operate credit card verification systems. For a monthly fee plus a per-transaction fee, a seller can use this system to have on-line access to credit card verification data. The seller enters the customer's card number into the system, which then checks for invalid cards, canceled cards, and accounts that have exceeded their credit limits (or that would do so with the transaction being verified). If the transaction is allowable, a verification number is sent back to the merchant. This number is the merchant's protection. Accepting a transaction without that number could mean that the merchant would have to pay back the amount of the transaction if the customer could not pay. Depending on the system used, verification could take several minutes to complete. In high-volume stores, the delay may mean lost business. Newer hardware and advanced networks are making the verification process faster, so that even fast-food chains are beginning to accept credit cards. We will return to a discussion of the use of credit cards for payment in collection systems in Chap. 6.

Debit Cards

Debit cards differ from credit cards in one primary way: with a debit card purchase the customer's account is debited very soon after the transaction occurs. In addition, the debit takes place automatically without the customer initiating a payment. A debit card is associated with a bank account, whereas a credit card does not necessarily have an associated bank account. There are two basic types of debit card systems.

Debit Card Systems On-Line with Banks.   Some debit card systems are associated with one specific bank or a consortium of banks. A customer makes a purchase with a debit card, and the merchant enters data about the customer account number and transaction amount. The data flow directly to the bank, and the customer's account is verified and debited that day. These debit card systems are somewhat limited because the merchant and customer would have to be using the same bank or consortium of banks.

Debit Card Systems Using the ACH.   A more general system uses the nationwide electronic payment network called the Automated Clearing House. Data about the purchase and the customer's account number are entered into a credit card–like inquiry system. If the transaction is verified, then the system creates an ACH debit (see Chap. 4 for details) and the debit is sent through the ACH network to the customer's bank. Any bank that can handle an ACH debit can be used, and, therefore, this system is more universal than the one just discussed.

Under both systems the customer's account is debited either the same day or the next day. A debit card does not extend credit and permit the customer to pay later.

Summary

Coin and currency probably account for the majority of payment transactions in the United States. While such transactions are convenient and inexpensive, coin and currency pose major problems for corporations: risk of loss and lack of control. Because value is stored directly in the medium, coin and currency systems must have careful safeguards built around them. These problems make this payment mode unattractive for larger-dollar transactions.

Checks represent the most common way to move money between businesses and between many consumers and businesses. Because banks are involved, there is a third party to each transaction and therefore a record is kept. Checks do not represent value—rather, they represent the order to transfer value between parties using one or more banks. It is important for the cash manager to understand the time delays involved in check transactions. Not only are checks delayed by the mails or other delivery system, but bank processing can cause delays of up to six calendar days. While checks are more secure than coin and currency, checks also present problems because they may be returned or may be misused. Regardless of which physical payment system is used, care must be taken to prevent theft and provide for adequate controls.

Credit and debit cards represent a viable way of moving money between consumers and corporations. Although fees are taken out by each intermediary, credit and debit card payments offer consumers great convenience.

Self-Test

1. Explain when cash would be available to you from a deposit that has the following characteristics. Assume the bank's cutoff time is 4 p.m.
   a. Coin and currency deposited and counted by 11 a.m. Monday.
   b. Coin and currency deposited at 11 p.m. Monday.
   c. A check deposited and processed by 7:30 a.m. Monday when the check has an 8 a.m. deadline for one-day availability.
   d. A check deposited and processed by 9:30 a.m. Monday when the check has an 8 a.m. deadline for one-day availability.
   e. A check deposited and processed by 9:30 a.m. Thursday when the check has an 8 a.m. deadline for one-day availability.
   f. A check deposited and processed by 9:30 a.m. Thursday when the check has an 8 a.m. deadline for one-day availability and the following Monday is a bank holiday.
   g. A check deposited and processed by 9:30 a.m. Wednesday when the check has an 8 a.m. deadline for two-day availability.

2. Acme Sales receives $3 million on average in check payments every month. Acme currently processes its own checks and takes them to Small Local Bank for deposit. Small Local Bank gives an average availability of two business days. Acme is considering Large National Bank as an alternative. Customers would mail checks directly to a post office box at Large National. This would save two days' average processing time at Acme and give one-day better availability over Small Local Bank. Large National Bank would be more expensive, with net additional costs of about $200 per month. If Acme considers its opportunity costs to be 10 percent per annum, what is the annual net benefit or net cost to Acme? You may assume other costs will remain the same.

4
Electronic Payment Systems

Introduction

Branham Plastics pays its employees on a biweekly basis. Several years ago, supervisors noticed that each payday the productivity at the plant nose-dived as employees took long lunch hours or left work early in order to cash their checks in town about 20 miles away. That has changed thanks to electronic payments. Branham no longer has productivity problems on paydays because employees are paid through direct payroll deposit into their bank accounts. Employees are happy because they know they will be paid on time even if they are out of town. Supervisors are happy with higher productivity, and accounting is happy because it doesn't have to wait for checks to clear.

There are two primary types of electronic payment systems in the United States: Automated Clearing House payments and FedWire transfer. In addition, there are several ways to transfer cash across international borders.

Automated Clearing House Payments

An ACH payment is analogous to a paper check, but the information, instead of being carried on a piece of paper, is stored in computer data files. The data files are transmitted between banks via a communication network. The advantage of moving information via computers and telecommunications rather than paper is that the sorting and transmitting processes are much faster, less error-prone, and less expensive. In addition, the timing of electronic payments is considerably more predictable than that of paper checks.

The term *ACH* has evolved over time to take on several different meanings. ACH is short for ACH payment. It may also refer to the entire system of moving payment information. But strictly speaking, an ACH is the regional organization of people, procedures, and computer hardware and software that receives, processes, and sends payment information to other parties (banks and other ACHs). So don't be too confused if someone says to you, "We'll use the ACH to send you an ACH."

Originating in 1972, this system is the newest payment system in the United States. ACH payments were initially designed with social security recipients in mind. Their use has now expanded to cover almost any type of consumer or corporate payment from direct deposit of payroll to large corporate-to-corporate payments. While the government was the largest user in the past, corporations now account for about 60 percent of total transaction volume.

Operation of the ACH

The Federal Reserve is the primary operator of most of the 20 or so regional ACHs, but financial institutions are actually the owners. Of the approximately 13,000 commercial banks in the country, about 12,000 are members of an ACH. Many savings and loan associations and credit unions are also ACH members. The National Automated Clearing House Association (NACHA) is the member-run organization that sets policies for the ACHs and performs other functions such as product design, research, pilot programs, and marketing.

Relative Costs of an ACH Payment

A check may cost $0.10 to $0.50 in bank charges; an ACH transaction can be much less expensive, say, $0.02 to $0.05. In contrast, a corporation would pay about $10 to $30 for a wire payment. The reason ACH payments are less expensive than checks is that no physical medium need be moved from one location to another. This can also be said for wire transfers, but wire transfers are generally one-at-a-time, labor- and security-intensive transactions. ACH payments are usually batch-processed. This means that many transactions (even tens of thousands) are processed in one batch. Hence, labor costs are very small on a per-transaction basis. By the way, if you want to send just one ACH payment, it may cost you as much as a wire transfer would cost.

Steps in an ACH Credit Payment

To illustrate how a corporation would use the ACH system to make a batch of payments to a group of vendors, let's follow through the sequence of

steps from the payor in Boston to many payees including one payee in San
Diego using ABC Bank of San Diego. As shown in Fig. 4-1, the example
accomplishes the same result as the check transaction we discussed in
Chap. 3. Assume the payment instructions are sent on Monday for settlement Tuesday.

1. The payor in Boston prepares a computer file containing payment
   instructions. The file contains information for each payment including
   the payment amount, receiving bank's transit routing number, sending
   bank's transit routing number, settlement date (when the cash should
   go into the receiving bank), payee's account number, payor's account
   number, and code indicating that this is a credit transaction. The format for this information is defined by the bank and firm working
   together. It may be in an ACH format, or it could be in the bank's proprietary format.

2. The payor transmits the data file to its Boston bank. Of course, it doesn't
   matter where the bank is located if the firm's computer has a modem
   and a telephone line. This bank is called the originating financial institution (OFI). Suppose this takes place on Monday.

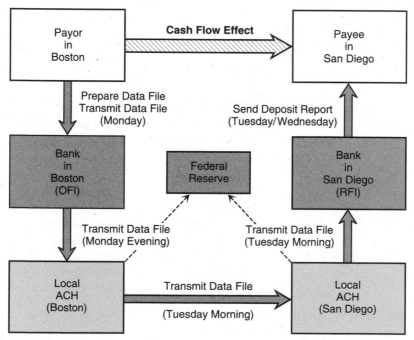

Figure 4-1. ACH credit transaction.

3. The OFI generates a batch of ACH-formatted transactions from the information received from the payor. The OFI checks for errors and prepares summary information for the payor. The OFI sorts out any on-us transactions (transactions involving the OFI or its own branches and processing affiliates) and debits these accounts on Tuesday.

4. The OFI merges the payor's transactions with transactions the OFI has received from other firms. Monday night a combined data file (minus on-us transactions) is transmitted to the local ACH of which the OFI is a member.

5. The local ACH sorts out all transactions pertaining to its member financial institutions and sends the remaining transactions to other ACHs around the country. This process takes place Monday night and early Tuesday morning. Each ACH in the system combines all transactions it receives into a data file for each financial institution in its region. This data file is transmitted to each receiving financial institution (RFI) Tuesday morning.

6. The ABC Bank of San Diego receives its ACH file from its local ACH Tuesday morning and posts transactions to each account.

7. On Tuesday each ACH in the system notifies the Federal Reserve Bank in its area of the amounts to debit and credit banks receiving ACH payments.

8. Also on Tuesday, cash value is subtracted from the payor's account at the Boston bank and cash value is added to the payee's account in the San Diego bank.

Timing of ACH Settlement

In this example, the ACH credits are initiated on Monday, while value is transferred or settlement occurs on Tuesday. The custom is to speak of settlement rather than availability for ACH payments although the effect is the same. ACH transactions are initiated one day and settled some time in the future. The shortest a delay can be is overnight. For payroll, banks require at least two days for settlement. While there is usually a higher charge for one-day settlement, the reason at least one extra day is allowed for direct deposit transactions is that banks don't do things in real time. When they receive an ACH data file on Wednesday morning, that information may not be posted to individual accounts until very late Wednesday night. An employee expecting cash in her bank account on a Wednesday payroll day would have it but not know about it or be able to withdraw it until Thursday. This would lead to frustrated employees. So a Wednesday settlement day for payroll must be initiated on Monday. Tuesday morning the transaction comes through to the employee's bank, but the payment specifies a settlement date of Wednesday. This enables the bank to *memo-post* the employee's account Tuesday evening, noting that funds will be available Wednesday morning.

Why would the firm want to pay for payroll Monday? It doesn't have to. In an ACH transaction, the payor's account is not touched until the settlement date, and so it doesn't matter really when ACH payments are initiated. We are only concerned about when the settlement date occurs. Of course, some banks want to make sure we have enough money in our account when we initiate ACH credit payments—or we better have a credit line arranged to cover payment in case something goes wrong with our cash flow by the time the settlement date rolls around.

ACH Credit Applications

How would you use ACH credit payments in your organization? The largest corporate application is in the area of direct deposit of payroll. There are many other applications for ACH credits. The government uses the ACH to make social security and other transfer payments. Some corporations are using ACH payments in place of checks to pay vendors. ACH credits may be used for moving cash from a concentration bank to a disbursement bank. Dividend and coupon payments sometimes make use of credits. Many states have begun requiring firms to pay state taxes via ACH (however, most applications here are ACH debits, discussed later). In the future, you may experience pressure from large vendors to pay electronically since it helps them save check processing costs.

Organizations may benefit from direct deposit and other forms of ACH credit payments in the following ways:

1. *Convenience to payee.* Most employees, for example, come to see direct deposit as a fringe benefit since they don't have to spend time and money traveling to a bank to cash a check. They are paid even if they are not in town to pick up their checks. (Of course, you may find some employees who want a check so they can cash it and never have to tell their spouse how much they make!)

2. *Lower administrative costs.* Many firms find that it is cheaper to send ACH payments than it is to prepare, sign, and distribute checks. Some of this advantage is negated because employees and other payees must be given some form of documentation explaining the payment amount and detailing deductions, etc. For corporate payments, as we see later, this can also be done electronically.

3. *Lower error rates with electronic systems.*

4. *More certain cash flows.* The ACH settlement date is specified in advance so there is no uncertainty about cash flow timing.

5. *Fewer escheated checks.* What's that? When you send a check to someone and they don't cash the check for a period of time (the time differs by state), the amount of the check becomes the property of the state. This happens with any check that goes uncashed whether misplaced, mismailed, etc. With ACH payments, if an account has been closed, the payment quickly comes back to the payor. ACH payments are automatically "cashed" on settlement date or returned. Hence, the escheat problem is eliminated.

ACH Debit Payments

An ACH debit transaction is identical to an ACH credit transaction except that the payor and payee change places. The instructions the payee sends to the bank include a designator that the transaction is a debit instead of a credit. The result is the reverse cash flow from the RFI to the OFI. Figure 4-2 shows the steps in a simplified ACH debit transaction in which the payee in San Diego initiates a debit payment drawn on the payor in Boston.

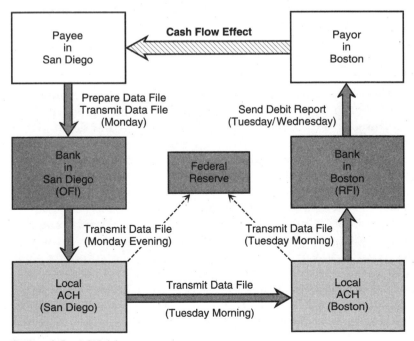

Figure 4-2. ACH debit transaction.

Of course, it wouldn't work to permit just anyone to send through a debit transaction drawn on your bank account without your permission. NACHA has established a procedure specifying that the payor must first give permission before the payee can draw debits against the payor's account.

ACH Debit Applications

Where can you use debit transactions? One of the fastest-growing corporate uses is for cash concentration. Concentration is used when you have more than one bank receiving your deposits. Suppose you own seven retail stores located in seven different cities. Each store makes daily deposits into a local bank located near the store. You could instruct your primary or concentration bank to draw ACH debits against each of the seven deposit banks. The following morning, the cash would be moved into your concentration bank from which you can more effectively manage the combined pool of cash. Chapter 6 describes this process in more detail.

You may also use ACH debits to collect payments from distributors, from dealer networks, and from customers. For example, insurance companies use debits to collect premium payments, and mortgage servicers collect monthly mortgage payments using ACH debits. ACH debit systems achieve a higher degree of customer acceptance when the payment amount is constant from month to month. Consumers hesitate to permit vendors to have open access to checking accounts.

ACH Formats

Format refers to how payment information is organized in a computer file. There are several different formats for various ACH applications. The most commonly used format is the preauthorized payments and debits (PPD) format, which is used for direct deposit of payroll, government transfer payments, and consumer debits. Cash concentration and disbursement (CCD) is the most common corporate-to-corporate format. It is used for cash concentration and payments that do not require accompanying remittance information. In recent years, NACHA developed what is called the corporate trade payments (CTP) format, which allows a firm to send remittance information with the payment. It is essentially a CCD payment with addenda records attached. A newer format called the corporate trade exchange (CTX) format is designed to combine electronic data interchange (EDI) remittance information with a payment. It is much like a CTP payment, but the addenda records are formatted in a commonly accepted standard [an American National Standards Institute (ANSI) X12 820 transaction]. That means that the receiver of the remittance information can use EDI translation software to automatically apply the payment to accounts receivable (more on this in Chap. 5). Some fairly large firms pay their suppliers using CTX payments. The main drawback is that many banks can't process a CTX. In the future, you may have firms approach you about the possibilities of getting paid or paying using CTX. Don't panic. It's quite analogous to direct deposit of payroll for your employees. The advantage of CTX is that the accompanying information will be computer-processible. Or you can just ask your bank to print out the remittance information and send it to you on paper.

What to Watch for in the Future with ACH

New ACH services are being introduced each year that make the ACH system more suitable to corporate needs. For example, there is currently a proposal (that may well be implemented by the time this text is published) to have ACH settle transfers the same day they are initiated. This means that you could use much less expensive ACH transfers in many cases where you now use very expensive wire transfers.

The ACH system continues to evolve as user needs and technology change. The rate of growth in ACH payment volume is far faster than the growth in paper checks. Some of the newer corporate ACH payments (CTP and CTX) are growing at a rate of over 100 percent per year. Each year more and more banks are able to handle the various formats, and more large firms are pushing smaller trading partners into the ACH world for corporate-to-corporate payments. It is inevitable that your firm will sooner or later be faced with a major trading partner that requests your participation.

Wire Transfers

Wire transfers enable you to move cash from one bank to another very quickly—within a few minutes or hours. There are several kinds of wire transfers in the United States. The most commonly used transfer for corporations and consumers is FedWire. A second kind is used by New York City banks and foreign banks having offices in New York City. This transfer system is the Clearing House Interbank Payment System (called CHIPS). There are other wire transfer systems for moving cash between countries. We spend most of our time discussing FedWire since you will be more likely to use that kind of wire.

FedWire

The FedWire system is operated by the Federal Reserve. Recall from our discussion about banks in the last chapter that each financial institution must maintain cash balances at a Federal Reserve Bank. FedWire is a real-time communication system in which one bank instructs the Fed to move some of that bank's reserve balance to another bank. The message goes through the Federal Reserve communication system that same day—usually within a few minutes after instructions are sent.

Steps in a FedWire Transfer.   Figure 4-3 illustrates the steps in a Fed-Wire transaction. Suppose a payor in Boston wants to wire $5000 cash from a bank in Boston to a payee in San Diego. The transaction would proceed with the following steps:

1. The payor in Boston instructs its Boston bank to make the transfer by giving the account number from which the cash is to be withdrawn, the transit routing number of the receiving bank, the account number of the payee in San Diego, and the amount of the transfer. There are several ways the payor could send these instructions:
   a. Written instructions.
   b. Telephone instructions (which would be verified by giving identification codes and/or confirming return calls from the bank to the payor).

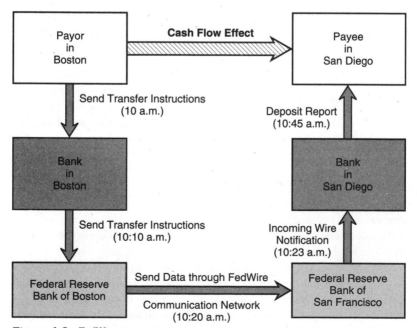

Figure 4-3. FedWire transaction.

c. Computer message to the bank's wire transfer computer (again verified by identification numbers and/or callback procedures). Sometimes wires are "preformatted," meaning that the sender has set up in
advance a list of accounts and banks it intends to pay in the future.
Only wire instructions to accounts on the list are permitted without
specific authorization from a designated officer of the sender's firm.
This reduces the possibility of unauthorized wires.

2. The sending bank checks the sender's available account balance to make
sure it is greater than the amount of the wire. If the wire request exceeds
the available balance, the bank then checks to see if the sender's available credit line will cover the wire. If not, the wire transfer people check
with the sender's relationship officer (lender) to get approval.

3. Assuming all is in order, the bank takes $5000 cash from the sender's
account and uses a telecommunication link to transmit wire instructions
to the Federal Reserve wire transfer computer system. The Fed sends
back a confirmation number, which can be used as a tracer to find mis-
directed wires.

4. The Fed deducts $5000 from the sending bank's reserve account and
adds the same amount to the receiving bank's reserve account. If the
receiving bank is in a different Fed district, then the message is sent to
that Fed and that Fed adds $5000 to the receiving bank's account. A
complication arises if the sending bank does not have enough cash in its
reserve balance. There are rules governing such a "daylight overdraft,"
but they usually don't have any apparent effect on corporate transfers.
Occasionally a transfer request is delayed until the bank has incoming
transfers that build up its Fed reserve account.

5. The receiving bank in San Diego adds $5000 to the payee's account and
notifies the payee. This is done through a monthly statement, balance
reporting system, electronic message, or some other type of communication agreed upon by the payee and receiving bank.

All these steps take place on the same day (except perhaps the notification of the payee by the receiving bank).

Issues Involving FedWire

Cost.　Because they are one at a time, labor-intensive, and highly secure,
FedWires cost corporations from $10 to $30 per transaction. Preformatted
wires are less expensive than free-format transfers since the bank bears less
risk with preformatted wires. Both the sending and the receiving institution impose a charge, but charges for receiving are usually less than for
sending. Considering costs at both banks, the total cost of a wire may be
from $15 to $40.

When would this high cost be justified? If the interest lost by moving a cash balance by a slower mechanism is more than the added cost of the wire transfer, then the wire should be used. For example, suppose you learn of a $40,000 deposit that has just arrived at one of your deposit banks. You have no need for the balance at that particular bank, and you could earn 9 percent if you moved the cash into your concentration bank from which the $40,000 would become part of your investment portfolio. You have the choice of transferring the cash using an ACH, which would take one day and cost $1. Or you could transfer the cash using a FedWire, providing immediate access to the cash, but at a cost of $30. Which mechanism would be best?

The cost of the wire would be $29 more than the ACH, but the wire would enable you to earn extra interest for one day. How much is that worth?

$$\$40,000 \times (0.09/365) \times 1 \text{ day} = \$9.86 \text{ savings}$$

In this case using a wire is not justified. The extra $29 cost of the wire is not justified by the extra $9.86 in interest earned by getting the cash in one day earlier.

Remittance Detail. FedWire allows for only about 240 characters of ancillary information to accompany payment instructions. This is sufficient for many transactions but may not be sufficient for transactions requiring extensive trade information such as payments involving partial shipments, trade and cash discounts, damaged goods, or complex terms. It is not uncommon for a firm to receive a wire transfer from some party and then not know how to apply the payment to its receivable system.

Confirmation and Notification. While the Fed provides a confirmation number, that does not confirm that a transaction actually reached its destination. That number only gives a means to trace an errant wire. In addition, the receiving party may not be notified of an incoming wire until a monthly statement is sent weeks after the transaction. Both of these features cause wires to be less useful than they might be for corporate payments.

Debit Transaction. FedWire can also be used to draw cash from a bank account. Such transactions are called *wire drawdowns.* Of course, as in the case of ACH debits, for such a transaction to take place, the bank to be debited would have to have permission from the payor.

Conclusion about FedWire. FedWire transfers are useful when you need to move a large amount of cash from one place to another and you can't anticipate the need to do so in advance. If you know in advance you have to move $50,000 from one bank to another, an ACH transfer could be used. An ACH costs much less than a wire transfer (especially when done in large batches) and settles on a day that is known with certainty. Sometimes, wires are required by contractual arrangement such as closing on real estate transactions. However, since FedWire is quite expensive compared with other transfer mechanisms, a good rule of thumb is "Use wires only for emergencies, contracts, and surprises."

Clearing House Interbank Payment System. CHIPS actually transfers greater dollar volume than FedWire. It is an electronic communication system that connects most major financial institutions in New York City and that is operated by the New York Clearing House Association. The system is essentially a netting system, meaning that only information and not value is transferred during the day. At the end of the day, net amount due to or from each member institution is computed. For example, if Chase Manhattan Bank owes $20 million to Chemical Bank and Chemical owes $18 million to Chase, then at the end of the day only $2 million need be transferred from Chase to Chemical. With many banks in the system, the net position of each of the 20 or so main banks is computed at the end of the day and the net transfers are reported to the Federal Reserve Bank of New York, which then debits and credits appropriate accounts. Nonsettlement banks settle through correspondent balances with the larger banks. Most dollar-denominated foreign transactions actually settle through CHIPS.

For all practical purposes, if you ask your bank to send cash through the wire transfer system, the bank may use either CHIPS or FedWire, and it won't matter much to you which one they use. Charges are usually the same for either. Some times of the day, your bank (if it can use CHIPS) may find it easier to get a wire through CHIPS than FedWire or vice versa.

International Wire Transfers

If you are growing like most firms, you may find yourself having to send or receive international wire transfers. There is no Federal Reserve at the international level and therefore no reserve balances to move about making FedWire and CHIPS possible. Instead, international wire transfers depend on correspondent balances to move cash. Remember that correspondent balances are just demand deposit accounts that banks keep with each other.

Suppose you want to send $5000 from your bank in Kansas City to Barclays Bank in London, England, to pay for some imported machinery. You would notify your bank that you wanted to make the transfer. Your bank would check to make sure you have $5000 in available balances. It would then check to see if it had a correspondent relationship with Barclays. Let's suppose it does have such a relationship. Your bank would send a message to Barclays via a telex, fax, TWX, or other means indicating that $5000 should be moved from the Kansas City correspondent account with Barclays into the payee's account. The Kansas City bank would also deduct $5000 from your account. Barclays would notify the payee that a $5000 deposit had been received.

This process may not be so simple if your bank does not have a correspondent relationship with Barclays. Suppose your bank does not. Then it
must find a bank with whom it does have a correspondent relationship and
which also has a correspondent relationship with Barclays. That bank might
be, for example, First Chicago. Your Kansas City bank would send an electronic message to First Chicago, telling it to subtract $5000 from its corre-
spondent balance and then to send instructions to Barclays to add $5000 to
the payee's account.

In the past, this type of transfer was frequently subject to errors, especially when the transfer involved countries where other languages were spoken. To solve the error problem and to provide consistent formats for wire
instructions, banks got together to form the Society for Worldwide Interbank Financial Telecommunications, quite a mouthful. SWIFT, as it is more
easily called, is a communication network that connects banks and allows
well-structured financial messages to be sent. Since the messages are structured, it doesn't matter which language is spoken by the person processing
a SWIFT message. The recipient's account number is always in the same
field, the amount is always in the same field, etc. So every party to the transaction knows exactly what to do. Settlement is still through correspondent
balances, but many fewer mistakes are made with SWIFT.

SWIFT also handles other messages such as balance reporting, security
transactions, inquiries, and certain trade documents used in banking transactions. In the future it may handle other trade documents such as invoices,
bills of lading, and purchase orders. But, at the moment, SWIFT only carries bank-related transactions.

Legal Liability and Electronic Payments

Over the past several years, most states have adopted a new section, Section
4A, of the Uniform Commercial Code (UCC). UCC 4A defines who is liable
and to what extent when an electronic payment is made. The law applies to
wire transfers and ACH credits but not to ACH debits and also not to consumer transactions. Consumers are protected under Regulation E of the
Federal Reserve regulations. In its most elementary form, UCC 4A says that
if the bank is using commercially reasonable security and commonly
accepted banking practices, then the bank is not liable for any consequen-
tial damages caused by errors that may enter into transaction systems. If the
bank is proved negligent, then the firm could obtain a refund of transactions charges and lost interest income but no damages caused by lost business or other expenses the firm might have to incur.

For example, suppose you send wire transfer instructions to your bank,
requesting that $10,000 be sent to your account in Kentucky. A hacker is
able to intercept the instructions and insert his own account number in the

field that shows where the transfer should be sent. As long as the bank used commercially reasonable security measures to protect against fraudulent use of its computer system, the bank would not be liable for returning the lost $10,000.

As another example, suppose you instruct the bank to wire $10,000 to a vendor. The bank through its negligence loses the transfer instructions and fails to perform the wire. As a result, the vendor is not paid and cancels a large contract with your firm, causing you to seek another vendor who happens to charge much more for the same product. Your loss is $100,000. Must the bank cover your loss? No—the bank may be liable to refund to you the price of the transfer and any interest you lost in not moving funds into an interest-bearing account. But the bank would not be liable for the $100,000 in consequential damages.

Of course, a bank and its customer can enter into a business contract that spells out responsibilities more favorable to the customer than UCC 4A. The contract would supersede UCC 4A. It would be helpful for you to sit down with your banker and have her explain what would happen under various scenarios. If you are concerned, you may want to modify your electronic transfer agreements with the bank.

Summary

Chapters 3 and 4 are designed to build your understanding of the payment systems in the United States. This information is essential groundwork for understanding how cash moves from place to place. We build on this foundation in later chapters where we explore how to improve your organization's collection, concentration, and disbursement systems.

Electronic transactions provide a useful alternative to paper-based transactions and for many corporate purposes are superior to paper. ACH transactions are generally much faster than paper-based payments. In addition they are usually much less prone to errors and are far less labor-intensive than paper payments. Wires are useful in moving cash about very quickly. While wires are generally quite expensive relative to paper and ACH payments, wires are important in moving large amounts of cash when cash flows cannot be anticipated with any accuracy.

What is the "best" payment mechanism to use? That, of course, depends on the nature of the transaction in question.

Self-Test

1. Given each of the following situations, indicate which payment mechanism(s) would overall be the most effective in terms of lowest cost, best information, best security, etc. Explain your recommendation.

a. Many small consumer payments mailed to a corporation on a monthly basis

b. Payment of $10,000 to the state government for sales tax on a date known well in advance

c. Payment of $5000 to another corporation for 34 invoices, each involving cash discounts and disputed amounts

d. Payment of $1350 to a salaried employee

e. International payment for $35,000 to a Kenyan firm

f. Concentrating cash from 22 retail outlets depositing cash and checks into 22 small, suburban banks

g. Monthly life insurance premiums from policyholders.

h. Dividend payments to stockholders that are institutional investors (e.g., pension funds, bank trust departments)

2. Suppose a wire transfer of $20,000 arrives at one of your deposit banks without warning. You already have excess balances in that bank, and so the $20,000 will not earn you anything of value. You would like to transfer the amount into a concentration bank where you would invest it at 10 percent annual interest rate. Possible transfer mechanisms are (a) a paper check costing $0.25 and taking three days to become available, (b) an ACH debit costing $0.10 and taking one day to settle, and (c) a wire transfer costing $35 (total costs from both banks) and settling immediately. Considering both transaction cost and lost interest, determine how much each payment alternative costs.

3. You have a balance of $60,000 in a deposit bank that pays an effective earnings credit rate of 3 percent per annum. If you move the cash into your concentration bank, you could earn 10 percent per annum. You could use either an ACH transfer that would settle in two days or a wire transfer that would settle immediately. The ACH costs $1.50, and the wire $11.50. Which transfer mechanism would be best?

5

Electronic Data Interchange and Bank Information Systems

Introduction

Stoermer Devices, Inc., produces plastic wire guides for large computer companies. Stoermer has always received paper purchase orders from customers, mailed out paper invoices, and received checks in payment for its products. One day Stoermer's largest customer announced that, starting in three months, purchase orders would no longer be mailed but would be sent via EDI. Invoices from Stoermer would be expected also to be sent via EDI, and payment to Stoermer would be made via electronic funds transfer (EFT) payments through the ACH payment system. Stoermer's cash manager was asked to learn about EDI and its impact on the firm's cash flows and information systems. How could the company comply with this important customer's request? What is involved in doing EDI and EFT?

Most businesses today are very paper-intensive. Purchase orders, shipping documents, catalogs, price lists, quotes, invoices, remittance advices, and payments are all paper-based. Information to produce the paper document is frequently stored in a computer, printed on paper, mailed to the receiver, and then keyed into another computer. A recent survey showed that almost 80 percent of the documents transacted between firms use paper as the medium to carry the information. The remainder are mostly phone and some facsimile transactions. According to Federal Reserve statistics, 97.3 percent of all payments are by paper check. Paper implies the need to key and rekey information and transport the paper from one location to another. Compared with electronic alternatives, paper transactions are slow, labor-intensive, error-prone, and uncertain.

EDI and its subsidiary technology involving payments, EFT, offer an alternative to paper-based business documents and paper checks. The impact on firms—both small and large—can be significant. EDI documents can move faster and with greater accuracy; labor costs may be reduced; inventories can be lowered; payments are more certain, and customer-vendor relationships can be strengthened.

The reason you may be interested in EDI is that more and more of your customers and suppliers are pushing their trading partners to engage in EDI transactions with them. The automotive, grocery, transportation, warehouse, and retail industries are all very advanced in the use of EDI. Some firms are mandating EDI. Others specify EDI as a prerequisite to maintain primary-supplier status.

You may think that small businesses are immune from pressures to use EDI. This is not true. Small suppliers are under constant pressure to satisfy the needs of large customers that demand EDI. Besides, there appear to be benefits for even small firms that implement EDI. This chapter clarifies what we mean by EDI and EFT and shows how EDI is applied to financial transactions. In addition, we discuss how you get information—much of it also electronic—to and from your bank. Bank information is vital to a cash manager in determining cash balances, cash inflows into various accounts, cash outflows from disbursing accounts, bank compensation, and information about bank loans.

Electronic Data Interchange

Definitions of EDI, EFT, and Financial EDI

Electronic Data Interchange. EDI is the movement of business data electronically between or within firms in a structured, machine-retrievable data format that permits data to be transferred without rekeying from a business application in one location to a business application in another location. A business application as defined here is a computer program that performs a business function such as purchase order processing. Essentially what you are doing is sending a document like a purchase order to a vendor, but the purchase order data are in the form of a computer data file and not on a piece of paper.

Electronic Funds Transfer. EFT can be seen as a subset of EDI in which the two parties to the transaction are financial institutions and the result is value transfer from one financial institution to another. We already discussed EFT in Chap. 4, but we wanted to put EFT in the context of EDI. As discussed there, ACH and FedWire are the two most commonly used forms of EFT in the United States.

Financial EDI. You may hear the term *financial EDI*. While some people use this term for EFT and invoices, strictly speaking, financial EDI refers to EDI messages between a payor and its bank or a payee and its bank. Such messages include debit or credit notifications, remittance data collected by the bank for the payee, balance data, returned-check data, and lockbox information. Some of these items are discussed in later chapters.

Figure 5-1 illustrates the relationship among "ordinary" corporate-to-corporate EDI, EFT, and financial EDI.

Relationship of EDI to Other Electronic Messaging

To clarify our concept of EDI, it is useful to compare EDI with other forms of electronic messaging. Figure 5-2 arrays the various forms of electronic messaging along a continuum from totally unstructured data to highly structured data. Facsimile transmission, on the far left of the continuum, represents the transfer of totally unstructured data. Any information that can be reduced to paper can be faxed. Fax is simply the digitized image of the business document. While fax gets the data to the receiver rapidly, the

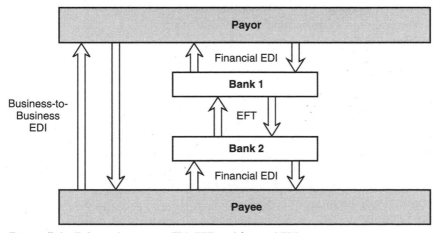

Figure 5-1. Relationship among EDI, EFT, and financial EDI.

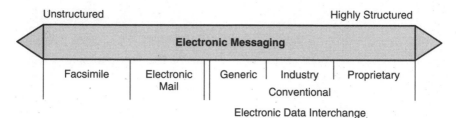

Figure 5-2. EDI and electronic messaging.

receiver would not be able to enter the image directly into a business application without, at worst, manually keying in the printed image or, at best, manipulating a character file that is produced by scanning the fax sheet. Electronic mail also moves business data electronically but generally uses a free format rather than a structured format. While an E-mail message is computer-processible, an E-mail purchase order would have to be manually edited before it could be processed by an order entry application program. EDI is more highly structured data, so that the information sent from one firm can be entered into a business application automatically without rekeying. Data from another firm can be treated the same way. We see below that standardized formats make this automation possible.

How an EDI Transaction Works

An EDI transaction generally follows the sequence of steps illustrated in Fig. 5-3. This transaction might represent how one of your largest customers might deal with you and how you might respond. We assume that purchase order data are stored in your customer's computer in a format unique to your customer. If the customer were to send these data directly to you, you would not understand them. So the purchase order data are first translated into one of the standard formats such as ANSI X12. To enable your computer and your customer's computer to talk to each other, the EDI message might be sent through a value-added electronic mailbox (or VAN, which stands for value-added network). You have your EDI software call the VAN several times a day to see if there are any messages in your mailbox. Upon finding this message, the EDI purchase order is downloaded to your computer and, with the use of your translation software (explained below), the data are reformatted to produce an electronic purchase order in the format you need for processing in your order entry system. The information from the purchase order forms the basis for all remaining documents.

After you receive the purchase order, an electronic acknowledgment is produced by your translation software and sent back to the customer. The

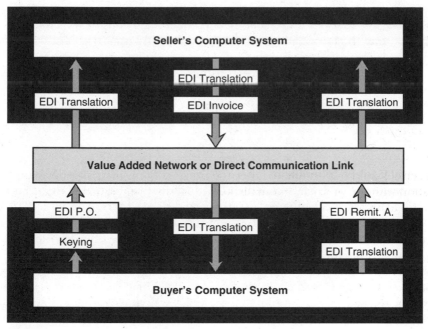

Figure 5-3. Data flow using EDI.

acknowledgment tells your customer that the purchase order has been received and was technically okay. This is called a functional acknowledgment and is a very important feature of EDI. Your order entry system then generates instructions to the warehouse or service center regarding the order. The order entry application may also feed into ("bridge into") the invoicing application so that you can prepare and send an electronic invoice. When the customer receives an EDI invoice, similar steps are followed. Your customer can now easily match your electronic invoice with the customer's purchase order. A payment advice and payment can then also be made through EDI/EFT.

The result of this kind of data exchange in comparison to a paper-based transaction system is faster response to customer needs, lower labor costs from keying, fast acknowledgment of an order, reduced error rates, and better management information. An important derivative benefit from EDI is that inventory may be reduced due to a faster reorder cycle.

Supporting Infrastructure for EDI Implementation

How would you actually do EDI? As a computer technology, EDI is very simple: all it really involves is the transmission of a data file from one computer to another. While firms have been capable of performing such a task for over 30 years, EDI has only recently become a major business factor. The reason is that the infrastructure to help you do EDI has only recently fallen into place. This infrastructure includes three components: generic formatting standards for handling most business documents, readily available translation software you can purchase off the shelf, and VANs to help your computer talk to anyone else's computer. Of course, another important factor is the emergence of low-cost microcomputers, but we will not dwell on that point.

Generic Format Standards

Proprietary EDI.   EDI started out with individual, usually large firms wanting to send electronic data to their trading partners. The large firm would define the structure of the message and impose it on its trading partners. The trading partner would have to comply in order to remain a supplier of the large firm. The small firm had to develop a software program to read the large firm's messages. You can understand how this approach would become problematic if the small firm had to service many large firms, each having a unique proprietary system. Proprietary data formats work well enough when you deal with only one, two, or a small number of partners, but the value is lost when you need to exchange data with a wide number of firms. It should be clear that widespread implementation of EDI could not proceed without the development of data format standards that would enable many different firms to send data using the same format.

Generic EDI.   Starting in 1968, representatives from the railroad industry, and later other transportation industries, got together and worked out a way to send electronic documents using generic EDI message formats. This is a powerful, yet simple, idea. With a generic standard, everyone who subscribed to that standard would be able to read the message. Out of this early effort, a number of standards bodies have arisen, some in the United States and others in Europe and in other parts of the world. To date, formats for over 200 different documents have been defined in North America. The definition of each document is generic enough to accommodate the needs of virtually all potential users. Records are typically variable in length and contain many optional fields and extensive code lists.

The primary body in the United States that defines standards is the American National Standard Institute's Accredited Standards Committee X12 (ANSI ASC X12, or simply X12). In Europe, another standards body works on standards under the auspices of the United Nations: EDI for Administration, Commerce and Transport (EDIFACT) to develop worldwide standards. This group has defined about 40 standards to date, and many more are planned.

Industry Conventional EDI. Some industries have adapted generic EDI format standards to make EDI easier to implement within the industry. These conventions are simply customized formats of the more generic standard EDI formats. Examples are the automotive, chemical, petroleum, utility, electric, grocery, and electronic industries. Each uses its own variant of ANSI ASC X12 standards. If your firm is in one of these industries, your industry group may help you implement EDI by providing implementation guides, seminars, newsletters, etc.

What Is an EDI Format Standard? Standards specify how the data are to be organized and sent to trading partners. You will want to be familiar at least with the terminology of EDI standards. The starting point of an EDI standard message is a fundamental building block called a *data element* (see Fig. 5-4). A data element is one piece of information such as price, unit of measure, name, or quantity. Data elements are defined in a *data dictionary,* which defines how many characters a data element should contain, what type of data it is (floating point, alphanumeric), etc. Related data elements are grouped together into *data segments.* A line item on an invoice is a data segment that might consist of the elements of quantity, unit of measure, price, product code, item description, and source of price. Data segments are defined in a *data segment directory.* Data segments are strung together into documents, or *transaction sets.* A purchase order is a transaction set, as is a functional acknowledgment.

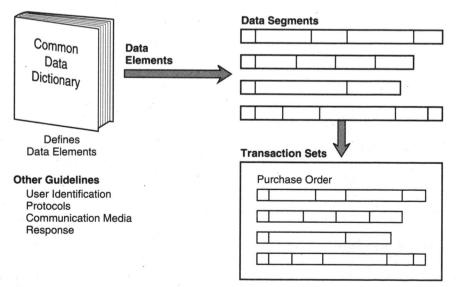

Figure 5-4. How standards organize data.

Each transaction set carries a three-digit identification number. Here are just a sampling of some of the transaction sets that have been defined in the X12 group of standards:

810   Invoice

812   Credit/Debit Adjustment

813   Electronic Filing of Tax Return Data

820   Payment Order Remittance Advice

822   Customer Account Analysis

823   Lockbox Deposit Information

830   Planning Schedule with Release Capability

850   Purchase Order

855   Purchase Order Acknowledgment

856   Ship Notice/Manifest

997   Functional Acknowledgment

As you can see, many different kinds of documents have been standardized. This is only a partial list of the 200-plus EDI documents.

Translation Software.   Fortunately, the EDI format standards are becoming very easy to use because EDI translation software handles the task of translating your data into standard EDI message and back again. Translation software actually has three functions, shown in Fig. 5-5. First, *data mapping* takes data stored in your firm's business application in a unique format and reformats the data for input into the EDI formatting software. Second, *EDI formatting* software operates on these input data and translates them into the desired EDI format. Third, *communications* software dials the trading partner or communication network and sends (or receives) the EDI formatted data to (or from) another party's computer.

Over the past five years, at least 70 software firms have developed off-the-shelf EDI translation packages available at costs ranging from several hundred to several thousand dollars that support EDI translation on a microcomputer.

Value-Added Networks.   When firms first began using EDI, most communications went directly between trading partners. In recent years, a service has been developed that solves some of the problems of direct communication. Direct computer-to-computer communication with a trading partner requires that both firms (1) use similar communication protocols, (2) have the same transmission speed, (3) have phone lines available

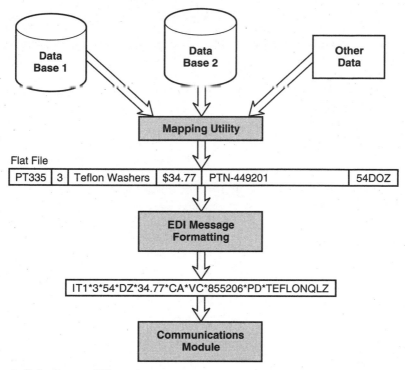

Figure 5-5. Steps in EDI translation.

at the same time, and (4) have compatible computer hardware. If these conditions are not met, then communication becomes difficult if not impossible. A VAN can solve these problems by providing services that enhance the basic phone network.

VANs provide you with the following kinds of services: *Mailboxing* permits you to send EDI messages to your customer or vendor where the messages will be stored until your trading partner is ready to retrieve them. This means you don't have to worry about when your trading partner's computer is up. *Protocol conversion* means that your firm can use a communication package with one transmission protocol and yet communicate with a trading partner that uses another protocol. Some VANs offer *standards conversion,* meaning that a transaction set could be received in one format and then translated into another format before being sent to a trading partner. VANs may provide *implementation assistance* in the form of consulting, software, and training of trading partners. All VANs permit *line-speed conversion,* so that messages may be received and sent at whatever line speed the user requires. Most VANs also *gateway* with other VANs, so that a firm can communicate with trading partners that do not use the VAN used by the firm.

Financial EDI and Corporate Payments

The Problem with Payments.   When a consumer pays an electric utility bill, the payment is usually accompanied by a "turnaround document" or bill stub that tells the utility how much is owed. The bill stub and payment almost always match, and often the bill stub is computer-readable. So it is relatively easy for the utility to apply the customer's payment to the appropriate account receivable. Likewise, when a consumer makes a mortgage payment, the transaction is a simple one, and there is usually no question about the purpose of the payment. On the other hand, corporate payments are not so simple. One payment may cover several invoices and may involve cash discounts or deductions for other purposes. Hence, a remittance advice is usually desirable for a corporate payment.

The problem arises when a corporate payor wants to pay via one of the EFT methods. As we discussed in Chap. 4, most formats (FedWire, CCD, PPD) do not permit very much in the way of ancillary information. Thus there are other alternatives you may consider for making corporate payments.

Alternatives for Using the ACH with Financial EDI

1. *Pay with ACH (CCD format) and send remittance information to the payee through your VAN or other connection.*   In other words, do not send the remittance information through the bank. Communicate electronically to the bank only simple payment information and include perhaps a reference number to the remittance advice sent through other channels. This works well because virtually all banks can process CCDs. The main problem is that the supplier will have to match up the payment from the bank with the remittance advice through EDI channels.

2. *Pay with a CTP.*   The CTP format for an ACH payment permits many addenda records (see Chap. 4) that could contain remittance information. The payment and remittance detail flow together, and the receiver doesn't have to match up payment information with separate remittance detail. The drawbacks are two: many banks can't process CTPs, and a vendor receiving a CTP would have to manually process it.

3. *Pay with a CTX.*   A CTX, as we discussed in Chap. 4, is a CTP but the addenda information can be formatted like an X12 820 remittance advice. If the receiving firm is used to handling EDI transactions, it can run the 820 through its translation software and automatically apply the remittance information to its receivable system. The advantage is the potential for automation, but the drawback is that most banks can't process a CTX.

4. *Pay with ACH debits.*   The three methods above assume the payor initiates the payment. An alternative is to have the payee initiate the payment. Since very few corporations want other corporations initiating ACH

debits on their accounts, another method had to be devised giving the payor control of payment. In a system first used by General Electric, the supplier (payor) sends General Electric an 820 remittance advice when the supplier is ready to pay an invoice. Then GE initiates an ACH debit (CCD) drawn on the supplier's account. In this method, remittance detail flows outside the banking system from payor to payee, and the payee initiates the transaction only when the payor agrees to it. In contrast to the one-at-a-time ACH payments implied in alternatives 2 and 3, which are actually quite expensive, this alternative provides the economies of scale of a large batch of ACH transactions. A large electrical manufacturer receives payments from its customers via this method.

Other Forms of Financial EDI

Payment Orders.   In the four examples above, the corporation initiating payment generally communicates with its bank via electronic communications. Most of these electronic communications use the bank's proprietary communications systems. Some banks facilitate communication through dumb terminals. The payment initiator would then have to manually enter payment instructions into the terminal. More advanced systems facilitate data entry via microcomputers or larger computers. Using a computer for communicating with a bank permits the sender to transmit data files created by the firm's accounts payable system rather than having to manually enter data. Many banks provide software to accomplish this data transfer. Some banks are equipped to receive payment instructions using ANSI X12 standards. For example, the 820 message is a standardized format for payment orders. Firms using EDI already will find this method of communication to be similar to other EDI messaging.

Balance Reporting.   Many large banks provide their customers with balance reporting services. Often this is in the form of a terminal that gives the firm the ability to look at ledger and available balances, balances scheduled to become available over the next two business days, and other balance-related information. If you deal with more than one large bank, your lead bank can probably provide you with key balance information in your other major banks in addition to balance information at the lead bank. Unfortunately, small local and regional banks usually do not make balance information available since they do not have the information systems required. More and more banks are moving away from terminal-based information systems since terminals don't let you download the information so you can store it in a computer for later retrieval and manipulation. There are even EDI standards for balance information, account analysis reports, and many other forms of information a bank may provide you.

Deposit Information.   Banks, of course, provide you with a monthly statement that includes detailed deposit information. But that information is not nearly current enough for a cash manager to deal with. For any but the smallest companies, daily deposit information is very helpful, especially if the bank is processing deposits that come directly from customers and others who mail you checks and make other deposits. When the bank processes deposits for you, we call it *lockbox service*. We'll talk about that in more detail in Chap. 6. The bank should be able to tell you about each item deposited into your account(s). If you want more information, such as who wrote the check that was deposited, then you have to pay the bank to capture that information for you. The bank can, for example, photocopy each check that is deposited into your account and then mail you the photocopies. Alternatively, if you need the information faster, the bank could capture the MICR line of the check, store the information in a computer file, and then transmit the information to you via EDI or bank proprietary format. This would give you the bank and account numbers of the party paying you and the amount paid—perhaps enough to know who that party is and therefore enable you to apply the amount to the account receivable. Or you could ask the bank to visually read each check; key in the name, account, and account number of the party making the payment; and transmit that information to you. Large banks provide you with whatever deposit information services you need to help you do your job. Just remember that you must pay for the services and therefore must decide the cost-benefit trade-off.

Paid Check Information.   One of the tasks of the cash manager is to reconcile the firm's checkbook. This means you need to keep track of checks that haven't yet cleared the bank. If you write a large number of checks, you may want your bank to help you automate this task. A bank can transmit to you a listing of paid checks. Combining this with your computer list of written checks, you can determine which checks haven't cleared.

Stop-Payment Services.   Another electronic service your bank may be able to provide you is an on-line stop-payment service. Suppose you write a check for some goods you later find out you didn't receive. If you discover the error soon enough, you may be able to transmit a stop payment to your bank for that check. This means the bank would enter that check's number into its check processing computers. When that check comes through in a presentment, the bank will automatically reject the check and you won't have to pay it. Of course, you could alternatively call the bank with that information, but communicating via computer is more accurate and faster.

Account Analysis.   Large banks will be able to provide you with an account analysis (discussed in Chap. 2). This report shows average ledger and available balances in each account, total value of services billed for the month, earnings credits on the free balances, adjustments, and excess or deficit balances. While this information is available on hard copy, it is often useful to have the data transmitted in computer-readable form so that you can enter the data into your own computer files. This way you can keep track of target balances and more effectively manage your banking compensation arrangements and compare alternative banks. There is an ANSI standard for account analysis.

As you can see by the above, there are a number of useful electronic data services your bank may be able to provide you. We have listed only a few to give you a flavor of possibilities. You should realize that smaller banks may not have the information capabilities to provide some or all of these services.

Taxes and EDI/EFT

One of the many overhead burdens a firm faces is the necessity of filing and paying taxes. State, local, and federal government entities all claim their share of tax money and information. In recent years, a majority of states have started programs to collect tax payments electronically. Not all taxpayers are required to use electronics, but most states mandate that payments over some minimum amount (say, $100,000) use EFT. Generally, states allow one or more alternatives in the form of EFT that can be used: ACH debit, ACH credit, or FedWire. The most common payment method chosen is ACH debit. That way the taxpayer does not have to have any kind of a system to do ACH. The taxpayer would just file a return and tell the government entity the bank and account number to be debited. The government entity does the rest. A new ACH format called TXP has been developed to accommodate tax payments. The federal government has a program in place, aimed at large businesses, that will launch electronic payments starting in 1993 and that will continue expanding to smaller and smaller businesses over the succeeding years.

Perhaps even a more onerous burden corporations face is the requirement to file tax information. While states and the federal government are slower in implementing electronic filing than electronic payments, progress is being made. Nationwide efforts are under way to ensure that states use common formats for filings. This would make it unnecessary for a firm doing businesses in 50 different states to have to complete 50 different filing formats.

Summary

EDI is computer-to-computer communication of business information. The benefits are a reduction in the errors and time delays that characterize manual processing. EFT and financial EDI are subsets of EDI. EFT is the electronic transfer of value between financial institutions. Financial EDI is the exchange of information between a financial institution and its client that results in a transfer of value.

The use of EDI requires the ability of trading partners to communicate in a common framework. EDI has evolved from proprietary standards, where one trading partner dictated the format to all other trading partners, to generic EDI, where all trading partners use an accepted standard format.

Financial EDI includes the initiation of corporate payments, bank reporting of balance information, stop-payment services, and account analysis. The standardized format allows the treasurer to establish automated systems to gather and analyze the information.

Self-Test

1. EDI should be able to help firms reduce accounts receivable. If a firm has sales of $1.2 million/day on average and is able to use EDI to bill and get paid three days sooner, how much would this be worth to the firm? Assume an annual opportunity cost of 10 percent.

2. EDI may also save inventory by shortening lead times and removing uncertainty about orders. If a firm has inventory of $50 million (60 days) and EDI can save five days' worth of inventory, how much would the firm save per year? Assume financing costs of 10 percent and inventory storage and other holding costs of an additional 15 percent.

3. Explain why ACH payments using the CCD format are all right for simple payments but not appropriate for complex corporate-to-corporate payments. What other electronic mechanisms would be better for corporate-to-corporate payments? Name three and explain how ancillary payment information goes between parties for each of the three. List the pros and cons of each of the three methods.

4. Explain why a VAN helps facilitate EDI communications. Why might you not want to use a VAN with some trading partners?

6

Collection Systems

Introduction

During a refreshment break at the meeting of the California Treasury Management Association, Edward Alvarez approached the speaker, who had just finished her presentation on cash collection systems. He said, "Hi, my name is Ed Alvarez, and I am Vice President, Finance, for Alvarez Office Supply, a chain of six office supply stores. I was very interested in your discussion of the difference between over-the-counter and mailed collection systems. We seem to have both types of collection problems. We sell to several large business clients. These clients all buy on credit, and we bill them once a month for all of their purchases during the month. Our general retail walk-in business involves sales of one or two items at a time. Generally, these people pay by cash, check, or credit card. I am wondering if we need to have two different systems or if we can effectively use the one system that we currently are running." Before the speaker could answer, the conference chairperson tapped the speaker on the shoulder and said, "I am sorry to interrupt, Ms. Collins, but we are waiting for you for the photo session with the rest of our speakers." As Ed walked toward the refreshment table to get a cup of tea, he wondered if he would be able find Ms. Collins later to discuss his collection system problems.

In this chapter we address the problem of converting sales into value for the company. We examine the difference between collections where the customer pays at the time of the sale and where the customer pays later in response to a bill or an invoice. We will concentrate primarily on paper-based systems, although we will briefly discuss the changes that electronic payment systems may bring about. We start our discussion of a collection system with the customer initiating payment and continue through the transfer of value to the company. (We leave for a later chapter the discussion of how we might encourage credit customers to initiate the payment process.) We also examine how the design of the company banking system may influence the need to concentrate funds from multiple collection sites into a central set of bank accounts.

Purpose of a Collection System

The primary purpose of a collection system is to mobilize funds, that is, to move funds from the hands of those paying the company, usually customers, into a deposit account. While it is tempting to say the purpose is to collect funds as fast as possible, the real goal is to collect funds as fast as is economically feasible. The benefits from faster collection must be balanced against transactions costs to achieve that speed. The cost of negative customer relations from faster collection is balanced against the benefits from receiving the funds sooner. In addition to receiving funds quickly, a well-designed collection system provides timely and accurate information. This information updates sales and receivables files so that the company can carry out its marketing function.

Costs and Benefits in Collection System Design

A collection system is the set of institutional arrangements, procedures, and banking arrangements that transfers value from payors to the company. The predominate payors for most companies are customers. As we saw in Chap. 5, value is transferred when the available balance increases. Thus, a collection system includes getting the funds from the customer to the company, processing the payments within the company, transporting the funds to the bank for deposit, and receiving availability credit at the bank. Designing or establishing a collection system involves a trade-off between several types of costs, including opportunity costs of float, transactions, and other collection system costs; losses through fraud or theft; the value of payment information; and the value of the relationship with the customer. The objective is to establish a collection system that will minimize the total of all these costs. We can express the objective in collection system design as to minimize the following:

Total costs = float costs + transactions and operating costs

+ fraud and theft costs − value of payment information

− value of customer relationship

Opportunity Cost of Float

The primary function of a collection system is to convert customer payments into value to the company in a timely manner. A delay in receiving value is a major cost in all types of systems. Suppose Alvarez Office Supply receives a check of approximately $25,000 from a customer once a month. Six days elapse between the time the customer writes and mails the check and Alvarez receives availability credit at the bank. If the opportunity cost to Alvarez is 10 percent per annum, the float cost for this customer is $25,000 × 6 days × (0.10/365) × 12 months/year = $493.15.

Collection System Costs

If the firm receives collections directly, either presented at the time of the sale or mailed in later, company personnel must process the payments. Proper security arrangements must be in place. The amount of the payment must be reconciled against sales, and against invoices and accounts receivable if it is payment for a credit sale. Finally, the funds must be deposited in the bank, and service charges are incurred for the bank's processing of the transaction. The costs of these arrangements depend on what type of payment is used, what information system the company has, and whether the company handles its own collection or uses a third party.

Cost of Fraud or Theft

It takes only a small amount of fraud or theft to offset the benefits from an otherwise efficient collection system. The obvious cost of fraud or theft is the value of funds absconded or misapplied. There may also be costs associated with the effect on morale or the image of the company if the incidence of theft is widespread or commonly known. Theft prevention security measures are particularly important in over-the-counter systems that collect coin and currency.

Value of Payment Information

There are two dimensions to the need for timely and accurate payment information. First, delayed information on timely payments results in a lag in crediting customers' accounts. Accounts receivable will appear larger than they really are. Information on sales patterns is delayed. Second, if information on the amount and timing of value transfer is not timely, the financial manager will likely act as if the funds are not there. Consequently, the company does not fully realize the "value" from reduced float.

Value of Customer Relationship

Damaged customer relations may result from delays in applying payment information. Credit managers may reject orders or delay shipments if it appears a customer is over the credit limit. The collection department may send letters or make phone calls requesting payment even though the check has been received. Damage to customer relations can ultimately lead to a loss of sales. As well, as a reaction to poor credit information, the company may err in the other direction. It may ship an order even when a customer is above the established credit limit. It may delay dunning slow-paying customers.

Over-the-Counter Collection Systems

Retail businesses use over-the-counter collection systems. In the most common version, such as a department store or restaurant, customers pay at the same time the goods are delivered or service is performed. Other companies, such as insurance or utility companies, bill customers for the amount owed but allow hand delivery of the payment to a field office or third-party collector. The decision elements in an over-the-counter collection system are the type of payment to be accepted, the number and location of field offices, funds handling and processing procedures, the number and location of deposit banks, and an information reporting system. Figure 6-1 presents a diagram of an over-the-counter collection system.

Collection System Design

Type of Payment Accepted.   The type of payment accepted from customers influences the delays that may occur in value being received. In addition, the nature of the security issues varies with the payment mechanism accepted.

Coin and Currency.   Coin and currency are *bearer instruments;* the value belongs to the holder, and they are negotiable without endorsement. Since they are bearer instruments, there is no need to verify the identify of the bearer. Coin and currency transfer value immediately, that is, as soon as they are placed into the cash register drawer. And handling costs per transaction are very low. These features make coin and currency the payment mechanism of choice for businesses engaged in small, frequent transactions, such as vending machine companies or fast-food restaurants. They are the preferred medium of exchange where an audit trail is undesirable, such as the underground economy.

However, there are some significant disadvantages to accepting cash and currency for payment. The most obvious is the physical security require-

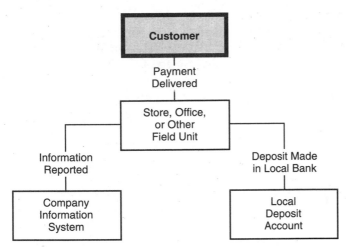

Figure 6-1. An over-the-counter collection system.

ments when dealing with bearer instruments. These instruments are difficult to trace through a series of transactions. Reconciliation of the flow of value and sales requires a dual information flow. For example, it would be very easy for an unscrupulous employee in a restaurant to skim some of the cash inflows. To counter this problem servers receive checks in numerical order and must account for all of them. Cash register receipts are matched to check numbers, and a duplicate copy is made. Most businesses accepting coin and currency assign separate individuals the tasks of recording the sale, recording the receipt of funds, and entering the deposit. While these procedures do not ensure nonpilferage of funds, at least they make it more difficult since all the parties involved would have to agree to committing an illegal act, and the more people involved, the less likely that will happen. The sales reporting system is frequently separate from the cash flow reporting system. This provides a second set of data as a check on the amount of the deposits. An additional disadvantage of coin and currency is that few companies use coin and currency to pay their bills.

Keep in mind that even though value transfer technically occurs with the receipt of payment, the currency must be deposited in the banking system before the company can use the value to pay bills or invest.

Checks. Accepting checks for payment adds another potential cost of delay. Value is not received until the available balance is credited for the deposit. The availability delay is in addition to the processing delay of recording the checks and transporting them to the bank. Identification is required to ensure that the person presenting the check is the one authorized to issue the check. The risk of insufficient funds in the account to pay the check when presented to the bank still exists. And although it is a little more difficult for employees to steal checks than currency, it is still possible.

Recently an employee in the Department of Motor Vehicles in Indiana established a company called D.M.V., Inc. An audit of shortages in the office where the employee worked revealed that checks made out to D.M.V. were deposited in the company's account instead of the state's account.

Instruments such as certified checks, traveler's checks, and money orders are a little safer to accept than personal checks. Although it is still necessary to verify identity, there is minimal, if any, risk of nonpayment of a properly verified item.

Credit Cards. Many retail establishments accept third-party credit cards, such as bank cards or travel and entertainment cards. Verification usually entails ensuring that the card is not on a problem list. Today this is usually done by swiping the magnetic strip on the card, or by calling a card center and reporting the credit card number. Obtaining proper authorization relieves the merchant of the responsibility of the card being used fraudulently. Funds' availability ranges from one day to several weeks, depending upon (1) whether the merchant uses electronic or paper reporting and (2) what the contract with the issuing financial service provider specifies. The financial service provider charges a fee as a percentage of the amount of the transaction. The amount of the fee depends upon the average size and the volume of transactions. Fees range from less than 2 percent to more than 6 percent. Electronic reporting is usually 1 percent to 1½ percent cheaper than paper documents with physical imprinting.

We do not consider company-issued credit cards, such as department store cards, as an over-the-counter payment. Rather, the cards are just a convenient method of issuing credit sales. The actual payment occurs when the credit card holder pays the monthly bill, usually with a check mailed into the company.

Electronic Payment. Electronic payments in over-the-counter systems are predominately through point-of-sale (POS) or debit cards. The clerk runs the card through a magnetic reader connected to an electronic network. The funds are transferred electronically from the card holder's account to the merchant's account. The merchant pays a fee and may have to buy equipment to use this system. POS or debit cards eliminate most of the problems connected with accepting coin and currency or personal checks for payment while providing about the same effective timing on value transfer. While debit cards have been touted as the coming thing in handling payments, they have not been as readily accepted either by merchants or by consumers as expected.

Location of Collection Site. It should be no surprise that collection system considerations are not the primary criteria in choosing the sites for an over-the-counter system. Rather, issues such as the attractiveness of the location, local transportation patterns, zoning ordinances, and proximity to customers are the driving forces in field office or store location.

Location of Deposit Bank.   The location and number of deposit banks are financially driven decisions. The location of a deposit bank close to the field office is the primary consideration. The payment items must be physically transported to the bank for deposit. A bank, or branch office, close to the place of business is usually chosen to minimize security problems and delay in the transfer of funds. An employee or an armored courier service may deliver the funds to the bank, depending upon the volume of funds involved.

Collection System Costs

Float Costs.   In balancing the costs for a collection system we are interested in total *collection float*. Collection float is the delay from the time the customer initiates payment until the bank credits the available balance. As shown in Fig. 6-2, the components of float in an over-the-counter collection system are ones that we identified as part of deposit float in Chap. 5. The internal processing includes the time the payments reside in the cash register (for a retail store) or the business office (for an insurance company) before the receipts are totaled and readied for deposit. Many retail stores do a large portion of the day's business in the late afternoon or in the evening. Frequently, funds are not received until after the bank's cutoff time. There will usually be one business day's delay in receiving ledger credit. Of course, Friday deposits will have a delay of three calendar days, even though it is only a delay of one business day. Any additional delay for bank float depends upon the form of payment accepted. Banks should credit available balances at the same time they credit ledger balances for coin and currency. Checks may have an additional delay, depending upon the location of the drawee bank. As shown in Fig. 6-2, the total collection float for an over-the-counter system may be as much as six days.

Let's use Alvarez Office Supply as an example for calculating the float cost for over-the-counter receipts. Alvarez Office Supply sells an average of

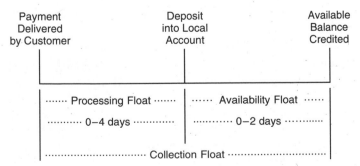

Figure 6-2. Float components in an over-the-counter collection system.

$10,000 per day to its retail customers. Approximately 20 percent of the dollar amount of sales is in coin and currency, 40 percent in credit card receipts, and 40 percent in personal checks. The office manager of each store prepares the deposit after the store closes at 5 p.m. A clerk endorses each check with the company stamp and prepares a three-part deposit ticket for the coin and currency and the checks. The original deposit ticket goes to the bank, the second one goes to the cash receipts file, and the third goes to internal audit for comparison with the sales record. The clerk prepares a separate duplicate deposit ticket for credit card sales. The original is filed with the copies of the credit card tickets, and the duplicate copy goes to internal audit. The store manager places the deposit in the night deposit box on his way home. The bank grants next-day ledger credit for the deposit. Three-fourths of the checks, either on-us items or checks drawn on local banks, receive availability credit on the same day as the ledger credit. The remaining checks receive a one-day delay in availability. Alvarez Office Supply is linked electronically with the credit card network. The actual charge is recorded at the time of the sale, and the company receives a one-day delay in the receipt of funds. The bank requires Alvarez to maintain copies of the tickets to resolve any potential disputes. Thus, Alvarez Office Supply receives availability credit for the credit card receipts on the day after the sale. Alvarez has a 10 percent cost of funds. The average daily float cost for Alvarez Office Supply for Monday through Thursday is calculated as follows:

Coin and currency	$= 0.2 \times \$10,000 \times 1 \times 0.1/365$	$= \$0.55$
Same-day checks	$= 0.4 \times 0.75 \times \$10,000 \times 1 \times 0.1/365$	$= \$0.82$
One-day checks	$= 0.4 \times 0.25 \times \$10,000 \times 2 \times 0.1/365$	$= \$0.55$
Credit cards	$= 0.4 \times \$10,000 \times 1 \times 0.1/365$	$= \underline{\$1.10}$
Total float costs Monday through Thursday		$= \$3.02$

On Friday the float costs are three times as much because the next business day is Monday, which is the third calendar day. Thus, the total float costs for the week are $4 \times \$3.02 + 3 \times \$3.02 = \$21.14$. Annual costs are $1099.28.

Transactions Costs.   Transactions costs depend largely on the form of payment accepted. Businesses usually pay a charge for each check deposited. Banks usually assess one charge per deposit for coin and currency. However, if the amount of coin and currency is substantial, there may be a charge for coin counting. In fact, for large depositors of coin and currency, such as vending companies or transit systems, banks may count the coin and currency only periodically during the week. They may require the presence of a representative of the company. This may cause an additional delay in granting ledger and availability credit. Credit card deposits are subject to a fee that is a percentage of the amount of the charge. Banks charge either originators or receivers, or both, for electronic payments. The party promoting the increased use of electronic payments usually pays the charges.

Collection System Operating Costs. Collection systems incur operating costs for collecting funds, preparing payments for deposit, transporting deposits to the bank, maintaining security, and applying the payment through the information system. Many accounting systems do not recognize these over-the-counter systems' costs as separate costs. Rather, they bury them in the costs of running the business. For example, in a restaurant the costs of collecting and recording payments in the information system are part of the cost of the servers, the hostess, and the cashier. Some of the operating costs may also be a function of the type of payment accepted. Because of the time required to verify identification or the validity of a credit card, service time is greater for customers using personal checks or credit cards than for those paying with coin and currency. However, it is difficult to break out these types of costs in analyzing the desirability of accepting these forms of payment.

Value of Information. There are two general categories of information in operating an over-the-counter collection system: (1) sales-related information and (2) cash flow information. Most cash registers today are actually terminals or computer work stations that just happen to have a cash drawer. The information input by the clerk updates sales by product code and dollar amount, adjusts sales forecasts and inventory records, and updates purchase plans. More sophisticated systems may capture information on customer purchase patterns for future marketing initiatives. Cash flow information may also be collected. If the system captures information on the type of payment and the company follows strict policies regarding deposit of funds, the short-term estimate of future book, ledger, and available balances can all be updated automatically. Unfortunately, sales and accounting systems' requirements dictated the design of many systems in use today. The financial manager may find they do not capture the cash flow information in a readily usable way.

Let's return to our example of Alvarez Office Supply. When sales are recorded at the cash register, the product code, number of items, and sales dollars are automatically entered into the store information system. The clerks ask if the items are being purchased for a business, and obtain the phone number if the answer is yes. If a phone number is keyed in, the system updates the customer information file. Periodically, the marketing staff views the output from the customer file for special promotional efforts. Each evening the information from the daily files for each store is uploaded to the company's main information system. The amount of the deposit—subtotaled by coin and currency, checks, and credit card receipts—is also uploaded to the main information system. This information is used both to check against the daily sales receipts and to inform the corporate financial manager of the amount of funds deposited into the account at the local bank.

Improving the Collection System

Designing or improving a collection system involves a trade-off among the various types of costs. For example, suppose Alvarez Office Supply is examining whether to require payment by coin and currency instead of accepting checks and credit cards. On the one hand, the following costs might decrease. Float cost from checks would be reduced. Decreased customer service time, from not verifying identification or the validity of the credit cards, might generate labor savings. Bank fees would be smaller by eliminating the deposit and encoding charges for checks. Credit card fees would be eliminated. On the other hand, the following costs might increase. The handling, theft, and security costs from an increased amount of coin and currency might increase. The mix of items purchased might change to more low-dollar items and fewer high-dollar items. Customers placing a high priority on the use of checks and/or credit cards, whether for delayed payment or for convenience in keeping their own accounting records, might shift their business to competitors.

The basic evaluation method is to identify the costs incurred under each alternative being considered. This result is a comparison of the costs between the two alternatives. A list of the factors not easily quantified is made for each alternative. If the dollar cost factors and the nonquantifiable factors favor the same alternative, the decision is easy. If not, a subjective trade-off is made between the quantifiable and the nonquantifiable factors.

Collecting Mailed Checks

Sales made on credit, whether on open account, by specific purchase order and invoice, or through a company's own credit card, require that payment be made sometime after the sale. The most common form of payment is a mailed paper check. In this section we identify the elements and costs in designing a mailed payment system to be run by the company. In the next section we consider the use of third parties to perform some of the collection activities on a contract basis. A diagram of a mailed collection system is given in Fig. 6-3.

The first step in a mailed collection system is to receive the incoming mail. A separate post office box should be used for receiving payments. Orders, complaints, etc., are directed to a different location and so will not interfere with the efficient operation of the collection activities. A post office "delivery" schedule for the post office box is used to schedule the number and timing of trips to pick up the mail. Mail is usually delivered faster to a central post office than to a branch office. Speed and accuracy of processing are the focus in the collection center. Clerks immediately open the envelopes. The clerks match checks against invoices or other return documents, and note the amount of the check and any exceptions on the document. They endorse the checks, complete the deposit, and take the deposit to the bank as soon as possible to minimize availability delays. After being separated from the checks, the return documents are forwarded to the credit or accounts receivable area to update the files and deal with any exceptions or problems. Only in rare circumstances where there is some implied liability should checks be held out of the deposit to reconcile problems before deposit. The steps in a mailed collection system are shown in Fig. 6-4.

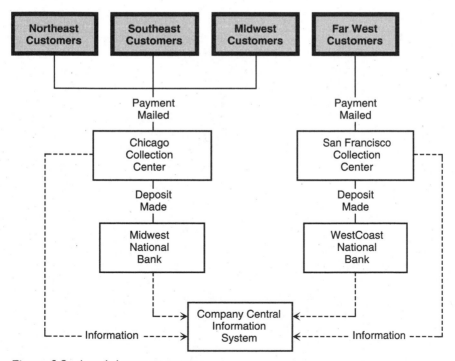

Figure 6-3. A mailed payment system.

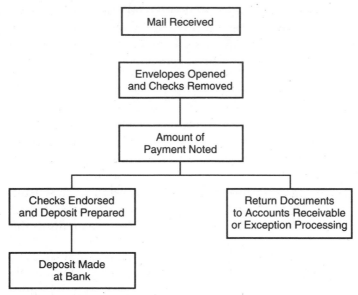

Figure 6-4. Operations in a mailed collection system.

Collection System Design

Type of Payment Accepted.   Basically, the only acceptable payment form is the paper check. However, procedures must be established to handle other types of payment, such as coin and currency, that occasionally may come through the mail.

Location and Number of Collection Sites.   The number and location of collection sites for over-the-counter payments for Alvarez Office Supply were dictated by the store location. Those constraints do not apply to mailed collection sites. Five of the six Alvarez stores are in the Bay Area, while the sixth store is in Los Angeles. How many collection sites should Alvarez have for the mailed payments, and where should they be located? The minimum possible number is one, to which all payments are mailed. Where should this be located? Would Alvarez be better off with a second collection site, and if so, where should it be located?

To answer these questions, the financial manager first must identify potential collection sites. For Alvarez, there are two obvious locations: the Bay Area and Los Angeles. However, within the Bay Area there may be alternative locations. The collection site could be located at the headquarters in Concord, or at the downtown San Francisco store. Second, the financial manager must identify the costs of each of the collection sites. There are three major types of costs: float costs, operating costs, and information costs. To determine the float costs, customers are grouped by geographic location and the average number and size of payments. Operating costs are a function of the procedures used to process payments and make the deposit. Information costs involve processing the payment information and applying it to the proper account.

Assignment of Customers to Collection Sites. If the system contains only one collection site, all customers are instructed to mail their payments to that location. If the system has multiple sites, individual customers are assigned to a specific location. Each customer is directed to send payment to the site with the lowest total float and processing costs.

Location of Deposit Bank. It is still desirable to use a deposit bank located close to the collection site for ease in making the deposit. Customers from a wide geographic area will be sending their payments to the collection site. There is now a trade-off between the convenience in deposit and the availability granted on checks deposited. If a company locates the collection site at its headquarters, the lead or headquarters bank is usually the logical choice for the deposit bank. However, if the firm has a multi-bank system, or if the collection site is not located at headquarters, it may be necessary to use another bank. In this case, the analysis should include the cost of transferring funds from the deposit bank to the headquarters bank. We will return to this issue toward the end of this chapter when we discuss concentration of funds.

Updating Accounts Receivable. All payments are against prior credit sales. It is necessary to record the payment in the correct account. This is sometimes called application of cash payments. There is an obvious need to apply this information as rapidly as possible to make sure that the accounts receivables files are current. However, the check should be separated from the return document as soon as possible and be deposited, not accompany the return document to the receivables processing area.

Collection System Costs

Float Costs. The calculation of float costs for mailed collection systems is similar to that for over-the-counter systems. However, as we can see from Fig. 6-5, there is an additional element in the total collection float: mail float. Float in the collection system starts when the customer releases payment, i.e., when the customer writes and mails the check. The mail delay is a source of float since the company does not have access to the value of the payment during this time. (The mail delay also gives rise to the much dreaded statement, "The check is in the mail.") Only after the check is received can we know with certainty how long it took to get there. We can,

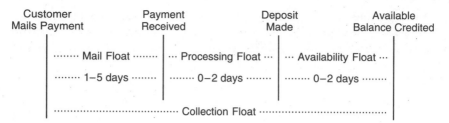

Figure 6-5. Float components in a mailed payment system.

however, estimate the length of time it takes for the payment to arrive, particularly for repeat customers.

Customers should be instructed to direct payments to one location and all other correspondence to a second location. The location, either a post office box or a company office, should be chosen based on the sorting and "delivery" time of the post office, and the mail should be picked up based upon post office activity.

Processing float in the collection system is a function of the way the company processes items after receipt. The company should process the mail containing payments immediately upon arrival. After the envelopes are opened, the amount of the check should be compared with the amount due. Any exceptions due to returns, allowances, or disputed items should be noted. The checks should be immediately prepared for deposit, and the deposit should be conveyed to the bank as quickly as possible. This will increase the fraction of the checks meeting the availability cutoff times. If the processing is completed as quickly as possible, the processing float will be minimized.

The availability float is a function of factors both within and outside the firm's control. By making deposits to meet the bank's cutoff times for availability credit, the firm saves one day (three days on Friday) in availability delay. Arguably, this addition to availability float could be considered processing float. Usually processing is considered finished when the bank grants ledger credit. If the deposit meets the ledger credit deadline but not the availability deadline, the delay is considered availability float. Two other factors affect availability float: (1) the drawee bank and (2) the deposit bank's availability schedule. While the company cannot directly control these factors, it can work to reduce availability float. By comparing the availability schedules from different banks, the treasurer can determine whether it is receiving the best availability possible. By locating its collection center(s) near customers, the company may reduce both mail float and availability float.

The total cost of the float is calculated by summing the cost of the individual float components (mail, processing, and availability). The product of this total float, the average daily checks received, and the daily interest rate results in the float cost for an average day. To obtain the cost of float for the period of analysis (say, a month), multiply the daily cost by the number of days in the period.

Transactions Costs. Transactions costs for mailed payment systems consist largely of the per-check charges for encoding and depositing checks at the bank. In a later section of this chapter we cover electronic payments and discuss how transactions costs for electronic payments differ from those for paper payments.

Collection System Operating Costs. Operating costs for a mailed payment collection system include all the labor, computer, and direct overhead involved in performing the collection functions. This includes costs to rent the post office box, pick up the mail, process the checks internally, and pay bank service charges. In many companies, particularly smaller companies, running a "collection center" may involve part of several people's time rather than a dedicated full-time staff. Separating joint costs to identify the collection system costs is difficult. However, it is critical if the company is going to investigate alternative collection procedures, locations, or the use of third-party contract processors.

Improving the Collection System

Improving a mailed collection system involves the same process as the over-the-counter system. The analyst identifies the costs for the current system and for each proposed alternative. The system is changed if the total cost for an alternative being considered results in cost savings over the current system. Let's use Alvarez Office Supply to illustrate how to evaluate a proposed change.

Under current operating procedures, Alvarez Office Supply bills each credit customer once a month. The company includes a blue return window envelope with the bill. Alvarez operates a single collection center at its headquarters location in Concord, California. The mail is delivered at approximately 12:30 p.m. each day. The mail clerk separates the blue envelopes from the remaining mail and immediately routes them to the collection processing clerk. After this initial sort, the mail clerk opens the remaining envelopes. Some of these envelopes contain checks along with copies of invoices. The clerk separates these payments from the rest of the mail and sends them to the collection processing clerk. The collection processing clerk opens the envelopes, records the amount of the check on the bill, and stamps the checks with an endorsing stamp. Photocopies are made of each check, and the checks and photocopies are arranged in batches of 50 checks. A deposit ticket is made out for each batch, and a duplicate is attached to the batch of photocopies. Each batch has an eight-digit batch number. The completed deposits are taken to the bank by 3 p.m. The bills with the notation of the amount paid are sent to accounts receivable so the customers' accounts can be updated.

Ed Alvarez has pulled together some information on the characteristics of the company's credit customers. The company has a total of 6000 customers spread fairly evenly over the six stores. These customers order an average of $500 per month. From a study of the last three months' collections Ed has determined that the average customer's check is in the mail for four days. The checks are deposited on the same day received, and so there is no processing delay. The average cutoff time for the checks being deposited is 9 a.m., so the company generally misses the availability cutoff. Based on the bank's availability schedule, about half of the checks have transit routing numbers that are eligible for immediate credit. The other half receive a one-day delay. Because the early cutoff time is missed on most of the checks, there is an extra day's delay.

Ed is considering moving the collection activity to the store in downtown San Francisco. In discussions with the post office, Ed was told that the mail would be available in a post office box by 7:30 a.m. In that case, a clerk could pick up the mail on the way into the office, process the collections, and deliver the deposits to the bank in San Francisco by 10 a.m. Ed estimates that this would allow the company to meet the cutoff on three-fourths of the checks. Internal processing costs would be about the same whether done at the Concord or the San Francisco location. The San Francisco location is currently being used for deposit of over-the-counter receipts. The charges for check deposits are the same as those charged by the bank in Concord. There would likely be a delay of one day in posting the payments to the accounts receivable files, and Ed was not sure how this would affect any customer relationships.

The differences between the current system and the proposed system are basically in float. Currently mail float is 4 days, and availability float is an average of 1½ days. The company receives an average of $100,000 per day. If the collection center is moved to San Francisco, the average availability delay will be ½ day on 75 percent of the items and 1½ days on 25 percent of the items. This will be an average availability delay of 0.75 day. We can see from the calculations in Table 6-1 that the float costs per month will be $3904 versus the current $4520, for a savings of $616 per month. Ed will need to weigh these savings against any potential problems caused by a delay in applying the payments to accounts receivable.

A second alternative might be considered. Alvarez Office Supply could establish a second collection center in Los Angeles to process the payments from customers in southern California. This second collection center would reduce mail float and probably reduce availability float. The offset

Table 6-1. Savings from Modifying the Collection System for Alvarez Office Supply

Item	Current system	Proposed system
Dollar amount/day	$100,000	$100,000
Mail float	4 days	4 days
Availability float	1.5 days	0.75 day
Total float	5.5 days	4.75 days
Daily opportunity cost	0.1/365	0.1/365
Daily cost	$150.68	$130.14
Monthly cost	$4520	$3904

would be the additional operating costs of a second collection center and the cost or delay in applying the payment information to accounts receivable. Banking costs would likely not increase since Alvarez is using a bank in Los Angeles for deposit of over-the-counter collections. Likewise, transfer costs to move the balances from Los Angeles to the headquarters bank would not be an issue, since the company currently has to move the funds from the over-the-counter collections. Let's assume that the company could save three days' float on the Los Angeles items. If the Los Angeles customers represent one-sixth of the total funds collected, the company would receive float benefits of $100,000 \times (\frac{1}{6}) \times 3 \times (0.1/365) \times 30 = 411 per month. The increase in costs to operate the second collection center would be subtracted from these float savings to determine whether there would be any net savings from this proposal.

Third-Party Collection Products

As an alternative to performing its own collection activities, a company can contract with a third-party financial service provider to perform some of the collection system functions. The most commonly used third-party collection product is credit cards. We discussed the use of bank or travel and entertainment credit cards in the section on over-the-counter collections. Third-party credit cards should not be viewed only as a way of speeding collections, since they provide a credit function as well. The most common bank product that is used strictly to facilitate collections is a lockbox.

Bank Lockboxes

A bank lockbox performs all the steps that a company performs in running a mailed payment collection. The bank picks up the mail at the post office, processes the checks, records the deposit, enters the checks into the check clearing system, and sends or transmits the return document information to the company. The bank has several advantages that it can exploit to create savings for the company. Because of the volume of items being processed, the bank will make multiple, perhaps as many as 20, trips to pick up the mail from the post office. Many large active lockbox banks even have their own ZIP code, which speeds sorting of the mail. The bank will process the items for the lockbox soon after it has retrieved the mail. Since much of the mail arrives at the central post office at night or in the very early morning, most of the bank lockbox processing is done at night. Since the lockbox processing area is usually located close to the check processing area, the checks are run through the reader/sorter as soon as they leave the lockbox processing area. The result is many more checks are processed in time to make the cutoff for expedited availability. Finally, because of the volume of processing done by the bank, the bank can afford to have specialized equipment, such as automatic encoders or image processing equipment, and a specialized work force. The bank may be able to process the checks at a much lower cost than many companies.

Two different types of lockbox processing are available. A *wholesale lockbox* is designed for a relatively low volume of large-dollar receipts. Many of the processes are manual and designed specifically for the individual company. The focus is on reducing float costs, with operating costs a secondary consideration. A *retail lockbox* is designed for a high volume of relatively low dollar receipts. The bank uses standardized and highly automated processing. The focus is on reducing operating costs, with float a secondary consideration.

Credit Collection Agencies

Credit collection agencies are generally thought of as a last resort to collecting delinquent accounts. While they definitely serve this purpose, some collection agencies are expanding beyond their original function. Some credit agencies will assist in designing a collection system, particularly the portion that deals with customer contact. In addition, some will handle all collections on an ongoing basis. So far they have had the largest impact in dealing with small firms with poor collection habits. Since this is a custom-designed service, the pricing can vary widely and is negotiable.

Multibank Collection and Concentration

In a startup phase most companies can function adequately with only one bank. As a company grows, it may find that it needs more than one bank. This magnifies the problems of monitoring and controlling the company's cash. The size and scope of the banking system are a function of both the company's activities and the structure of the banking system. In the United States, banks can perform certain functions (primarily deposit activities) only in limited geographic areas. This may force a company to use more banks than it would otherwise find desirable. However, a company may also use multiple banks to foster a sense of competition among its suppliers of money. There is a trade off between the cost of maintaining a banking rela tion and the perceived benefit of the competition. When a company uses multiple banks, one of the banks is considered the lead, or headquarters, bank. Generally, the treasurer wants to concentrate as much of the cash as possible in the headquarters, or concentration, bank.

The Need for Multiple Banks

Banks face a number of limitations on the geographic location of their services. Branching restrictions limit a bank's physical presence to a particular state, or within a state to county or other political boundaries. While these geographic limitations theoretically affect many services, the practical effect is most severe on a bank's provision of deposit services for cash and currency and possibly credit cards. As we saw above in the discussion of over-the-counter collection systems, one of the primary criteria in choosing a deposit bank is the proximity to the place of business. In a state with very restricted branching, each field office may deal with a separate deposit bank. Statewide branching should cut down on the number of banks required. But even in a state with statewide branching, the preferred bank may not have a branch close to the location of a particular field office. If the company has locations in different states, it will be forced to use different banks. Even though the United States now has "multistate banks," they must be operated as separate legal entities and cannot take out-of-state deposits. Thus, a company with multiple field offices, particularly ones that are located in more than one state, faces the problem of maintaining and managing a multibank system.

Concentration

Concentration of funds is the action to move funds from multiple deposit banks into the headquarters, or concentration, bank. Again we address a cost trade-off in designing the concentration system. As before, we will try to minimize the total cost of the system. The cost function for a concentration system consists of the following items:

Total cost = opportunity cost of idle funds + transfer costs

+ operating and administrative costs

+ security costs − value of information

Reasons for Concentration.   One of the jobs of the treasurer is to manage the cash resources of the company efficiently. As we saw in Chap. 5, balances may earn credits to pay for some bank services. However, it is usually
cheaper for a treasurer to pay cash fees for services and invest the balances
in marketable securities. The costs of managing and investing from a number of small balances can be quite high. In addition, it is usually possible to
get higher rates on larger investments. Thus, if the treasurer can consolidate, or concentrate, the funds in the banking system into one account, he
or she can make investments in larger blocks. This should cut costs as well
as generate higher returns. A side benefit is that efficient concentration of
funds requires accurate and timely information. Most treasurers take a conservative approach of acting as if funds are not available if they have no
timely information about their arrival. Thus, the lack of good information
about funds in deposit accounts results in excess funds existing in those
accounts which could be invested to earn a return. For security reasons the
ability to disburse funds from accounts is limited and tightly controlled. It
is easier to control disbursements from a single headquarter's bank account
than from several deposit bank accounts at field locations. Figure 6-6 presents a diagram of the deposit and concentration banking system for
Alvarez Office Supply.

Concentration Mechanisms.   Concentration involves nothing more
sophisticated than moving funds from one account at one bank to another
account at the concentration bank. Regular checks are not generally used

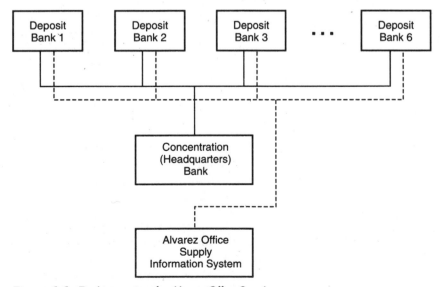

Figure 6-6. Banking system for Alvarez Office Supply.

for concentration because of potential security problems. Frequently the account at a deposit bank serves only one purpose: a place to deposit funds to be transferred later to the concentration bank. To deter a misdirection of funds into unintended accounts, such as numbered offshore accounts, disbursements are limited to moving the funds to the concentration account. Three mechanisms are used to transfer funds: (1) a depository transfer check, (2) an ACH transfer, and (3) a wire transfer. Each has its advantages and disadvantages.

Depository Transfer Check. A depository transfer check (DTC) is a check that is valid for only one purpose: to move money from one account in a company to another specific account. Because of its limited use, it requires no authorizing signature. Other than that, it looks, acts, and clears like a regular check. To use a DTC for concentration the treasurer, or an agent at the concentration bank, receives information on the amount of the deposit and/or the amount of the transfer from each deposit bank. The amount of the transfer is entered onto the DTC, and the DTC is deposited into the concentration account and entered into the check clearing system. The availability delay depends upon the transit routing number of the deposit bank, the availability schedule, and the time the DTC is deposited. Usually, everything is properly synchronized and the DTC is presented for payment at the deposit bank on the same day the funds are available in the concentration bank. However, things do not always go as planned. If the concentration bank has established a very aggressive availability schedule, the DTC may sometimes be presented for payment one business day after the funds become available. On these happy occasions the company has funds available in both the deposit account and the concentration account. These dual balances earn credits at the deposit bank while they also either earn credits at the concentration bank or are withdrawn and invested. If the concentration bank has a very conservative availability schedule, the DTC may be presented at the deposit bank one business day before funds are available at the concentration bank. On these unhappy occasions the company has funds in neither account. These negative dual balances provide cost-free funds to one of the two banks in the system. Unfortunately, the days on which dual or negative dual balances occur are very hard to predict. Continued progress in the Fed clearing system is making their occurrence less frequent than had been true in the past.

The cost of using a DTC for concentration includes the cost to convey information to the treasurer or bank, the cost to fill out the DTC, and the cost of the deposit. The actual cost in dollars and cents is fairly cheap. Some estimates put it in the range of $0.75 to $1. The disadvantage of a DTC is in the delay in the transfer of funds. In addition, there is the uncertainty of each specific delay due to weather, etc.

ACH Transfer. Instead of issuing a DTC to transfer the funds, the treasurer or the agent bank can originate an ACH transfer. The ACH transfer has a built-in one-day delay; thus, funds will be transferred one business day later. Although the delay is similar to that of DTCs, there is less uncertainty with ACHs. The ACH is also cheaper to use than a DTC. Many companies have software that allows them to generate an ACH transaction on a terminal or a personal computer and automatically transmit it to the bank. The advantage of the ACH is the cost, perhaps $0.25 per transaction, and the certainty of knowing when the transfer of value will take place.

Wire Transfer.   A wire transfer is an electronic transfer that results in an immediate transfer of value. Thus, the funds are available in the concentration bank on the same day the transfer is originated. The trade-off is the cost of the transaction. Wire transfer costs can range from $10 to $20. In a transfer to concentrate funds the company is both the receiver and the originator of the wire. Many banks charge both for sending and for receiving wires, and so the cost may be double.

Concentration Scheduling.   The choice of transfer mechanism and schedule for transferring funds to a concentration account is made by attempting to minimize the total concentration costs. At best, funds left in a deposit account earn the earnings credit rate. The correct opportunity cost rate is the difference between the earnings credit rate earned if the funds remain in the deposit account and the rate they would earn if forwarded to the concentration account. The opportunity cost rate is the investment rate on securities only if the funds exceed the amount needed to cover all service charges. The opportunity cost is calculated by multiplying the opportunity cost rate times the delay times the amount.

The transactions cost is the cost of the transfer mechanism chosen times the number of transfers made in the period of analysis. It is tempting to compare the difference in cost between wires and an ACH with the cost of delay to determine a minimum transfer amount so the extra transfer cost will offset the opportunity cost of the delay. There is a flaw in this line of reasoning, though. If the company can forecast with a fair degree of accuracy, it can originate an ACH one day in advance of the desired transfer date and achieve the same timing as with the use of the more expensive wire. The risk may be minimal if there is a level of balances in the deposit account as a cushion against errors.

Reducing the number of transfers decreases concentration transactions costs. Most banks use average available balances to determine the earnings credits generated. Instead of daily transfers to meet this balance exactly, it may be better to transfer less often with the balance above the desired level on some days and below it on other days. This idea is illustrated by the example shown in Table 6-2. Flows into a deposit account are $3000 for each of four days. With a daily transfer schedule we start the week with a beginning balance of $10,000. Each day's transfer is the amount of the deposit, $3000. The transfer is by wire at a cost of $20, and so the transfer cost for the four days is $80. The average ending balance is $10,000 over the four days. What happens, however, if, instead of a daily transfer, the transfer is made at the end of the third day? That gives us the situation shown in the two right-hand columns in Table 6-2. The beginning balance on Monday is $8500. One transfer of $12,000 is made on Wednesday, and so the total transfer costs are $20. The average ending balance for the four days is still $10,000. Thus, the new transfer schedule has maintained the same average balance but at a transfer cost of one-fourth the cost of the daily transfer. Of course, with this simple a situation, we could reduce the transfer costs even more by arranging for an ACH on Tuesday, which would be effective on Wednesday. Now the transfer costs would be less than $1 versus the daily cost of $80. The calculations are more difficult for an irregular deposit flow pattern and for weekends. But the concept still is applicable: averaging about a target balance and reducing the number of transfers rather than doing a daily transfer to get to the target balance. Administrative costs may be higher because of the extra attention needed to schedule transfers instead of the automatic daily transfer, and these costs would be a partial offset to the savings.

The larger the number of deposit banks in the banking system, the more important the concentration becomes. Alvarez Office Supply, the example used throughout this chapter, would likely have five transfers, one from each deposit. If it could cut its transfer costs by approximately $80 per week per bank, it would save almost $20,000 per year in transfer costs. If the additional administrative effort required four hours per week (probably a very high estimate), it would still save approximately $100 per hour of time spent. This is not a bad saving for time invested.

Table 6-2. Concentration Scheduling Example

(All Figures in Thousands)

Day	Deposit amount	Daily transfer		Transfer Tuesday	
		Amount	Ending balance	Amount	Ending balance
Monday beginning balance			$10		$ 8.5
Mon.	$3	$ 3	$10	$ 0	$11.5
Tues.	$3	$ 3	$10	$ 0	$14.5
Wed.	$3	$ 3	$10	$12	$ 7.5
Thurs.	$3	$ 3	$10	$ 0	$10.5
Total amount transferred		$12		$12	
Average ending balance			$10		$10.0

Electronic Collections

Point-of-Sale Collections

There are two types of POS cards in use today: a merchant-issued card and a bank (ATM-type) card. Both cards debit the user's account and credit the merchant's account automatically, but the mechanisms by which they operate are slightly different.

Merchant-Issued Card. In a merchant-issued card the merchant has the customer fill out an application for the POS card. The application includes the information necessary for transfer, such as the bank and the bank account number. This information, captured along with sales information when the card is used, is used to generate an ACH debit to the customer's account. The merchant usually checks the card against a negative file—a file listing lost, stolen, or otherwise problem accounts. As long as the negative file is clean, the merchant will honor the card. The funds are transferred the next day. The merchant absorbs the risk, similar to a check, that there will be insufficient funds available the next day or that the customer will put a stop payment on the account.

Bank-Issued Card. A bank-issued POS card is essentially an ATM card. The card and sales data are read into the network on a real-time basis. The funds are subtracted from the customer's account immediately. The merchant has little risk that the transaction will not go through. Settlement occurs between banks on an end-of-day net transfer of funds. A critical issue in the use of this payment form is whether the merchant is willing to pay for the necessary equipment.

Automated Payments

Automated payments are increasing for regular, fixed payments, such as mortgage or insurance payments. The customer authorizes his or her bank to allow an ACH debit by the company of a set amount on a specified day each month. The customer saves time, checking account charges, and postage to mail the payment. The merchant usually pays the ACH charge but saves all the administrative costs involved with handling a paper check. Cash application to accounts receivable is faster because it is completely automated. Both parties receive increased certainty of when the value transfer will occur. Acceptance of this form of payment has been low for variable payments, such as utility bills, because of the uncertainty of the amount of the payment. One solution has been the spread of "budget plans," where the transfer is at an estimated fixed amount for 11 months of the year, with the final payment of the year at an amount to cover the estimation error.

Electronic Corporate Payments

Electronic corporate payments have increased substantially over the past few years, largely because of the push from several large players such as the federal government, state taxing authorities, General Motors, Sears, and General Electric. The greatest acceptance to date has been by the major trading partners, many of whom conduct business electronically through EDI. As the experience from EDI and electronic funds transfer increases, many of the fears associated with a new technology will disappear. It is likely that electronic linkages for orders, data, and payment will be the way of life for frequent trading partners in the next decade.

Summary

A collection system is the set of activities designed to efficiently transfer value from payers (usually customers) to a company. The objective is to minimize the sum of all costs involved in the collection system. The relevant costs include opportunity costs for delay in receiving value, operating costs, security costs, value of customer relationship, and value of information provided by the collection system. Factors such as the type of payment accepted, the number and location of the collection points, the operating procedures used, and the use of third-party processors affect the cost of the collection system. A multiple-site collection system employing multiple banks has the added dimension of concentration of funds into the lead bank. The increased use of electronic payments simplifies the collection and concentration system design.

Self-Test

1. CDR, Inc., receives an average of $20,000/day from its customers. By examining the postmark date on the envelopes, the financial manager has determined that payments take an average of four days to be received by the company. The payments are processed internally and are taken to the bank for deposit late in the afternoon after their receipt. Most of the checks are local checks and receive same-day availability. The opportunity cost for CDR is 12 percent per annum. Determine the total collection float, the float cost for an average day, and the float cost for an average month for CDR. (For simplicity, ignore any difference between business and calendar days and assume a 30-day month and 360-day year.)

2. Alpha Supply currently collects all the receipts from its credit customers internally. The account officer at the bank has suggested that Alpha start

using a bank lockbox for the collections. Discussions with the account executive indicate that Alpha would probably have access to funds approximately one day faster with the lockbox. The primary time savings would come from a better mail pickup time and quicker entry of checks into the clearing system. The bank would charge a fee of $200 per month and $0.30 per item to operate the lockbox. This would include courier delivery of return documents the day after they are received by the bank. Alpha uses about one-half a full-time employee, at a cost of about $800 per month, to process the checks and make the deposit. Since Alpha is downsizing its staff, the financial manager believes the savings would actually be realized. Alpha receives approximately 3000 checks per month of an average size of $500 from customers. The bank currently charges Alpha $0.08 per check deposited into its account. Alpha has an opportunity cost rate of 12 percent per annum. Determine the amount of savings, or extra cost, for Alpha to use the bank lockbox service. What nonquantifiable factors should be considered before making a final decision?

7

Payables and Disbursement Systems

Introduction

Maggie McGovern walked into her office as her phone started ringing. As she answered the phone, her mind was still on in the discussion over the last hour with the accounts payable manager. They had been trying to outline the criteria to use to decide when to pay suppliers. "Hello, this is Maggie McGovern."

"Hi Maggie, this is Brian. I just wanted to make sure you received the company history that I compiled."

Maggie riffled through the mound of papers on her desk, found the envelope, and said, "Yes, I have it right here, but I haven't had a chance to look at it."

"I think you'll find it interesting. I was intrigued by the impact that changes in technology and communication have had on the way we have done business since great-great-grandpa started the company in 1870. Maggie, I've got to run. I have a golf game with Gerry from Georgia Supply in an hour."

"Thanks, Brian. I'll try to read your report tonight after dinner. Check with Sally and see if you can come over for dinner next Saturday."

Later that evening, as Maggie read the report, she reflected on the fact that most commercial purchases in the United States have generally been made on credit. Historically, the supplier has helped provide the customer with financing. In the early days of commerce in the United States, credit terms were six months to a year. This corresponded to the time that it took

103

the merchant to complete the circuit of customers and make a return trip. Essentially, the customer would pay the merchant for the prior purchase before the merchant would sell him any more goods. Most transactions were done on a face-to-face basis, and so disputes were easily resolved. Payment was also on a face-to-face basis, made in currency or with a local bank draft.

As transportation and communication changed, merchants shortened the billing period and credit terms. Today credit terms vary across industries, with 30 days being common. Many firms are willing to negotiate nonstandard payment terms for large-volume or specialty purchases. As companies became larger, the face-to-face nature of the transactions disappeared. Systems of controls were established to ensure purchases were properly authorized and only bills not under dispute were paid.

In this chapter we develop a procedure to analyze the choice between payment options. We also examine how to ensure payments are made only for those items that are valid expenses. Finally, we discuss some banking products that can assist management in operating an efficient disbursement system.

Disbursement System Costs

The broad objective of the design of a disbursement, or payment, system for a company is the same as that for other cash management tasks: minimize the total cost of the system. The total cost includes the following elements:

$$\text{Total cost} = \text{operating costs} + \text{security costs} + \text{fraud costs}$$

$$+ \text{ supplier relationship costs} + \text{cost of lost discounts}$$

$$- \text{ opportunity cost of delay} - \text{value of information}$$

The total cost of a payment system has many of the same elements that we examined for a collection system. There are, however, a few differences. The delay in payment is a benefit instead of a cost. Failure to take a discount offered is a cost. Intentional delay of payments may result in a cost due to damaged supplier relationships. This cost might appear as a reduced willingness for a supplier to handle special orders, reduced service, reduced credit available from the supplier, or, in the worst case, a damaged credit rating with all suppliers. Increasingly, suppliers and customers view each other as *trading partners,* where both firms gain from the relationship, rather than adversaries, where one gains at the expense of the other. While some of the costs in a disbursement system may be hard to measure, they are real and should be considered in looking at total payment system costs.

Deciding When to Pay

When should a bill be paid? The simple answer is pay when the bill is due. However, as with most complex situations, the simple answer is usually not complete. Many credit arrangements between trading partners give the payor more than one option of a payment date. In addition, there may be circumstances under which payment should be deferred until disputes or questions on merchandise quality, errors in the order, or damaged goods are resolved.

Payables as a Financing Source

The use of accounts payable—generated by buying on credit—is a convenient, cheap, and effective form of financing. The supplier offers temporary financing to the customer. If a company maintains a short production cycle time and a high inventory turnover, accounts payable can provide most of the funds required for inventory. Accounts payable financing also offers the advantage of varying with the level of activity. As activity expands, more materials are required and the amount of funds invested in inventory increases. The amount of funds provided by suppliers in the form of accounts payable increases with the increased orders. As activity decreases, purchases decrease, funds invested in inventory decrease, and accounts payable decrease as payments outstrip new orders. Thus, the level of financing automatically adjusts to the operating activity level.

Why Suppliers Offer Credit.   Businesspeople, at least those that stay in business, are generally not altruistic with the company's funds. Credit is offered because it generates one of two benefits to the supplying company: (1) it increases sales, or (2) it lowers costs. A company buying on credit pays a lower effective cost than one paying cash. Buying on credit allows the buyer the use of funds during the credit period. It is almost as if the supplier has the buyer borrow the money to pay cash, and pays the interest payment incurred during the credit period. This can enhance sales either by increasing market share—if competitors don't offer the same credit terms—or by increasing the overall demand because of the lower effective price.

A second marketing advantage may exist in the form of an implied warranty when credit is offered. A supplier confident of the product quality is willing to allow the buyer an inspection period before payment is required. A supplier offering goods of questionable quality or value is prone to get the money up front and worry about adjustments later.

Credit sales may also reduce costs. This is most applicable where customers place frequent orders for small lots or where there is a contract extending over time. Instead of billing for each delivery or order, the supplier establishes a billing period and bills at the end of the period for all items ordered during the period. This reduces costs for billing, processing collections, and updating accounts receivable for the supplier. Payment once a month may also reduce payment system costs for the buyer. Cutoff dates for the billing period and the payment date may be negotiated between trading partners.

When Is the Payment Really Due?   Credit terms should be clearly stated on the invoice or billing statement, unless the trading partners have negotiated a payment date in their contract. The invoice is the primary evidence of the obligation. Credit terms usually start on the date of the invoice. If the terms are net 30 days and the invoice date is June 10, the payment is due July 10. What if the merchandise and the invoice don't arrive at the customer's until June 15? As long as the invoice date is the starting date, the bill is due July 10. Many suppliers are willing to extend the due date the additional days required for the goods to arrive. Rather than simply assuming the extension applies, the company should confirm the expected payment date with the supplier, particularly if a large amount is involved.

If a supplier offers split credit terms, such as 2/10, n/30, the due date is still 30 days after the invoice. However, the customer can pay within the first 10 days and deduct a 2 percent discount from the bill. If the invoice takes five days to arrive at the company, there remain only five days in which the company can make the payment and take the discount. Many companies have difficulty processing an invoice for payment in this period of time. As we will see shortly, missing discounts can be very costly. Therefore, it is critical to be able to process invoices for payment quickly.

Payment Cycle versus Invoice Date.   Some companies establish their own payment cycle for suppliers, rather than have the suppliers dictate the payment date. For example, some automobile manufacturers pay suppliers once a month for all shipments during the billing period. One-half of the suppliers are paid on the 10th of the month and the other half are paid on the 25th of the month. The cutoff for the payments might be the 5th and the 20th of the month, respectively, for payments on the 10th and the 25th. Usually these arrangements are made where the paying company is large, has many suppliers, and has a contractual arrangement with the supplier for the provision of materials.

When to Pay.   Bills should be paid on their due dates. Payment of a bill before the due date results in a transfer of value before it is necessary. Unless some unusual benefits accrue to the customer who pays early, there is no advantage to paying before the due date. The supplier has offered to provide financing at zero incremental cost for the credit period. Only if you have no other use for funds, in which case you probably would not be reading this book, should a bill be paid early.

Assume a payment of $10,000 for McGovern Enterprises is due on June 25. McGovern Enterprises currently borrows funds under a line of credit at a rate of 12 percent per annum. What is the cost to McGovern if the bill is paid on June 10 instead of June 25 when it is due? To pay the bill on the 10th, McGovern borrows the funds against the line of credit. On June 25, McGovern owes the bank the $10,000 and the interest for 15 days of $10,000 × 0.12 × 15/365 = $49.32. Thus, the net cost to McGovern of borrowing and paying early is that it owes the bank $10,049.32 on June 25, whereas it would only have owed the supplier $10,000.

The analysis of the early payment would be the same if McGovern were not borrowing, and instead had the funds invested in money-market securities. The interest rate might be different, but the result would be the same: there is an opportunity cost to paying early. We defer a discussion of paying late until after our discussion of discount terms.

Discount Terms

Some suppliers offer a discount for early payment. Frequently the discount applies if payment is made in 10 days, for example 2/10, n/30. We could debate whether this is truly a discount for early payment, or whether the "real" price is the discounted price and the net price includes a penalty for taking extended credit. The important aspect is that missing a discount has a cost. Some companies never take discounts because they cannot process the payment in the time allotted. Other companies always take discounts, regardless of the size. Still others take discounts only if they have excess funds in the checking account. We now look at how we can apply the basic opportunity cost concepts to determine the appropriate time to pay.

Cost of Missing Discounts.   The easiest way to express the cost of missing a discount is to calculate an effective rate of not taking the discount. Let's return to the example of the purchase of $10,000 by McGovern. The supplier offered credit terms of 2/10, n/30. For now, assume that McGovern is willing to consider either paying 10 days after the invoice date and taking the discount or paying 30 days after the invoice date and paying the net price. If the payment is made on the 10th day, the total payment is 98 percent of the purchase price, or $9800. If the payment is made on the 30th day, the payment is $10,000. The payment options are shown in Panel A of Fig. 7-1. To calculate the effective interest cost of missing the discount we can think of these options in the following way. The supplier has offered $9800 free credit for 10 days. If McGovern decides not to pay on day 10, the supplier will allow an additional 20 days of credit at an "interest" cost of $200. What is the effective interest rate of borrowing $9800 for 20 days and paying $200 interest? The percentage cost for the

a. Options for Paying Supplier

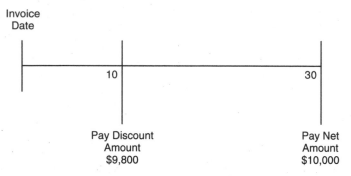

b. Borrow from Bank to Pay Supplier

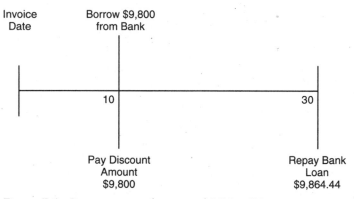

Figure 7-1. Payment options for terms of 2/10, n/30.

20-day period is found by dividing the interest by the amount of financing provided:

$$\text{20-day interest rate} = (\$200/\$9800) \times 100\% = 2.04\%$$

We customarily express interest rates in annualized percentages. We need to adjust the 20-day rate to a 365-day rate. We can make a simple interest (not compounded) adjustment by multiplying the 20-day rate by the number of 20-day periods in the year. This is

$$\text{Effective annual rate} = 2.04\% \times 365/20 = 37.23\%$$

We express the discount D as a decimal fraction and combine both of these steps into one formula as follows:

$$\text{Effective annual rate} = [D/(1-D)] \times [365/(\text{net day} - \text{discount day})] \times 100\%$$

The final step is to compare this effective annualized interest rate with the opportunity cost rate for the company. McGovern Enterprises can borrow from the bank on a line of credit at a rate of 12 percent per annum. Without question, it is cheaper for McGovern to borrow from the bank at 12 percent than it is to borrow from its supplier at 37 percent. McGovern should pay this bill on the 10th day after the invoice and take the discount.

Another way to view this decision is to compare the dollar payment on day 30 under the two alternatives. McGovern can pay the supplier $10,000 on day 30. McGovern can borrow $9800 from the bank on day 10, pay the supplier the discounted payment, and repay the bank on day 30. Panel B of Fig. 7-1 illustrates these payment options. If McGovern borrows $9800 for 20 days, it will owe the bank $9800 × 0.12 × 20/365 = $64.44 in interest. On day 30 it would pay the bank $9864.44. This is $135.56 less than paying the net price. We reach the same conclusion using either method of analysis: the bill should be paid on day 10 at the discounted amount. Whether we analyze the alternatives by using the effective annualized rate or by comparing the dollar payments is a matter of choice. Both approaches incorporate the opportunity cost of the money.

Choosing the Best Payment Time.   Until now we have not considered paying late. The logic was if the buyer agreed to the terms, the payment should be made by the due date. Of course, not all buyers choose to pay on the net due date. If payment is delayed, the effective cost of missing a discount declines. What if McGovern pays on day 45 instead of day 30? The $200 in lost discount pays for an additional 35 days of credit. (Remember, the supplier is providing 10 days of credit at no charge.) The effective interest rate is calculated to be

$$\text{Effective annual rate} = 2.04\% \times 365/35 = 21.27\%$$

While this is still higher than the 12 percent on the line of credit, the effective cost is quite a bit smaller. The longer the time elapsed before payment, the lower the effective rate. Figure 7-2 contains a graph of the effective annualized costs for different payment dates. Clearly, the longer the payment can be deferred, the lower the effective cost of missing the discount. However, a later payment date increases the cost of damaged supplier relations.

A treasurer can use the graph in Fig. 7-2 and a subjective estimate of the cost of damaged supplier relations to consider the cost trade-off. The treasurer of McGovern can compare the opportunity cost of funds with the graph in Fig. 7-2. It is necessary to defer the payment to approximately day 72, or 42 days past due, before the effective cost of a missed discount is as low as McGovern's opportunity cost. The treasurer can decide that McGovern can defer payment this long (or longer) without incurring significant

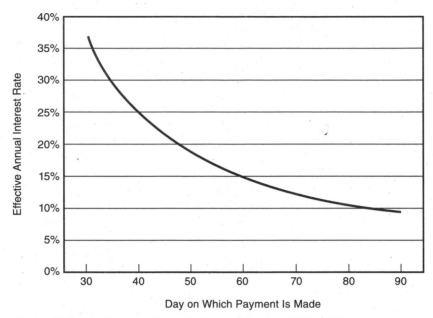

Figure 7-2. Effective annual interest rate for credit terms 2/10, n/30.

supplier relationship costs. If that is the case, it's cheaper to delay the payment. If not, the best alternative is to pay on day 10 and take the discount.

Although the graph in Fig. 7-2 is valid only for the terms of 2/10, n/30, it is easy to construct a similar graph using spreadsheet software for any other payment terms. The treasurer can then proceed in the above manner: determine the payment deferral necessary to achieve positive opportunity cost benefits and weigh these against the subjective cost of damaged supplier relations from payment deferral.

Determining when a supplier is to be paid is a policy-level decision. Once a standard payment time is established for each supplier, accounts payable should follow this standard unless there is a dispute with the supplier. Adhering to the payment standards not only ensures consistent supplier relations but also improves the cash forecast.

Electronic Payments

American businesses are slowly moving toward electronic payments. In the past the payor has resisted electronic payment because of the loss of float. A driving factor toward the use of electronic payments is the reduction in operating costs achieved by eliminating the delays and errors occurring in manual processes. Linking electronic payments with other EDI activities (see Chap. 4) results in significant cost reductions that more than offset the loss of float.

It is not necessary to lose float just because payments are made electronically. The move toward electronic payments is not a one-sided decision. There is negotiation between trading partners to determine, for example, what type of security is required, whether payment information will accompany the payment or will be transmitted separately, and whether communication will be direct or through a VAN. Negotiation should also include the effective date of the transfer of value. Careful timing can make the electronic transfer of funds float neutral; that is, value will be transferred on the same day as under a paper payment system.

Several years ago Sears Roebuck decided to start paying major suppliers electronically. It conducted a study of the amount of float in the paper payment system for each major supplier. It negotiated to keep the effective date of the ACH payment to be the same date as paper payments. Thus, everybody maintained the same float position that they had before. General Motors took a slightly different approach when it developed its electronic payment network. It measured the average float to be between three and four days for its payments. It negotiated a change in the payment date from the 10th and the 25th of the month to the 13th and the 28th of the month. On average, GM retained three days of the old float and gave up a fraction of a day. Of course, not all suppliers received the payment on the average date in the past. Those suppliers who were receiving value in less than the average three-plus days were hurt by the longer delay, whereas those who were receiving the payment in more than three-plus days were helped. After the change virtually all suppliers have the same float.

These two examples illustrate that, with negotiation, float involved in the move to electronic payments may not be an issue. If the opportunity costs are unchanged (because the date of value transfer is not changed), the analysis of a change to electronic payments can focus on the other elements in the cost function.

Direct Deposit.   Payers and payees have embraced one form of electronic payments: direct deposit of payroll. The paying firm loses float by direct deposit of payroll. However, other cost savings are felt to more than offset this loss of float. Many companies lose productivity on payday while employees take an extended lunch hour to cash their checks. Operating costs and bank charges for the ACH deposits may actually be lower than for paper checks. Employees may view the certainty of the availability of funds on payday, even if they are out of town, as a significant benefit.

Ensuring Invoices Are Valid

Significant savings on operating costs, opportunity costs, or supplier relations are easily undone by paying invalid invoices. The payables and dis-

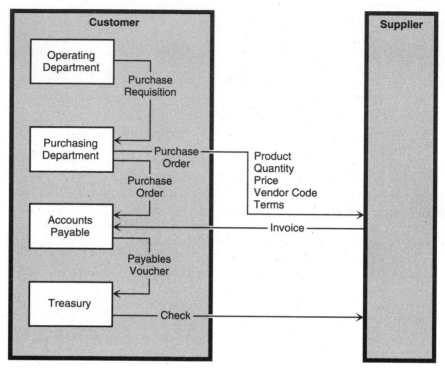

Figure 7-3. Accounts payables processing.

bursement system must ensure the original purchase was properly authorized, the goods or service were in the stated condition and properly performed, and the right amount of funds is disbursed to the correct vendor. Figure 7-3 contains a diagram of the steps in this process.

Purchase Authorization

The security of the disbursement system really starts with the proper authorization of the purchase and continues through the transfer of value. Most firms have a process that includes the following steps:

Requisition.   Operating departments submit requisitions for purchases to the purchasing department along with proper departmental management approval.

Request for Quote.   The purchasing department issues a request for quote to a qualified list of suppliers.

Purchase Order. The purchasing department issues a purchase order, which is sent out after receiving proper approval. The purchase order contains the name and address of the supplier, the specific product ordered, and delivery and payment terms. Purchasing assigns a vendor code to the vendor and instructs the supplier to include the vendor code on the invoice. The vendor code is a means of ensuring the invoice is valid and from the correct vendor, rather than a fictitious invoice from a company with a similar name. The purchase order may also trigger an update to the information system regarding delivery schedules, production schedules, and cash flow forecasts.

Processing Invoices for Payment

The supplier sends an invoice for the goods shipped or services provided. The invoice triggers the process to pay the supplier. The process includes some or all of the following steps:

Match Invoice with Purchase Order. The invoice is compared with the purchase order and with any shipping documents accompanying the shipment. Any discrepancies, such as a difference in quantity or price, or a missing or incorrect vendor code, cause the invoice to be handled on an exception basis.

Generate Accounts Payable Voucher. Once any exceptions are corrected, an accounts payable voucher is generated. The accounts payable voucher may be a paper document, or it may be an electronic file. The accounts payable voucher is the piece of information that authorizes scheduling the check to be written. Scheduling the payment should be in accord with the discount standard established for the supplier. The voucher also updates the cash forecast.

Release of the Check. Only authorized treasury department personnel can distribute checks. For control, each account has a designated signatory who must sign the check for it to be valid. In a system where the checks are automatically signed, the authorization is usually in the form of a password or code, changed frequently, necessary for the checks to be processed by computer. Electronic funds transfer systems use similar security measures to guard against unauthorized disbursement.

Disbursement Locations

When a company uses more than one bank, the treasurer must decide which bank or banks will be used for disbursements. If more than one bank is used for disbursement, payees are assigned to individual banks. The decision process involves the same type of analysis used in collection system design in Chap. 6.

Disbursement System Costs

In a collection system, float is a cost. In a disbursement system, float is a benefit since the company has the use of funds until the checks clear. The value of the float is determined by the now familiar process of multiplying the amount of the disbursement times the days' delay times the opportunity cost rate. In addition to the float benefits, the design of the disbursement system most directly affects the operating costs, the cost of supplier relations, and the administrative costs to manage the system.

Evaluating Alternative Disbursement Sites

Analysis of Cost Trade-off.   McGovern Enterprises is headquartered in Philadelphia and uses the Third National Bank (TNB) as its lead bank. The company also uses a lockbox at South Western National Bank (SWNB) in Dallas to collect receipts from customers in the western half of the country. Currently, all disbursements are drawn on TNB. McGovern writes an average of $400,000 checks per day. The average disbursement float is five days.

The treasurer is considering using SWNB as a second disbursement bank. If SWNB is used for disbursements, approximately $300,000 per day will be disbursed to payees in the eastern half of the country. The treasurer estimates McGovern will gain an additional two days in disbursement float by using the second disbursement point. The use of a distant disbursement site with the idea of extending the disbursement float is sometimes called *remote disbursement.* The benefit of the additional float is $300,000/day × 2 days × 0.12/365 = $197.26 per day, or approximately $5900 per month. McGovern will incur additional costs to operate and administer this second disbursement point. The treasurer estimates these costs at about $1500 per month. It is tempting to say McGovern should establish the second disbursement location for a net savings of about $4400 per month. Before rushing to open the new account, though, we need to address some other factors that may offset part of these savings.

Other Factors.   If suppliers have multiple collection points, perhaps bank lockboxes, the anticipated savings may not be realized or may be short-lived. When suppliers notice the change in their collection float, they may direct McGovern to send its payment to the closest lockbox. If the new lockbox location is closer to Dallas than the old lockbox was to Philadelphia,

McGovern may find it has actually reduced disbursement float by a change in the disbursement point.

Some suppliers use receipt of funds or of value as the determinant of whether or not a discount is allowed. If the discount is disallowed, McGovern will lose much more than it would gain from the increased float. To continue to receive the discount, McGovern might have to initiate the payment earlier, which would defeat the purpose of changing the disbursement point.

The Fed and banks continue to try to improve the clearing system to decrease the float. Advances in clearing time will reduce the float savings.

Finally, some people feel it is not ethical to intentionally use disbursement float to extend the payment time. A number of years ago a national stock brokerage firm was using a San Francisco bank for checks for payments in the eastern half of the country and a New York bank for those in the west. After some adverse publicity, the firm discontinued the practice and issued all checks on the New York bank.

Controlled Disbursement

One of the issues in managing disbursements is maintaining the proper level of balances in the disbursement account. A treasurer knows when the checks are written but can only estimate when they will be presented for payment. Uncertainty in the check clearing system complicates maintaining the desired balance. If the treasurer could know the amount of checks being presented for payment early in the day, he would know whether he had excess funds to invest or a deficit to be financed. The earlier in the day the treasurer has this information, the more flexibility he has in making adjustments to the cash position. In addition, the short-term money markets are the more active and the investment rates are slightly better in the morning than they are in the afternoon.

Many banks offer a product called *controlled disbursement* to assist treasurers in monitoring the balances for the day. Banks receive an early morning (usually 8 a.m.) presentment of checks from the Federal Reserve. If a bank can be sure there will be no other presentments during the day, it can process the checks and notify the account holder by late morning, say, 11 a.m. The treasurer then has time to make adjustments in the cash position. If the bank receives presentments later in the day, say, noon, it will be mid to late afternoon before the bank can notify the treasurer.

The Fed makes an early morning presentment to all banks. For Federal Reserve city banks, or active large banks, the Fed makes a second presentment, perhaps as late as noon. Large banks can get around this later presentment by maintaining their controlled disbursement accounts at an affiliate with a transit routing number that designates it as a non-Federal

Reserve city bank. Thus, they are assured of receiving only the early morning presentment. Any checks not available for the early presentment are held to the next day's presentment. The treasurer thus gains both the value of the early notification of the presentments and a delayed presentment on some checks.

Note the difference between remote disbursement and controlled disbursement. Remote disbursement is done primarily to extend the check clearing float. The disbursing bank is frequently located a significant distance from the bulk of the company's payees. Controlled disbursement is done primarily to receive early notification of the presentment of checks for the day. The account is maintained at the lead bank, rather than at some geographically remote location. Although there may be some delay in the check clearing because of the lack of a second presentment, that is not the primary focus.

As might be expected, the Fed is not excited about any attempt to increase the check clearing float. If the volume of presentments exceeds a specified level, currently $10 million per day, the Fed may make a second presentment, regardless of the transit routing number of the bank. Banks offering controlled disbursement accounts are dealing with this situation by receiving an electronic report from the Fed concerning the later presentment. The electronic report includes information on the vast majority of the presentments that will be included in the second presentment. Thus, the bank can still provide the treasurer with an early report that has just a slightly greater uncertainty than the more traditional controlled disbursement report.

Zero Balance Accounts

All but the smallest companies have multiple disbursement accounts. Multiple accounts serve at least two purposes: (1) control of disbursements and (2) efficiency in accounting. With multiple accounts a company can authorize certain individuals to issue disbursements from only one type of account. For example, an insurance company may have a separate account for payroll and for claims reimbursement. It can authorize an agent to issue checks for claims settlement of less than $500. The agent does not have authorization to disburse funds from the payroll account. A person authorized to issue payroll checks may not be authorized to disburse funds from the travel account, which may require a different authorization procedure. This division of control makes it easier to limit fraudulent expenditures and to assign responsibility for specific types of disbursements. Multiple disbursement can also ease the accounting and check reconciliation burden. Many companies have separate disbursement accounts for different divisions or business units. With separate accounts it is easy to track material, equipment, or labor expenditures for each business unit. In addition, some regulations require different reporting for salaried and hourly employees. Separate payroll accounts for these two classes of employees simplify reporting.

The simplest approach is for a company to open a separate account for each of these purposes. But as is usually the case, the simplest approach is not always the best. The treasurer has to arrange for funds to be placed in each of the accounts to cover expected presentments. To guard against creating overdrafts, or even worse, having checks returned because of insufficient funds, the company will maintain balances in each account. In addition, a company may receive a separate account analysis for each account. Fortunately, there is a better way. Banks offer a product called *zero balance accounts* (ZBAs) which simplify the operation of multiple disbursement accounts. Several recent surveys indicate that over 80 percent of the companies in the United States use zero balance accounts for disbursement.

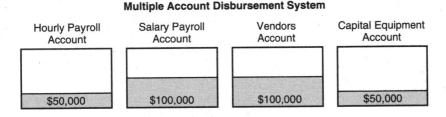

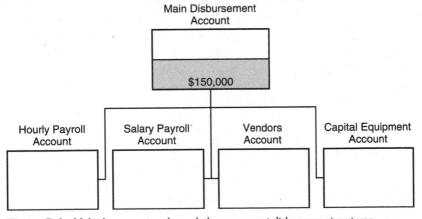

Figure 7-4. Multiple account and zero balance account disbursement systems.

How Zero Balance Accounts Work

With a ZBA system a company has one main account. This main account houses all balances kept at the bank. The ZBAs are all linked to the main account. Each ZBA starts the day with an opening balance of zero. When a check is presented for payment against one of these accounts, it is paid even though this drives the intraday balance negative. At the end of the day, when the bank posts its accounts, it automatically initiates an internal transfer of funds from the main account to each ZBA for the amount of checks presented. The ending balance in each of the ZBAs is zero. Figure 7-4 shows a comparison of a system with separate accounts and a ZBA system.

Usually a ZBA system is all at one bank. It is possible, though, for some of the zero balance accounts to be set up at correspondent banks of the bank maintaining the main account. The individual accounts are funded by ACH or wire transfers. This complicates the funding of the ZBAs as well as increases the cost.

Advantages of Zero Balance Accounts

Lower Balances.   With separate accounts, the treasurer maintains balances in each account. In the example in Fig. 7-4 the treasurer maintains average balances of $50,000 in the hourly payroll and equipment accounts and $100,000 in the salary payroll and vendor accounts for a total of $300,000 in balances. Presentments against these accounts are not perfectly correlated. For example, vendor payments are not likely presented on the same days as hourly payroll. With a ZBA system the treasurer can take advantage of the differences in the timing of these presentments and carry a lower level of balances in the main account than the total in separate accounts. Perhaps the treasurer can provide the same level of overdraft protection with $150,000 in the main account in a ZBA system as was provided by the total of $300,000 in the separate account system. The other $150,000 is now available for investment elsewhere in the firm.

Automatic Funding.   With a system of separate accounts the treasurer has to fund the individual accounts by transferring funds from securities or from the main disbursement account into the other accounts in anticipation of presentments. In our example the treasurer has to make four separate funding decisions, and possibly four separate transfers. In the ZBA system the treasurer only has to transfer funds from securities to the main account.

Account Analysis.   Since the ZBAs are all part of the same account system, the bank provides a single account analysis report which consolidates the activities. This simplifies managing the banking relationship and determining compensation for services.

Data Collection for Forecasting.   The flow of presentments to ZBAs is a source of information the treasurer can use in preparing cash forecasts. Different types of payments, such as payroll or vendor, have different patterns in presentment. If the company has only one disbursement account, the treasurer has to separate the disbursement by type to identify patterns. With a ZBA the bank has already sorted these presentments and provides the company the information in its account reporting. A treasurer can use the report from each of these accounts as the information base for a forecast.

Summary

Disbursement systems have many of the same cost components as collection systems. Float in a disbursement system is a benefit since the paying firm retains the use of the funds until the check clears. Because of the opportunity cost, bills should not be paid before due. Discounts offered for early payment should be analyzed and compared with the opportunity costs before deciding whether to take the discount. The analysis can be done either as an effective annual rate or on the total dollar payment under the different options. Electronic payments simplify the payment process and eliminate some of the operating costs and errors of manual systems. Many trading partners are negotiating electronic payment terms to be float-neutral, which overcomes one of the major objections to paying electronically. A carefully designed process should be in place both to ensure that all payments are for items that were properly authorized and to ensure that all invoices are valid. A controlled disbursement account can provide a treasurer with information on presentments early in the day, which allows more flexibility in funding decisions. Zero balance accounts, a frequently used disbursement product, capture the information and control aspects of having a number of separate accounts without sacrificing the advantages of maintaining consolidated balances of one account.

Self-Test

1. Barelli's Construction Company purchased $15,000 of materials from a supplier on terms of 2/15, n/45. Barelli's, a typical undercapitalized construction company, borrows funds from a bank at an interest rate of 15 percent per annum. Determine whether Barelli's should pay on day 15 and take the discount or pay on day 45 and pay the net price. If Barelli

thinks he can delay payment until day 60 without incurring significant supplier costs, when should the bill be paid?

2. Michitah Manufacturing has operations in Michigan and in Utah. Currently it uses a local bank for payroll disbursements but disburses all vendor payments from the Michigan bank. The account representative at the Utah bank suggested Michitah use a controlled disbursement account to disburse payments to its vendors. It has vendor disbursements of approximately $5 million/month. Currently it keeps a balance of $50,000 in its vendor disbursement account because of the uncertainty of when the checks will be presented for payment. The treasurer estimates that Michitah could reduce the balance to an average of about $10,000 with the controlled disbursement account. In addition, disbursement from the Utah bank would add one day of float. The Utah bank will charge $1500/month for the controlled disbursement account. Michitah has an opportunity cost rate of 12 percent per annum. Determine the amount of the savings that Michitah would have by using the controlled disbursement account in Utah.

8

Short-Term Investments

Introduction

At 11 a.m. Katrina Graff, treasurer of the Phoenix Company, receives the daily report from the company's controlled disbursement account. The report indicates a total of $150,000 in checks will be paid out of the account today. Glancing at the balance report, she finds yesterday's ending available cash balance was $25,000, and an additional $80,000 in ledger balances will become available today. From the cash forecast she expects that an additional $175,000 in immediately available funds will be deposited today. This would leave Phoenix with an ending available balance of $130,000. The treasurer tries to maintain an average available balance of $20,000 to cover unexpected transactions activities and to provide partial compensation for tangible services supplied by the bank. She pulls up the portfolio management module on her computer so she can see how close the portfolio composition comes to meeting the investment policy guidelines. She also gets out the list of approved brokers so she can start calling to determine the best options for placing the excess funds. She looks at her watch and thinks, "I have a half hour before the executive committee meeting, which will probably last until about 2:30. I better get these funds placed before the meeting because the money market will be fairly inactive by the time the meeting is over."

In this chapter we examine liquidity management and marketable securities investment. First, we look at how liquidity is measured, both by outsiders and by insiders. We investigate the factors that should be considered in determining how much liquidity is desirable. We also examine the characteristics of marketable securities that serve as a temporary store of liquidity and look at how different securities are priced.

121

Measuring and Managing Liquidity

Definition of Liquidity

An asset is considered *liquid* if it can be converted into cash quickly at little loss of value and at minimal transactions cost. This concept of liquidity determines the value of an asset if a company disposes of it rather than maintaining ownership to generate income. Most managers view a firm, particularly the one employing them, as a going concern. Clearly we must use a different definition for the liquidity of a firm than we do for the liquidity of an asset. A *firm* is considered liquid if it can meet its obligations when due.

Primary Liquidity. *Primary liquidity* consists of cash either that is currently in the available balance or that will be available at the time a payment must be made. This includes cash inflows that will occur during the time of analysis. These cash inflows may be from maturing securities, which are fairly certain cash flows; or from collections from receivables, which are slightly less certain; or from cash sales, which are much less certain.

Secondary Liquidity. *Secondary liquidity* consists of liquid resources that can be called upon to make payments. In the normal course of business the company does not plan on using these secondary sources of liquidity, but they are available if needed. Secondary liquidity sources include items such as securities which will not mature until after the payment time and unused credit capacity.

Measuring Liquidity

A variety of parties have an interest in measuring the liquidity of a firm. Creditors are concerned about the ability to be paid on time. Managers are concerned about the ability to conduct their jobs in a nonpanic environment. Stockholders are concerned about the ability of the firm to maintain ready access to funds to finance desirable investments.

External Measures. Many of the common measures of liquidity are used by people outside of the firm. While managers may have better ways to measure liquidity internally, it is important for managers to know how the firm appears to outside parties. The appearance of a low level of liquidity may result in a higher cost of credit, or worse, unavailability of credit.

Outsiders generally have limited information on the financial position of a firm. Financial statements provide their primary data for estimating liquidity. The two most common measures, the current and quick ratios, are constructed from balance sheet data. The current ratio is defined as

$$\text{Current ratio} = \frac{\text{current assets}}{\text{current liabilities}}$$

The quick ratio (sometimes called the acid test ratio) is defined as

$$\text{Quick ratio} = \frac{\text{current assets} - \text{inventories}}{\text{current liabilities}}$$

Current assets are those which presumably could be converted into cash within a year. Current liabilities are those obligations due within a year. Both the current and the quick ratios are static measures with a nominal one-year horizon. They do not consider the firm as a going concern. They measure the value of funds that could be generated from disposition of the current assets (or current assets minus inventories) as a multiple of the amount needed to pay off the current liabilities.

There are several problems with these measures of liquidity. (1) The book value of the assets may not be realized if a firm shuts down and the assets are eliminated. (2) The timing of the conversion of the assets into cash may not match the due date of liabilities. (3) The measures ignore any additional funds available from or obligations due to continuing operations. (4) They ignore both the ability of managers to make compromises to meet the obligations and the consequences of those compromises.

Some creditors use a second set of measures, which are a combination of balance sheet and income statement items. Two popular measures are the times interest earned and the fixed-charge coverage. The times interest earned is defined as

$$\text{Times interest earned} = \frac{\text{earnings before interest and taxes}}{\text{interest payments due}}$$

The fixed-charge coverage is defined as

$$\text{Fixed-charge coverage} = \frac{\text{earnings before interest and taxes}}{\text{interest} + \text{principal} + \text{lease payments due}}$$

These measures are also beset with problems in measuring actual liquidity. They ignore charges not appearing on the statements at the current time that may be generated in the very near future. They relate accounting earnings to the amount of the obligation. While accounting earnings may be roughly equal to cash flow in the long run, accounting earnings may have little resemblance to cash flow in the short run. These measures may not reflect the ability of the company to meet its interest or fixed-charge obligations.

Internal Measure of Liquidity.   Managers of a firm have access to much better information to measure liquidity than do outsiders. As defined above, the liquidity of a firm is the firm's ability to meet obligations when due. In designing an internal liquidity measure it is instructive to think about the process by which a manager attempts to meet an obligation as it comes due. The first source is the available cash balance when the check is presented for payment. This is not the current cash balance; rather it is the future cash balance. The amount of cash available is a function of other checks that will clear and deposits that will become available before the check is presented for payment. If these funds are sufficient to cover the payment, no other action need be taken. If these funds are insufficient, the manager may look to the sale of securities. If these are insufficient, the manager may look to an unused capacity in a line of credit. Perhaps, the manager will consider delaying paying some other bills until additional funds become available. Depending upon the lead time and the anticipated duration of any payment problems, the manager may defer expenditures for items such as research and development, marketing, or new equipment.

The process we are describing is one of estimating cash flows and, if necessary, rearranging cash flows. Only after the manager has exploited all easy sources of funds will she consider an abnormal liquidation of assets, such as receivables or inventories. Thus, any attempt to measure liquidity should take into account real potential sources of funds used to meet obligations. We define *liquid resources* as the sources of funds available in the time frame necessary to meet obligations. The items that qualify as liquid resources vary with the time frame of the analysis. Cash available is always a liquid resource. Marketable securities and unused credit lines also qualify as liquid resources. Accounts receivable and inventory are included through the cash flow forecast. Accounts receivable expected to be collected during the period of analysis are liquid resources. Those that are not expected to be collected are not. Similarly, inventory serves as a liquid resource only if the product is expected to be sold and payment received in the time frame of the analysis.

If all of a firm's cash flows are certain, it is easy to measure the liquidity of a firm. The firm is liquid if the liquid resources are sufficient to cover the obligations in the time period of analysis, and illiquid if not. Unfortunately, the world is not so simple. At least some of the cash flows are uncertain. The assessment of the liquidity of the firm is related to the likelihood the liquid resources are sufficient to meet obligations. Liquidity can be measured by relating the expected liquid resources to the uncertainty of the cash flows during the period of analysis. This can be represented as follows:

$$\text{Internal liquidity ratio} = \frac{\text{expected liquidity resources}}{\text{uncertainty of cash flows}}$$

The higher this ratio, the greater the likelihood the liquid resources will cover the actual cash obligations. In general, there is no absolute level that is good or bad. The level must be established by the judgment of the management with consideration of the cost of maintaining the liquidity and the consequences of having insufficient liquidity.

If the firm has many relatively small cash flows, the cash flows may approximate a normal distribution. Measuring the uncertainty as the standard deviation of cash flows results in this internal liquidity measure approximating a standardized normal distribution. A table of a standardized normal distribution (Z scores) can be used to approximate the probability of running out of cash.[1] For example, a Z score of 2 means the expected liquid resources are about twice the standard deviation of cash flows. Approximately 95 percent of the observations from a normal distribution are within plus or minus two standard deviations. There is approximately a 2.5 percent chance that the actual cash flow will be so negative that the amount of resources will be insufficient to cover the obligations. This is illustrated graphically in Fig. 8-1.

Suppose that the treasurer of Phoenix is trying to decide whether the firm has a sufficient level of liquidity. The treasurer has a one-week time horizon. Currently Phoenix has $50,000 in available balances. Marketable securities total $150,000. Phoenix currently is borrowing $400,000 against a bank credit line of $500,000. From the cash flow forecast Katrina estimates the expected cash flow for the next week to be a negative $50,000. The standard deviation of the weekly cash flow is estimated to be $150,000. The internal liquidity ratio has a value of

$$\text{Internal liquidity measure} = \frac{50,000 + 150,000 + 100,000 - 50,000}{150,000}$$

$$= \frac{250,000}{150,000} = 1.67$$

Let's assume Katrina is comfortable with a probability of running out of cash of 2.5 percent or less. The ratio must be increased from 1.67 to approximately a value of 2. In the short term there are only two actions the treasurer can take to effect this ratio. One is to defer some cash payments to make the expected cash flow less negative. For example, if she could arrange to defer payments of $50,000, the expected cash flow would be zero, and the ratio would have a value of 2. However, this deferral only serves to push the cash outflows off to the next week. If the expected cash flows in the next week are not sufficiently positive, this action would only delay the liquidity problems. A second potential action is to increase the bank line of credit to provide an acceptable level of liquidity. In the long

---

[1] A complete discussion of Z scores and probability distributions is beyond the scope of this book. The interested reader is encouraged to consult an elementary statistics book for a discussion of standardized normal distributions.

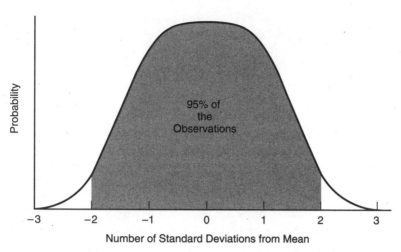

Figure 8-1. Standardized normal distribution.

term the treasurer could increase the cash balance or the amount of marketable securities to increase the level of liquidity.

Estimating Required Liquidity

In many firms it may not be possible to identify the distribution of cash flows and obtain an estimate of the probability of insufficient funds. However, some of the cash flows still have a random nature. The elements contained in the internal liquidity ratio are the items a treasurer must estimate and control in determining an adequate level of liquidity. As long as the cash flows have some degree of uncertainty, a treasurer cannot, and should not, hope to have sufficient liquid resources to cover all possible situations.

The following procedure can be used to determine the required level of liquidity.

1. Determine a maximum acceptable probability of having insufficient funds. (If this sounds too risky, then determine a minimum acceptable probability of having sufficient funds. It will just be 1 minus the probability of having insufficient funds.) Suppose the treasurer is dealing with weekly cash flows and feels that 1 chance in 50, or a 2 percent probability of having insufficient funds, is acceptable. At this probability level the treasurer would expect to have to take some emergency action approximately one week out of each year.

2. Estimate the amount of the net cash outflow that the firm has only a 2 percent chance of exceeding. This estimate can be obtained by measuring the net cash flow for each week for a prior time period, say, the

last two years. Rank the cash flows from the most positive to the most negative. The two most negative cash flows represent approximately the worst 2 percent of the cash flows over the last two years.

3. Arrange for total liquid resources that are sufficient to cover the third most negative cash flow. If the treasurer is willing to accept a higher probability, say, 5 percent, the level of liquid resources would not have to be as high. The treasurer would now arrange for liquid resources sufficient to cover the sixth most negative cash flow. The five more negative cash flows would represent the 5 percent of the time that the liquid resources were insufficient to cover the cash outflow for the week. A similar analysis could be done for other time periods, such as a day or a month.

An acceptable probability of insufficient resources is a function of several factors. Perhaps the most important is management's attitude toward risk. A very risk-averse management will want to minimize the probability of insufficient resources and accept the cost of maintaining a high level of liquid resources. A more risk-tolerant management will be unwilling to absorb the cost of maintaining liquid resources and will accept a higher probability of insufficient funds. A second important factor is the slack in the payment system. If the firm has been pushing its suppliers to the limit on payment, there may be very little flexibility in deferring payment. A firm that has been paying promptly can likely defer some supplier payments occasionally without adverse consequences. A third factor is the firm's activity in short-term funding markets. A firm that maintains a ready access to short-term funding, say, through regular sales of commercial paper, has more sources and more flexibility in raising funds than a firm that normally does not participate in raising funds on a short-term basis.

An analogy can be drawn between maintaining an inventory of materials for production and maintaining a portfolio of liquid resources for paying bills. The level of inventory held is a function of the uncertainty of the rate of usage, the cost of ordering in small quantities, the speed of delivery, the cost of carrying the inventory, and the consequences of running out of material. The trend in recent years has been toward reducing the level of both physical inventory and liquid resources.

The Form of Liquidity

Once a treasurer has determined the required level of liquidity, the focus of the decision shifts to the form in which the liquidity is maintained. A firm's liquidity portfolio consists of a combination of cash, marketable securities, and access to credit. The decision on composition of the liquidity portfolio is a function of the relative opportunity and conversion costs. Cash has virtually no transactions costs but a relatively high opportunity cost. The return earned on marketable securities results in a lower opportunity cost at an increased transactions cost. Access to unused credit has a fairly low opportunity cost until it is needed to be used; however, it may entail relatively high administrative costs. In the rest of this chapter we will discuss the marketable securities that fit in a liquidity portfolio. In subsequent chapters we will discuss short-term borrowing arrangements.

Characteristics of Money-Market Securities

The term *money market* usually refers to the market for short-term securities. The securities traded in these markets generally have a maturity of one year or less. The money market does not have a fixed location, such as the New York Stock Exchange. Rather, it is located anywhere there is a telephone. Thus, the money market is really a network of brokers and dealers who buy and sell money-market securities.

A portfolio of money-market securities is probably the most prevalent form of a company's liquid resources. In choosing securities for a liquidity portfolio, the financial manager must not lose track of the reason for investing the funds in securities: *to maintain easy access to funds while earning a return higher than holding the funds in cash.* The following characteristics are considered in choosing securities for this portfolio.

Liquidity

Liquidity is the primary consideration. When we speak of the liquidity of a marketable security, we use the definition of the liquidity of an asset. That is, the security must be able to be converted to cash quickly at minimal transactions costs and at very little risk of principal.

Marketability

The usefulness of a security as a liquid resource depends in part on the asset's marketability. A security with a strong, active secondary market is easier to convert to cash than one for which the treasurer has to search out potential buyers. In addition, securities with strong secondary markets tend to be priced closer to their "true" value than securities with a thin market. It is less likely that the action of any one investor, or a small group of investors, will have an impact on the price of the security.

Risk

There are two types of risk in marketable securities. The first is default, or credit risk. This is the possibility that the issuer of the security will not pay the interest or the principal when due. Most treasurers attempt to avoid default risk by restricting their investments to those issuers who have only the highest credit rating. In certain securities, where the market maker is critical to converting the security into cash, the credit risk of the market maker should also be considered.

The second type of risk is interest rate risk. The interest rate risk may affect the treasurer in two different ways: price risk and reinvestment rate risk. The price of a security is based on the terms unique to the security and the prevailing market interest rate. If the security is sold before maturity, its price may be above or below the purchase price. If rates have risen since the time the security was purchased, the price will have fallen; thus there could be a loss of principal. Security price fluctuations are directly proportional to the length of time remaining until maturity, that is, a security with a longer maturity has a greater fluctuation in price. The second way interest rate risk affects a firm is through the rate at which interim cash flows can be reinvested. If funds are available for a longer time than the maturity of the security, the rate at which the cash flows can be reinvested is uncertain.

During most economic climates the interest rate price risk is viewed as more costly than the interest rate reinvestment risk. Consequently, long-term securities are generally felt to be riskier than short-term securities.

Yield

The yield of a security is the rate earned. Usually it is a secondary consideration to liquidity, marketability, and risk. After acceptable levels of these other three factors have been met, the treasurer worries about maximizing yield. Unfortunately, there is generally a trade-off between yield and risk—you get a higher yield by being willing to accept more risk. Again, we must not lose sight of the fact that the primary reason for holding marketable securities is to provide a source of liquidity, not to maximize yield. If yield maximization becomes the primary consideration, and if the firm is particularly successful, perhaps it should consider getting out of its main line of business and becoming a financial institution.

Since longer-term securities are felt to have more risk, they usually offer a higher return. A graph of a typical relationship between yield and maturity for U.S. government securities is given in Fig. 8-2.

Taxability

Securities differ in taxability. Income from U.S. government securities is generally not subject to state taxes. Income from state and local governments' securities is generally exempt from federal taxes and may be exempt from taxes within the state of issue. Some special-purpose securities, such as

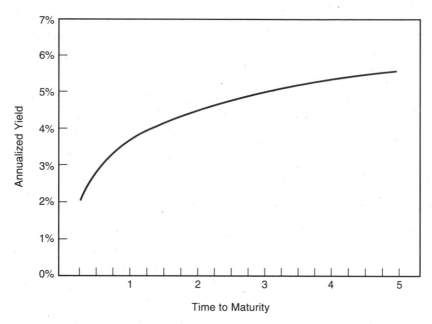

Figure 8-2. Yield curve for government securities.

pollution control or economic development bonds, may also be exempt from federal or state taxes.

Types of Securities

The majority of securities that qualify for a marketable securities portfolio are short-term debt securities. Debt securities have a set maturity, a contractual payment pattern, and a fixed maturity value. Equity securities are not acceptable for a liquidity portfolio. At one time all securities existed in physical form; that is, a paper document was issued. Increasingly money-market securities are moving to book entry form, where the "security" is simply a record in a computer system. This has reduced the transactions costs and increased the safety of transferring ownership of the securities.

Securities differ with respect to denomination, maturity, the number of days in a year on which the interest is calculated, and type—whether they are coupon-bearing or discount securities. Table 8-1 contains a listing of the features of a sample of money-market securities.

U.S. Government Securities

U.S. government securities, sometimes called *governments,* are debt instruments that are issued by the U.S. Treasury. There are three common types

Table 8-1. Summary of Characteristics of Some Common
Money-Market Securities

Security	Interest payment	Original maturity	Taxability	Interest year
		Government Securities		
T-bills	Discount	<1 year	Federal	360 days
Treasury notes	Coupon	1–10 years	Federal	365 days
Treasury bonds	Coupon	>10 years	Federal	365 days
		Agency Securities		
FHLB notes	Discount	<1 year	Federal	365 days
FHLB bonds	Coupon	>1 year	Federal	365 days
GNMA	Coupon	>1 year	Federal	365 days
Bank for Cooperatives	Coupon	6 months	Federal	360 days
		Municipal Securities		
Municipal notes	Discount	<1 year	Some state	360 days
		Bank Securities		
Bank CDs	Coupon	>30 days	All	360 days
Banker's acceptances	Discount	Variable	All	360 days
Loan participations	Coupon	Variable	All	360 days
		Corporate Securities		
Commercial paper	Discount	<270 days	All	360 days
ARPS	Coupon	>1 year	70% excluded	360 days
		Other Securities		
Repurchase agreements	Discount	1+ days	All	?

of government securities. *Treasury bills,* commonly called T-bills, are *discount securities.* T-bills are non-interest-bearing securities issued in denominations ranging from $10,000 to $1 million. They are issued at a price less than face value, and the holder earns a return through price appreciation. Although this price appreciation is a capital gain, it is treated as regular income for tax purposes. The pricing of T-bills and the calculation of the effective yield are discussed below. T-bills have original maturities of 13, 26, or 52 weeks and are issued at auction on a regular schedule. A designated fraction of the issue is sold to the highest-price (lowest-rate) bidders. The remaining portion is reserved for smaller purchasers who buy at the average auction price. There is a very active secondary market for T-bills, and so they are available with almost any remaining maturity less than a year.

Treasury notes and *treasury bonds* are coupon-bearing securities that pay interest semiannually. Treasury notes have an original maturity of between 1 and 10 years. Treasury bonds have an initial maturity of more than 10 years. Both notes and bonds are issued in denominations from $10,000 to $1 million. Longer-term notes and bonds may have too much interest rate price risk for a marketable securities portfolio. However, a 5-year maturity note issued 4½ years ago or a 20-year bond issued 19½ years ago both are now 6-month securities, and may be appropriate for short-term investments.

Agency Securities

Agency securities, also called *agencies,* are securities issued by agencies of the federal government such as the Federal Home Loan Bank (FHLB), the Federal National Mortgage Association, the Government National Mortgage Association (GNMA), Banks for Cooperatives, and Federal Intermediate Credit Banks. Securities issued by these agencies lack the full faith and credit of the U.S. government behind their repayment. As such, investors perceive them as having more risk. However, it is doubtful that Congress would allow any one of these agencies to default on its obligations, and so the risk and the yield are only slightly higher than governments.

State and Local Government Securities

Municipal securities, also called *munis,* are issued by state and local governmental units. These securities come in a wide range of maturities and denominations. Income from most municipal securities is exempt from federal taxes. For a corporation with a 34 percent tax rate, the after-tax return on a fully taxable security earning 8 percent would be only 5.28 percent. The return on a muni should be contrasted with the after-tax return on a fully taxable security for a valid comparison. That's the good news. The bad news is munis also come in a wide range of risks. The risk of a municipal security is a function of the local political and economic climate of the issuing municipality. Although outright defaults on munis are not common, there have been several scares in the past few years.

Corporate Securities

Commercial paper is an unsecured short-term promissory note of a corporation. As long as it is issued with an original maturity of less than 270 days and is used for working capital needs, commercial paper does not have to be registered with the Securities and Exchange Commission. Most commercial paper is issued on a discount basis and has an initial maturity of about 30 days. Commercial paper is negotiable, but the secondary market is limited and most investors hold the paper until maturity. Moody's Investors Service, Standard and Poor's Corporation, and the Fitch Investor Service rate the risk of commercial paper. Most commercial paper issuers plan to issue additional paper to obtain the funds to retire the original paper. To guard against a sudden change in the commercial paper market, most issuers maintain a bank line of credit as a backup to the commercial paper outstanding.

One other corporate security, *auction rate preferred stock* (ARPS), or a variant, *Dutch auction preferred stock* (DAPS), has gained acceptance in some marketable securities portfolios. ARPS is preferred stock whose dividend rate is periodically reset through an auction process. Generally, the rate is reset every 49 days to reflect changes in rates due to changing economic conditions and to comply with current tax regulations. A corporation that holds stock in another corporation for at least 46 days can exclude 70 percent of the dividend from taxable income. The effective tax rate is thus only 30 percent of the rate applied to income from a fully taxable security. For a corporation in the 34 percent tax bracket, the effective tax rate is only 0.3×34 percent $= 10.2$ percent. Theoretically, the rate adjustment process of ARPS and DAPS provides protection against interest rate price risk, and the auction process provides liquidity for the investor. However, if there are insufficient bids at the auction, an investor may be stuck with holding the security until the next auction.

Bank Securities

The most common bank securities are *certificates of deposit*. These are fixed-term securities with either a fixed or a variable interest rate. On larger-denomination CDs interest is usually paid only at maturity. CDs with a denomination of greater than $100,000 are negotiable; that is, they can be sold to another investor rather than being held to maturity. However, an active secondary market exists only for CDs from a few large banks and in a denomination of $1 million. The yield on the CDs varies with the perceived risk of the issuing bank.

Banks also sell *banker's acceptances*. Banker's acceptances are time drafts that result from financing commercial, usually international, trade. They come in a range of denominations and maturities. They are sold on a discount basis, and a secondary market is maintained by dealers.

Recently, a number of banks have started offering *loan participation certificates*. These securities come from loans that the bank makes to its customers, frequently under a line of credit. The buyer of the loan participation certificate is essentially buying a piece of the bank's loan. Care must be exercised to understand the relative position of the bank and the purchaser of the certificate in the event of a default on the loan by the borrower.

Repurchase Agreements

A *repurchase agreement*, also called a *repo*, is an agreement to buy a security with a commitment by the seller to repurchase it at a specified time and price. Banks and security dealers with a temporary oversupply of securities are active issuers of repurchase agreements. While it would seem to be a very safe way to invest, there are some risks. For very short term repos the securities are not transferred to the purchaser. Thus, the repo is essentially a loan collateralized by the security. Although a repo is usually quite safe, there have been a few incidents where an active repo dealer was using the same securities for multiple repos and the "collateral" was insufficient to pay off all the repurchase customers when the firm went bankrupt.

Money-Market Funds

Companies with a small amount of funds to invest in marketable securities may be at a significant disadvantage relative to larger investors. They may have to choose between paying higher transactions costs and receiving lower yields from investing in smaller-denomination securities or concentrating their funds in a limited number of securities. In addition, the cost to administer a small securities portfolio may be quite high. *Money-market mutual funds* may provide an attractive alternative. The manager of the money-market fund, either an investment management firm or a bank, invests in a portfolio of money-market securities. Investors buy shares in the fund. Most of these funds provide ready access to funds through check writing, wire transfer, or telephone transfer. The management of the fund charges a fee, usually a percentage of the value of the assets managed.

In addition to being an attractive vehicle for a diversified portfolio of securities, a money-market fund may provide a sanity check on an internal fund manager. If the internal fund manager cannot provide a return at least equal to a money-market fund of a similar average maturity and risk, the CEO should seriously question whether the internal fund manager should be replaced.

Managing the Investment Process

Establishing an Investment Policy

All companies should establish a written investment policy approved by top management and the board of directors. A carefully drafted policy can eliminate many potential problems, both for the firm and for the manager in charge of implementing the policy. The policy includes a description of the objectives of the portfolio, the resources available to manage the process, the investment strategy, acceptable financial instruments, and the relative composition of securities in the portfolio.

Objectives of a Marketable Securities Portfolio. Without clearly artic-ulated portfolio objectives it is easy for a portfolio manager to fall in the trap of trying to maximize the yield without proper consideration of the liq-uidity and risk of the portfolio. This is probably a more important problem in large firms where several people are involved in estimating and manag-ing cash flows and where many people rotate through the investment func-tion as a part of a career path. A well-documented policy helps to keep everybody on the same page of the play book.

Resources Committed to Managing Investments. The objectives and expectations for results should be consistent with the resources committed to managing the portfolio. One important resource is the people employed. A more sophisticated and aggressive investment approach requires people with specialized knowledge and an ongoing educational program to keep abreast of new instruments or new approaches to generating returns and managing risk. A second important resource is access to timely information. It is nearly impossible to try to squeeze the last few points out of the yield if the manager is acting on information that is hours or days old. The increased use of computer models to make automated investment decisions has dramatically reduced the time that a manager has to act on new infor-mation before it is captured in the pricing. An additional resource that sometimes is ignored is an accurate, timely company cash forecast. The lack of a good daily cash flow forecast forces the liquidity portfolio to have a very short maturity, to be turned over frequently, and to have lower returns.

Strategy: Aggressive or Passive. A very passive approach to a liquidity portfolio is to use a buy-and-hold strategy. The term of funds needs is esti-mated by a cash flow forecast. Securities are purchased with a maturity that matches the cash flow need. Only if unforseen circumstances occur will securities be sold before maturity.

A more aggressive approach to security investing involves the portfolio manager buying and selling securities to take advantage of special situa-tions. For example, if there is a bias toward longer-term securities having higher yields, the portfolio manager may buy securities with a longer matu-rity than the cash flow needs of the company require, with the intent of sell-ing the securities before maturity. An extreme example is a portfolio manager who buys securities based on what he or she perceives to be a mis-pricing in the market. The securities are then sold when the mispricing is corrected. Of course, this approach requires the portfolio manager be more astute than the average investor.

List of Eligible Securities. Specifying a list of acceptable securities is another way of protecting both the company and the manager. Some managers may find this approach restrictive. However, this is probably preferable to finding out after being terminated that the board was not willing to have the company funds invested in options on Eurodollar futures.

Portfolio Composition.   Portfolio diversification is the modern-day version of not putting all your eggs into one basket. The old adage is our forbearers' way of advising us to diversify our risks. Specifying a maximum percentage of the portfolio that can be concentrated in a particular type of security or a particular industry is one way of carrying multiple baskets. An observation from a recent trip to a developing country suggested an updating of the adage. A woman was riding a bicycle to market loaded with several baskets of eggs. She was hit by a motorbike, breaking almost all of the eggs. In diversifying your portfolio, make sure the separate baskets are not all on the same vehicle.

Security Prices and Effective Yields

Alternative money-market securities differ both in the way the interest is paid and in maturity. To make a comparison across securities the yield must be calculated on a consistent basis. The most common way to compare security yields is on a simple annual interest rate. Unfortunately this is complicated by the way that some rates are quoted and the differences in the number of days in an interest rate year. We examine the yield calculations for the two types of securities: discount securities and coupon securities.

Discount Securities

Security Prices.   Discount securities are purchased at a price below face value. At maturity the face value is paid to the holder of the security. Discount securities are usually quoted on a bank discount basis. The rate quote determines the amount deducted from the face value of the security. On U.S. securities the quote is for a 360-day year, although the amount of deduction from face value is based on the exact number of days remaining until maturity.

The amount of the discount is determined as follows:

Amount of discount = face value × rate quote × days to maturity/360

The price of a discount security is

Price = face value − amount of discount

Katrina Graff is considering the purchase of a $100,000-face-value, 91-day T-bill with a rate quote of 5.80 percent. The amount of the discount is

Amount of discount = $100,000 × 0.058 × (91/360) = $1466.11

The purchase price for this security is

Price = $100,000 − $1466.11 = $98,533.89

Although we have used a T-bill in this example, the price is calculated in the same way for other discount securities. The most common discount securities are T-bills, banker's acceptances, commercial paper, and municipal securities.

Yields. The calculation of the effective simple annual yield, sometimes called the *bond equivalent yield,* is done in two steps. (1) Calculate the holding-period yield. (2) Annualize the holding-period yield. The holding-period yield is calculated by dividing the income by the purchase price. The income is the total of the interest plus (minus) any capital gain (loss). The holding-period yield is

Holding-period yield = (total income purchase price) × 100%

If Katrina holds the T-bill until maturity, she will receive the face value of $100,000. For the T-bill there is no interest income. The total change in value comes from the change in price. Thus her total income is $1466.11. The holding-period yield is

Holding-period yield = ($1466.11/$98,533.89) × 100% = 1.488%

The annualized yield is determined by adjusting the holding-period yield to a yearly rate. The $1466.11 in income is obtained by holding the security for 91 days. The annualized yield is the holding-period yield multiplied by the number of holding periods in a year, or

Annualized yield = holding period yield × number
of holding periods per year

For the T-bill purchased by Katrina the annualized yield if it is held to maturity is

Annualized yield = 1.488% × (365/91) = 5.97%

The annualized yield, 5.97 percent, is larger than the yield quote, 5.80 percent, for two reasons. First, the yield quote is for a 360-day year, whereas the annualized yield is calculated for a 365-day year. Second, and more important, the discount is calculated on face value, but the investor pays less than face value. Fewer funds invested result in a higher effective yield. The difference between the yield quote and the effective yield on a T-bill with a discount of 5.8 percent with different maturities is shown in Fig. 8-3. We can see that the longer the maturity, the larger the difference between the yield quote and the effective yield.

Not all securities are held until maturity. Assume that 30 days have passed and Katrina now needs to sell the T-bill. The rate quote is now 5.75 percent. The amount of the discount is $100,000 \times 0.0575 \times (61/360) = \$974.31$. The selling price is $99,025.69. The total income is the capital gain, or the selling price minus the purchase price. This is $99,025.69 - \$98,533.89 = \$491.80$. The holding-period yield is

$$\text{Holding-period yield} = (\$491.80/\$98,533.89) \times 100\% = 0.499\%$$

The 0.499 percent return was obtained by holding the security for 30 days. The annualized return is the holding-period return multiplied by 365/30, or

$$\text{Annualized yield} = 0.499\% \times 365/30 = 6.07\%$$

Since the T-bill is being sold before maturity, the price depends upon the prevailing interest rates at the time of the sale. If interest rates are higher than 5.75 percent, the price will be lower and the realized yield will be less. The opposite is true if interest rates are higher than expected.

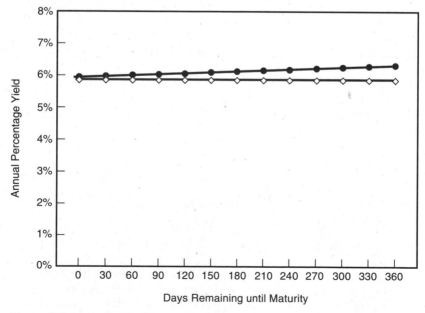

Figure 8-3. Annualized yield versus maturity.

Coupon Securities

Prices.   Money-market coupon-bearing securities usually pay interest once at maturity. Since the rate is set at the time they are issued, they are generally issued at close to face value. The price of the security at a time before maturity depends upon the coupon rate, the time to maturity, and the market rate of interest. The price is the present value of the cash flow at maturity.

Assume Katrina was considering the purchase of a bank CD as an alternative to the T-bill. The CD had a face value of $100,000, an original maturity of 180 days, and a coupon rate of 6.5 percent. At the time Katrina considered the purchase, the CD had 30 days remaining until maturity and was quoted at a rate of 6.60 percent. Unlike the discount quote on the T-bill, the quote on a CD is a simple-interest annual rate quote. The price of the security is determined using standard present-value calculations as follows. Determine the interest rate for the period remaining until maturity. In this case we have a 30-day period. Divide the cash flow at maturity by 1 plus this interest rate. We can represent this by a simple formula:

Price = cash flow at maturity/(1 + interest rate for remaining period)

Interest rates for bank CDs are quoted on a 360-day year basis. The 30-day interest rate is calculated by dividing by 360 and multiplying by 30. The 30-day interest rate is 6.60 percent × 30/360 = 0.55 percent. The cash flow at maturity is the principal of $100,000 plus the full 180 days of interest. The interest is based on the coupon rate of 6.5 percent. The total amount of interest to be paid at maturity is $100,000 × 0.065 × 180/360 = $3250. Thus, the total cash flow at maturity is $103,250. Using the above formula, we find that the price is

Price = $103,250/(1 + 0.0055) = $102,685.23

Yields.   If Katrina buys the bank CD and holds it until maturity, she will receive the full cash flow. The holding-period yield will be

Holding-period yield = ($103,250 − $102,685.23)/$102,685.23 = 0.55%

We annualize this yield to compare it with the annualized yield on the T-bill. We have

Annualized yield = 0.55% × 365/30 = 6.69%

Above we noted that the annualized yield for a T-bill (or any other discount security) is greater than the quote both because the quote is on the face value while the investment is less than face value and because the discount quote is on a 360-day year while the annualized rate is on a 365-day year. For the coupon security the difference between the annualized rate and the quoted rate is due only to the rate quote on 360-day year and the yield annualized on a 365-day year. If we multiply 6.6 percent by 365/360, we obtain 6.69 percent.

Assessing Relative Value

It is tempting to conclude that Katrina should purchase the CD since it offers an annualized yield of 6.69 percent versus 6.05 percent for the T-bill. Before jumping to this conclusion, though, we need to analyze other differences between the securities. First, at the time the T-bill is purchased, the selling price is unknown. Katrina may expect the rate to be 5.75 percent in 30 days, but it could be different. She has to accept interest rate price risk if she buys the T-bill and plans to sell it after 30 days. Second, the CD has some default risk. For a $100,000 CD, the default risk is minimal, assuming the bank is insured by the FDIC. However, for larger-denomination CDs there is a risk of default. (If you think that there is no risk of default, ask someone who had Penn Square Bank CDs when the bank was closed by the FDIC.) Third, the secondary market for T-bills is much stronger than that for bank CDs. If it should be necessary to sell the security earlier than planned, the sale of the T-bill would be much easier and transactions costs would be lower.

The treasurer should assess the differences in risk and determine if the extra return offers sufficient compensation for the higher risk. One way to gauge whether the difference in yield is sufficient to offset the greater risk is to compare the current spread between effective rates with a "normal" spread. By looking at historical patterns of rates and rate differences, we can determine whether the current spread is more than, about equal to, or less than the normal spread. Let's assume the normal spread between T-bills and CDs from this bank is 50 basis points. A basis point is $1/100$ of a percent, and 50 basis points are equal to $\frac{1}{2}$ of 1 percent. The current spread is 64 basis points. Thus, investing in the CD will result in a yield that is 14 basis points higher than average. As long as the treasurer cannot identify any special circumstances to explain this higher-than-average spread, the relative higher yield on the CD argues for investing in the CD.

Outside Investment Managers

Large companies have sufficient funds invested in marketable securities to justify a specialized and highly trained staff to handle investments internally. In small companies the controller or financial manager likely invests excess funds in his or her "spare" time. An alternative for both large and small firms to consider is the use of an outside investment manager.

Using Outside Managers

The first step in considering using an outside investment manager is to have a well-defined investment policy. Without a carefully articulated policy it is difficult both to provide the outside manager with the guidance on the investment objectives and to evaluate the performance. The choice of a manager involves a trade-off between the desire of the investment manager to have total discretion over the placement of the funds and the desire of the firm's management to limit the activities and instruments to those with which they are comfortable. Consistency in philosophy between the investment manager and the firm may be equal in importance to cost of the services. Before hiring a manager, both current and former customers of the investment manager should be interviewed to prevent surprises. Finally, definitive evaluation criteria should be developed prior to the engagement, and, in fact, even be included in the contract.

Outside Managers as a Benchmark

Even large firms with their own internal portfolio managers may use an outside manager for a portion of the portfolio. The outside manager provides a benchmark, or a comparison, for the yields obtained on the investments as well as the costs of managing the portfolio. In addition, the outside manager may be a good source of new securities or new techniques for managing the portfolio.

Small firms generally do not have a sufficient volume of investments to employ both inside and outside managers. For these firms, money-market mutual funds can serve as a benchmark. A portion of the funds placed in a money-market mutual fund allows an ongoing check on the yields on a professionally managed short-term liquidity portfolio and the management expenses charged. If the internal manager cannot do at least as well as the money-market fund, perhaps the internal manager's time can be better spent on other activities.

Summary

A firm must maintain a sufficient level of liquidity to pay its bills when they are due if it is to stay in business. Liquidity can be maintained either as a store of assets or as ready access to additional liabilities. The appropriate level of liquidity is a function of the distribution of a firm's cash flows, management attitudes toward risk, and the cost and availability of "emergency" funds. Because of limited information, outsiders tend to rely on ratios of financial statement data as liquidity measures. These ratios are not adequate for internal management of liquidity. Rather, managers should use liquidity measures that incorporate the forecast of future cash flows and the uncertainty of cash flows. One of the most common forms of secondary liquidity is marketable securities. The investment policy should carefully detail the goals of the investment portfolio and the type and concentration of acceptable investments. Alternative investments should be compared on the basis of after-tax annualized yields. The annualized yield is most easily calculated by first determining the holding-period return and then adjusting it for the number of holding periods in a year.

Self-Test

1. You submitted a noncompetitive bid for a 91-day T-bill at the auction held earlier this week. Your bid was for a $500,000-face-value T-bill. The average auction rate was 5.25 percent. Determine the price you will have paid for the T-bill, the holding-period yield, and the annualized yield if you hold the T-bill to maturity.

2. Assume that you plan to sell the T-bill in part at the end of 60 days. You anticipate the rate will be 5.10 percent at that time. Determine the selling price, the holding-period yield you will have realized for the 60-day time period, and the annualized yield.

3. As an alternative you are considering investing $500,000 in a negotiable bank CD. The CD would have a face value of $500,000, an initial price of $500,000, a maturity of 90 days, and a coupon rate of 5.75 percent. You anticipate you could sell the CD at a rate of 5.60 percent 60 days from now. Determine the selling price, your holding-period yield, and your annualized yield from investing the money in the CD and selling it after 60 days.

9

Bank Borrowing

Introduction

Earl Wilson makes high-quality log home kits to sell in the New England market. Early each winter he purchases large shipments of logs from timber companies and begins the long process of debarking, drying, cutting, planing, and shaping the logs to his design specifications. Most of his kits are purchased by do-it-yourselfers who spend a summer vacation on the construction task, and so sales usually do not pick up until late spring. Hence, Earl's business accumulates a cash outflow of about $180,000 from November through May and then receives healthy cash inflows through the remaining months. When Mr. Wilson started the firm, he was able to finance the physical plant with stock, bank mortgages, and equipment leases. But he depends on a credit line from his bank to provide seasonal financing to cover log inventory purchases and operating expenses during the lean seven months.

Most firms need short-term loans from time to time to cover such circumstances as unanticipated cash outflows (or lack of inflows), seasonal cash flow patterns (like Earl Wilson faces), and interim financing to cover the firm until more permanent financing can be secured. Short-term debt is considered any loan with a maturity of up to a year. There are many sources for short-term loans. Commercial bank loans represent a very large fraction of such loans to small and medium-sized businesses. In this chapter we consider bank-originated short-term loans, and in the next chapter we discuss nonbank sources of financing.

Types of Short-Term
Bank Financing

Various kinds of short-term bank borrowing are available today. They differ in purpose, repayment arrangements, and maturity. There are

143

also differences in interest rates and fees charged and in collateral requirements.

Single-Payment Loans

Features. The simplest bank loan is a single-payment loan, or promissory note. If your firm had a large quarterly tax payment coming due next week and you did not anticipate cash flows from operations being able to cover the payment until three weeks from now, you might arrange a two-week single-payment loan. You would sign a promissory note prepared by the bank. The note would specify the interest rate, fees paid, terms of repayment, and actions the bank will take if you don't repay. Some notes are *discount notes,* meaning that the bank gives you the face amount of the loan minus a discount rate. You repay the face amount of the loan, and so the discount is essentially the bank's interest. Most notes today include the interest payment at the end.

Interest on Single-Payment Loans. Interest is usually computed on a daily basis. If the note extends over several months, the bank might require a monthly or quarterly interest payment. Generally notes can be repaid before the due date without any interest penalty. The bank should charge you interest for only the number of days the note is outstanding. The interest rate is sometimes fixed for very short-term notes but is more often tied to the bank's prime rate, or base rate.

While the single payment, or "bullet loan," may be arranged with the bank for a one-time-only borrowing arrangement, it is much more common to see this kind of borrowing under a more general borrowing agreement with the bank, like a line of credit or a letter of credit.

Example. To illustrate a single-payment loan, suppose Mr. Wilson, from our example above, arranges a single-payment loan for one shipment of logs that will cost him $40,000. He plans on repaying the loan in 60 days, and the bank quotes an interest rate of "prime plus 2 percent." Suppose that the bank's prime rate is 7 percent and that the bank uses a 360-day year in computing interest. Interest is compounded monthly. After 30 days, the bank changes its prime rate to 6.5 percent. What will Mr. Wilson pay the bank when the promissory note is due in 60 days?

Mr. Wilson will repay the $40,000 plus interest. The complexity is that when interest is added the first month, it becomes part of the principal. So the second month's interest is computed by using the principal of $40,000 plus the first month's interest. We first compute the interest due by the end of the first month: $40,000 \times 30 \times (0.09/360) = \$300$. The total amount due is then $40,300. The second month, interest due includes the extra $300:

$40,300 \times 30 \times (0.085/360) = \$285.46$. Mr. Wilson would then pay back $40,300 + \$285.46 = \$40,585.46$.

Most banks, unfortunately for our computations, compound interest *daily*. This means that the first day's interest goes into the principal used to compute the second day's interest, etc. Fortunately, if you have a business calculator, you can compute this quite simply. You will have to read your calculator's instructions on financial computations if you are not already familiar with them.

Here's how you would do it. In the time value mode of your calculator, first put $40,000 into the present-value (PV) register. Then put 9/360 into the interest register and 30 into the N register. Compute the future value (FV) by pressing the FV button. This should give you $40,301.09. This is the amount that would be due to the bank in 30 days. Why is this number $1.09 higher than the $300 we computed above? That's the effect of compounding the interest. Now enter this amount into the register for PV, enter 30 for N, and enter 8.5/360 for interest. By pressing FV, you should get $40,587.54. This is about $2 more than our simpler computation above. But for larger amounts and longer periods, the difference can be substantial.

Credit Lines

Features of Credit Lines. If Mr. Wilson wants the bank to fund several different log purchases during the year and also help fund payroll and other cash flows until sales begin to materialize in the spring, he will be back to the bank many times with requests for single-payment loans. To ease the management and informational burden on both Mr. Wilson and the bank, Mr. Wilson will probably want to arrange a *credit line* with the bank. A credit line is an agreement under which a firm may choose to borrow up to a specified limit over a particular time period, usually a year. A credit line is sometimes called a *bank facility*. Credit analysis and much of the administrative approval and processing take place when the credit line is set up. Subsequent borrowing against the credit line is much easier and requires usually only the approval of the firm's bank relationship manager (loan officer). Loans taken out against the line are often formalized by a promissory note for that specific borrowing. The loans are repaid as the borrower's cash flows permit. Sometimes, however, the bank may specify that the borrower must bring the loan down to zero during some period of time like a month or two. The ability to pay off the line for part of a year shows the bank the customer is not using the bank's money for long-term investments. If that is the case, the bank would consider the risks to be different and want perhaps a different lending arrangement.

A credit line is usually attested to by a letter from the bank (or perhaps a more formal legal agreement) offering the credit line and specifying the terms and conditions of loans to be made. Although most lines are for a period of one year, credit lines represent an ongoing relationship with the bank and are often renewed at maturity, provided the borrower continues to represent an acceptable credit risk. When the line is renewed, the credit limit, interest rate, or other conditions of the line may be changed.

A *revolving credit line* is a credit line that extends out multiple years and often does not carry the requirement that the borrower have the line paid down to zero during the year. A revolving line gives the borrower assurance that the ability to borrow will be there next year unless financial conditions significantly change.

Repayment on Demand.   The terms and conditions of a credit line usually contain a clause stating that the bank has a right to demand repayment of borrowing against the line if the firm's financial picture changes. The degree of permissible changes may be specified in terms of financial statement ratios or other actions that might indicate problems with the borrower. However, even if a key ratio is violated, a borrower can often work with the bank and explain temporary problems and avoid repayment demands. It is important in any kind of bank borrowing to keep the bank informed of significant changes that may affect your firm's financial health. Bankers are not fond of surprises!

Compensating a Bank for a Credit Line.   When you work out a credit line with your bank, there are several forms of compensation you must pay.

Commitment Fee.   This is compensation for the bank's commitment to keep the line available for your use. Credit lines—even unused ones—are a scarce resource, and so banks charge for them, especially if the credit line is formalized into a legally binding credit agreement. For less formal, uncommitted lines there is usually no fee or at least a much smaller fee. The fee on a committed line may be stated as a percentage of the total credit line or as a percentage of the unused portion of the line. Typical fees are in the range of ⅛ to ½ percent (quoted in annual terms but payable monthly).

Suppose Mr. Wilson negotiates a $200,000 credit line with the bank and the commitment fee is ½ percent based on the unused portion of the line. During October, Mr. Wilson only uses $20,000 of the line, and so the bank would charge Mr. Wilson the following:

$$0.005 \times (200{,}000 - 20{,}000) / 12 = \$75$$

We divide by 12 because the ½ percent is an annual rate and we are computing the charges for one month.

Compensating Balances.   Your bank may also require that you keep demand deposits in the bank as part of your compensation for the credit line. While not as common now as a decade ago, some banks still charge compensating balances for small and medium-sized businesses. The balances are in the range of 5 to 10 percent of the amount of the credit line and typically earn no interest. The cost to the borrower is the opportunity cost that could be made by investing the balances elsewhere. The balance specified is an average balance over some period like a quarter. One month the balance may be far below that required—as long as subsequent months bring up the average to the required level. As with commitment fees, the balance requirement may be based either on the line or on the unused portion of the line.

If Mr. Wilson, with his $200,000 credit line, is also required to keep 5 percent of the total line in demand deposits (not 5 percent of the unused portion), his balance in October should average

$$0.05 \times 200,000 = \$10,000$$

The $10,000 is not a payment to the bank but only a bank balance that is left in the firm's checking account earning no interest. So the cost is not $10,000 but only the opportunity cost on $10,000.

Interest Rate. If Mr. Wilson does not borrow on the credit line, there would be, of course, no interest payment even though Mr. Wilson would have to pay commitment fees and perhaps compensating balances. Interest is charged only if loans are taken out against the credit line. The rate used is almost always tied to some variable rate like the bank's prime rate, the Treasury bill rate, the bank's CD rate, or the Eurodollar CD rate. The latter rate is called the *LIBOR rate,* standing for London Interbank Offered Rate. That's the market interest rate paid on CDs denominated in dollars and issued by large London banks. Some large U.S. banks fund some of their short-term loans through this market.

The rate usually depends upon the creditworthiness of the borrower. If you are a financially strong borrower with an excellent profit history and strong potential, you will get the bank's prime rate. Weaker borrowers get "prime plus 1 percent" or "prime plus 2 percent." The bank's prime rate is determined by the bank's executive committee and changed from time to time. Although each bank could set a different prime rate, most banks follow each other: when one major bank changes its prime rate, the others fall in line. The other rates to which credit line borrowing is sometimes tied are market-based rates that change daily or more frequently. Hence, each day the interest rate will be different. The advantage to the borrower in having a true market rate is that when rates are falling, the prime rate may lag behind. Of course, when rates are rising, the prime lags, too, and so the borrower benefits from the "stickiness" of the prime rate.

Collateral and Other Loan Protections. Credit line borrowing is often unsecured. In these cases the bank is willing to make loans to the firm on the basis of the firm's strong financial position. No specific assets stand behind the loan in the event of default. However, many small and medium-sized firms pose too much of a risk for unsecured lending. There are several ways a firm can still take advantage of the flexibility that credit line borrowing offers even if circumstances do not qualify the borrower for an unsecured line.

Collateral is a common way to secure a credit line. A secured loan is a loan that gives the lender a claim on specific assets in case of default. Usually short-term assets form the basis of the collateral. There are two basic ways to handle collateral in short-term loans: a collateralized loan and an asset-based loan.

Collateralized Loan.   With a collateralized loan the bank still views the loan primarily on the strength of the borrower's financial strength. The collateralized assets serve as an "escape hatch" in case the loan cannot be repaid. The bank does not expect to seize the assets—only to have them there in the event of problems. Accounts receivable and inventory are commonly used collateral for small and medium-sized businesses. Since these represent assets that may be on the books at a much higher value than the bank could receive if it took control of the assets, the bank will discount the assets in determining if there is enough collateral.

For example, suppose Mr. Wilson uses his accounts receivable as collateral and shows the bank his customer invoices that total $100,000 for April (some are from previous months' sales, too). The bank would examine the invoices and eliminate any that were too old (these could end up as bad debts). "Too old" is often defined as three times normal credit terms. If Mr. Wilson allowed people 30 days to pay, then invoices older than 90 days would not be counted by the bank. The bank also eliminates any invoices that are likely not to be paid for other reasons—perhaps the customer is known to be bankrupt, for example. The bank then takes a percentage of the invoices, a typical number would be 70 percent, and the resulting number would be the amount the bank would loan against accounts receivable. So out of $100,000, Mr. Wilson may get:

Total receivables, April	$100,000
Unqualified receivables	7,000
Qualifying receivables	93,000
Less 30%	−27,900
Maximum loan amount	$ 65,100

The same idea applies to inventory. The bank discounts the inventory to more accurately assess its value as collateral. One percentage may apply to raw materials inventory and another to work in process and yet another to finished goods inventory. In Mr. Wilson's case, the following illustrates how these percentages apply to April data:

Inventory type	Book value	Percentage	Loanable amount
Raw materials	$100,000	50%	$50,000
Work in process	80,000	10%	8,000
Finished goods	50,000	50%	25,000
Total	$230,000		$83,000

Mr. Wilson could then borrow a total of $65,100 plus $83,000 against his receivables and inventory. Mr. Wilson would supply the bank with inventory and receivables reports on a regular basis—usually monthly. Occasionally, a bank officer may pay a visit to Mr. Wilson to see the inventory and discuss receivables records.

Asset-Based Loans. While quite similar to collateralized loans, asset-based loans are often done in different departments of the bank or even by nonbank financial companies. With such loans, the bank does not look primarily to the financial strength of the borrower to protect the loan, but primarily at the value of the assets. Asset-based loans are for borrowers who are financially weak or who are relatively new and have limited financial history and yet have assets that are themselves quite salable. A new record store in a mall may have no credit history and may be quite weak financially and yet has a readily marketable inventory on which to base a loan.

To make sure inventory does not disappear, the lender may insist that inventory be stored in public warehouses where the lender can control inventory release. Some farm equipment dealers, for example, use this type of security arrangement. Where public warehouses are not practical, the lender may require that the firm physically segregate the bank's asset-based inventory from other inventory the firm may own. A bonded employee could then be given exclusive access to the inventory area and be responsible for its safekeeping. Asset-based lenders are known to move very quickly to seize inventory from a firm that is on the verge of trouble.

Such lenders will also sometimes make buy-back arrangements with suppliers who sell to the borrower. If the borrower can't repay, then the supplier agrees to buy back the goods.

If accounts receivable serve as the asset base, the lender may require the borrower's customers to send payments directly to the lender, usually through a lockbox at the bank. Thus, the customers may not know of the arrangement.

Key Executive Insurance. For many firms one or two executives are key to the success of the firm. If anything were to happen to those key people, the firm's operations could be endangered and, consequently, the bank's loan placed in jeopardy. Mr. Wilson is by far the most important driving force in the company. If he became ill or died in a car accident, the company would have no one who could quickly assume leadership responsibilities. To protect the lender from such consequences, the bank may require that the borrower take out a *key executive insurance policy* payable to the bank covering the amount of any outstanding loans.

Personal Guarantees.   It is quite common for banks to ask principal executives of small businesses to personally guarantee loans. While the corporate structure nominally protects owners from losses, this is one common area in which the protection breaks down. Banks feel that a small-business owner who is confident of her success will be willing to lay all on the line! The personal guarantee may include a second mortgage on the officer's house and pledges of other personal assets like securities, cars, and vacation homes. Generally banks stop short of asking for the firstborn child.

Computing the Effective Cost of Credit Line Borrowing.   Suppose Mr. Wilson's borrowing requirements are given in the following table:

Time period	Loan outstanding
October–December	0
January–April	$100,000
May–July	$180,000
August–September	$ 50,000

Mr. Wilson has negotiated a credit line of $200,000, which is compensated with a commitment fee of ½ percent (per annum) on the unused portion of the line, a compensating balance of 5 percent of the line, and a variable interest rate of prime plus 2 percent. Let's assume for simplicity that the prime rate is 7 percent and stays the same throughout the year. Assume also that Mr. Wilson could earn 10 percent per annum on the balances he has to tie up in the compensating balance.

To compute the effective interest rate on this credit line borrowing, we compute the total cash Mr. Wilson has to pay for the loan and divide this by the average loan Mr. Wilson gets to use from the bank. The cash he must pay for the loan consists of three separate costs: commitment fee, compensating balance opportunity cost, and interest payments.

Commitment fee.   This occurs in four parts.

Oct.–Dec.	$3 \times (200,000 - 0) \times (0.0025/12)$	= $125.00
Jan.–Apr.	$4 \times (200,000 - 100,000) \times (0.0025/12)$	= $ 83.33
May–July	$3 \times (200,000 - 180,000) \times (0.0025/12)$	= $ 12.50
Aug.–Sept.	$2 \times (200,000 - 50,000) \times (0.0025/12)$	= $ 62.50
Total commitment fees		= $283.33

Compensating Balance Opportunity Cost. Mr. Wilson will have to keep, on average, $0.05 \times \$200,000 = \$10,000$ on deposit with the bank during the year. At 10 percent opportunity cost, this is worth $1000 to Mr. Wilson.

Interest Payments. We have assumed the interest rate is constant. It would not be difficult to use a different rate for each month. The interest rate Mr. Wilson pays is 9 percent, 2 percent above the prime rate of 7 percent.

Oct.–Dec.	3×0	=	0
Jan.–Apr.	$4 \times 100,000 \times (0.09/12)$	=	$3000
May–July	$3 \times 180,000 \times (0.09/12)$	=	$4050
Aug.–Sept.	$2 \times 50,000 \times (0.09/12)$	=	$ 750
Total interest payments			= $7800

Effective Interest Rate. This is found by summing all out-of-pocket expenses Mr. Wilson incurs and dividing by the average loan. The average loan must be weighted by the number of months a given amount is outstanding:

Oct.–Dec.	3×0	=	0
Jan.–Apr.	$4 \times 100,000$	= $	400,000
May–July	$3 \times 180,000$	= $	540,000
Aug.–Sept.	$2 \times 50,000$	= $	100,000
Total		= $	1,040,000
Average (divide by 12)		= $	86,667

Total expenses incurred by Mr. Wilson are:

Total commitment fees	= $ 283.33
Compensating balance opportunity cost	= $1000.00
Total interest payments	= $7800.00
Total expenses for credit line	= $9083.33

The effective interest rate is then total expenses divided by the average loan:

$$\text{Effective interest rate} = \frac{\$9,083.33}{\$86,667} = 10.48\%$$

The effective rate is higher than the bank's quoted rate of 9 percent because interest expense is not the only factor in computing the effective rate. The effective rate also includes the compensating balance and the commitment fee. The effective rate is important to know because it permits you to compare rates across institutions, which may charge for credit lines differently. It also lets you compare credit line borrowing with alternatives like commercial paper (discussed in the next chapter).

Letter of Credit

A letter of credit (LC) is a document created by the bank that states that the bank will pay the borrower or another party approved by the borrower a certain amount at some specified day or over some specified time period as long as certain conditions are met. While they are used commonly in international trade, LCs are also used in domestic transactions when a seller seeks assurances that a potential buyer will, in fact, pay as promised. Some financially weak cities, for example, sell their municipal bonds with LC backing, thereby promising if the city can't pay back the bonds, a very large, trusted bank will honor the bonds. This assurance helps the bonds readily sell to the public.

LCs are particularly useful for importing and exporting because the buyer and seller typically do not know one another well, have few legal recourses if things go wrong, and face long time delays and high costs of international shipments. As described more fully in Chap. 14, an importer in the United States, for example, would ask its U.S. bank to issue a letter of credit promising to pay a German supplier $5000 for a shipment of electronic parts. The bank performs a credit analysis on the U.S. importer, and if the firm is deemed creditworthy, the bank issues a letter of credit to the supplier's bank in Germany. The German bank, trusting the creditworthiness of the U.S. bank, confirms the LC to the German supplier. In essence, the German bank now stands behind the transaction; and the German supplier, confident of getting paid, releases the electronic parts to the U.S. importer.

Some LCs, like those used in the import-export business, result in the bank paying to close the transaction. The buyer then pays the bank at a later time. Other LCs, like the ones issued to the city that sells its municipal bonds, are standby LCs that generally result in no cash flow from the bank unless the city can't pay. Standby LCs are also used in domestic credit purchases when a seller does not have confidence in a potential customer.

Banker's Acceptance Financing

Banker's acceptance financing is closely tied to letters of credit. Suppose your firm exports goods to an Italian importer. The Italian importer has had its bank send your bank an LC for $100,000 payable in 90 days. Your bank has accepted the LC and stands behind it. You now draw a time draft on the importer and present it to your bank. The bank stamps "accepted" on it, and it becomes a banker's acceptance. The payment is not due for 90 days, however, and you may need the cash now. You may sell the acceptance to the bank and receive the discounted amount immediately. The bank is providing short-term financing. Your bank may hold the acceptance itself for 90 days and receive the $100,000 from the Italian bank, or your bank could sell the acceptance in a marketplace that trades in acceptances. These are readily salable instruments backed by the importer's bank, the exporter's bank, and the Italian importer, and so an acceptance is a relatively safe security. The amount of discount applied to an acceptance sold before maturity depends on market forces. The discounts are usually close to rates on certificates of deposit. Banker's acceptance financing is widely used by importers and exporters.

Reverse Repurchase Agreement

This kind of borrowing is really just using securities in your short-term investment portfolio as collateral for a bank or broker loan. For example, suppose you have, some time ago, purchased a $50,000 Treasury bond that matures six months from now. You do not wish to sell the bond now because of its current depressed price. But suppose you need $50,000 for a few days to cover a temporary cash shortage. You could get your banker or perhaps a broker to buy it from you. You would buy it back, with interest, in a few days. This procedure gives the effect of a short-term loan even though it is technically a sale and repurchase. Often the underlying security does not even change hands.

Master Notes

A form of short-term financing used by very creditworthy borrowers is the master note arrangement. It is an agreement between the bank's trust department and the corporate borrower that the trust department (which invests cash for its clients and not for the bank itself), over the next several years, will purchase short-term notes of the borrower. It is like a credit line in that a maximum amount of financing is usually specified and the rate paid is variable. There might also be a minimum amount of borrowing stated. This arrangement is essentially like a private placement of commercial paper (see Chap. 10).

Longer-Term Bank Borrowing

While this chapter covers essentially short-term bank borrowing, we should also mention that banks provide longer-term financing as well.

Term Loans. Term loans extend out two to seven or so years. Banks are typically not interested in direct lending extending much beyond that time period because their deposits do not have maturities that extend beyond five to seven years. Term loans are often funded in the beginning and then paid off over multiple years. The repayment schedule could take the form of a constant monthly payment (like a car loan), a constant principal repayment with diminishing interest payments, or interest only with a balloon payment at maturity. Term loans frequently require collateral in the form of fixed assets like equipment, buildings, or real estate.

Lease Financing.   Banks sometimes have leasing subsidiaries that can arrange equipment leases, building leases, etc. The leasing company essentially buys the equipment for you, and you sign a long-term lease agreement that locks you into payments and assigns you most of the risk. But these are the risks you would have taken anyway had you borrowed under some other arrangement and purchased the asset.

Mortgage Financing.   Banks can also provide mortgage financing. A mortgage is a long-term loan secured by physical assets like real estate. Most banks, once a mortgage is arranged, sell the mortgage in a very well-developed mortgage market. The bank may continue to service the mortgage, meaning that it collects payments, handles problems, and processes information about the loan.

Working with Your Banker

What You Need to Know before Applying for a Loan

Banks Are Becoming More Risk-Averse.   When you approach your banker to inquire about a loan, it is helpful to know how a bank looks at prospective borrowers and what pressures the banking system in general is facing today. You probably know already that a bank is not an equity risk taker. Bank loans carry no provisions for the bank to make exceptional profits if the firm does exceptionally well. The proprietor, partners, or shareholders are the ones who benefit if the firm does well. The bank can, of course, generate more loan and service business, but there is a cap on the amount banks can make on any given loan. A bank can get back principal plus interest or anything less than this, down to and including zero (or even worse if you count administrative and legal costs). So a bank faces limited upside potential and lots of downside risk when it makes loans. Firm owners, on the other hand, can also lose everything, but they have enormous upside potential.

Over the past few decades, most banks, in fact, have made very little on their loan portfolios. Many of the nation's major banks are trying to recover from years of serious losses particularly in loans on real estate, farming loans, and loans to lesser-developed countries. In addition, recent changes in the Federal Reserve System could make banks even less anxious to make risky loans. Because of the S&L bailout and numerous commercial bank failures, the banking system must absorb tens of billions of dollars in increased insurance premiums. Higher capital requirements imposed by Congress put tremendous profit pressures on banks. In 1994, the Fed will divide banks into three major risk classes based on the riskiness of their loan portfolios and other investments. The most risky class of banks will have to pay the highest insurance rates. Not many banks want to be classified in the most risky class—that could be very bad for business in general. So, to clean up their acts, most banks are becoming more and more restrictive in their lending practices.

What Increased Bank Risk Aversion Means for Borrowers. With banks becoming more risk-averse, it means that you will have to make a better case to your banker to qualify for loans in the future. You will have to demonstrate a better understanding of your business and will have to be more persuasive in making your case to the bank. It means that banks may become less tolerant of marginal loans. That means you must do a more comprehensive job of keeping your banker posted on how your firm is doing. It means that banks will tighten loan covenants for most of their lending agreements. Perhaps never before will Will Rogers' quip about bankers be more applicable: "To get money from a bank, first you have to convince them you don't need it."

How Banks Look at Prospective Borrowers. In judging a credit application, a bank lending officer looks at many different factors. For years, these have been classified into five categories called the *five C's of credit*. Everyone seems to have a slightly different list telling exactly what the C's stand for. But that's all right—it's just a vehicle for discussing some key points anyway.

Character. A lender would prefer to loan money to a borrower who is honest, hard-working, and straightforward. Since character is difficult to determine in any quantitative way, the lender may try to assess this through personal interviews, character references, other bankers, and the borrower's reputation with customers and suppliers.

Capacity. Does the prospective borrower have the potential to service the loan—that means make interest and principal repayments? What are current borrowing levels? As we said above, banks are not interested in taking large, equity-style risks. They want to have the proprietor, partners, or shareholders absorb the major part of the firm's risk. To determine the firm's capacity for handling the requested loan, the lending officer will request the firm's (it is hoped, audited) financial statements. They will show how much debt the firm already has outstanding. Certain financial ratios help credit analysts assess the debt levels of the applicant. Debt to total assets measures total debt in the form of long-term debt (bonds, shareholder loans, etc.) and short-term debt (other bank loans, notes payable, and sometimes accounts payable). While payables are usually not included in total debt, many argue that payables are a form of trade debt.

While an acceptable ratio for debt to total assets is hard to determine, there are databases (such as the Robert Morris Associates listings of financial ratios) that give statistical information on ratios for various industries. Most banks would consider a 50 percent ratio to be fairly high.

Some banks also use the interest coverage ratio as a measure of ability to handle interest payments. Interest coverage ratio is defined in several ways, but a common one is

$$\text{Interest coverage} = \frac{\text{operating income (before interest and taxes)}}{\text{total interest payments}}$$

Total interest payments include interest on both old and proposed borrowings. The magnitude of this number gives the bank some idea of how well protected the bank's interest payment is. A large number means that earnings could drop significantly and the borrower could still make interest payments.

Of course, a better approach to answer the question of whether the firm could make interest and principal payments would be cash flows. We show in Chap. 11 that income, no matter how it is measured, does not adequately capture cash flows. To get closer to cash flows, some banks add depreciation (a noncash expense) back to operating income.

Any financial ratio has usually severe shortcomings. A better way to determine if the firm has the capacity to repay debt is to analyze pro forma financial statements. The well-prepared borrower will have carefully projected balance sheets and income statements to show the bank both the need for the loan and the ability to service the loan.

Collateral. If a loan is to be collateralized, the bank is interested in the quality of the assets backing up the credit. If accounts receivable will serve as collateral, the prospective borrower will want to show the bank details about its customer base. The bank may also be interested in personal guarantees and key executive insurance if the borrower is relatively new or financially weaker.

Cash Flow. While the bank will be interested in profitability, it will also want to see cash flow projections over the term of the loan. Again, pro forma financial statements can show the firm's ability to generate cash to service the loan. Pro forma statements also help convince the bank that you know your business.

Cautions. In this category fall all the miscellaneous concerns the bank may have about the firm. What risks does the firm face from competitors, from the economy in general, from substitute products, from lawsuits? In this category might also fall potential headaches for the bank. Is the potential borrower going to be easy to work with or difficult? With profit margins on loans relatively low, a banker does not have much time to spend with problem borrowers.

What to Prepare before Visiting Your Banker. Before you visit your banker to request a loan, you will want to prepare well. Here are a few ideas that may help you prepare.

Know the Bank. Is the bank itself having problems? Has it been profitable in the past? Is it under profit pressure? If you are a small business with relatively weak financial statements and a short history on which to base your case, you will likely have a harder time with a bank that is under profit pressure. What is the bank's reputation with firms your size and in your industry? Some banks have specialized lending groups within the bank that focus on servicing fast-food companies, energy companies, financial services, etc. Does your bank have any special interest in your particular industry? If so, it will understand your situation more easily and perhaps be more sympathetic to your needs. Will the bank be able to handle the other financial services you may need now and in the future? If you are a big customer of the bank in one area, that gives you leverage in other areas like getting loans.

To learn about the bank, you may want to examine its annual report and also read about how the bank is rated by one of a number of bank rating services available.

Know Your Financial Picture. Make sure you know how your firm works financially. To do this, it is very useful to go through the exercise of preparing pro forma financial statements (see Chap. 11) under a number of different scenarios. This will tell you where you are vulnerable from a cash flow position. It will also help you assess more realistically how much cash you need to meet expected circumstances. It is generally considered unwise to ask a bank for a credit line of $100,000 and then, three months later, go back to the bank and request an increase of $50,000 because you failed to understand what was happening in your business. This type of activity does not build the lending officer's confidence in your financial prowess.

Be Able to Make Your Case Convincingly. The bank officer you work with needs to understand your business and needs to obtain this understanding very quickly with a minimum of effort. That means you must prepare well and be able to convey to the bank officer key information about your products and services, production and delivery methods, customers, suppliers, management personnel, past performance, projected performance, and strategies for the future. Bankers are usually not impressed with generalities and vague ideas but want hard facts and evidence of detailed planning.

Dealing with Your Banker
after Closing a Loan

Keeping the Bank Informed.   Since banks will generally be much less tolerant of problem loans in the future, you will want to keep your banker constantly informed of your financial circumstances. The information you
provide should be agreed upon between banker and borrower. Your part is to
make sure the information is timely, accurate, and easy to understand. Your
banker will not appreciate first learning of your firm's problems by reading
the newspapers! As is happening in production between manufacturers and
suppliers, the relationship between borrower and lender needs to move more
toward a productive partnership rather than a battle between adversaries.

What Can Go Wrong.   If you do get into financial difficulties and are
unable to meet the terms and conditions of the credit line or other loan
agreement, there are several courses of action the bank might take. It could
do nothing. This is often the case for small problems. The bank may just
acknowledge that your firm is in technical violation of loan covenants and
ask you to move into compliance as soon as possible.

Stronger action would be to take control of the collateral. The bank
could seize inventory and sell it or take control of receivables, collect them
from customers, or sell them to another party.

Your bank could, of course, demand immediate repayment of your loan.
If you have been a very cooperative partner with your banker, this is less
likely to happen than if you have been adversaries.

Another option is for the bank to restructure the loan. For example,
Mr. Wilson may find that during a bad year with high interest rates, potential customers of his log homes can't get financing and his sales drop off
unexpectedly. Unfortunately he has purchased logs and processed them in
anticipation of a certain level of sales. He would be unable to repay his
credit line from reduced summer sales. He would have to sit down with the
bank and discuss the possibility of waiving the requirement to be out of
debt by October. Perhaps the credit line could be redefined as a revolving
credit line or even a term loan.

At the far end of the spectrum is forcing bankruptcy. The bank can go to
court and force Mr. Wilson to seek bankruptcy protection. There are two
primary forms of corporate bankruptcy: Chapter 11 and Chapter 7. Essentially, Chapter 11 permits a firm, under supervision of a judge, to restructure its financing. Creditors are held at bay until the firm returns to
profitability. A court would permit Chapter 11 if the firm demonstrates it
has a high likelihood of survival. The restructuring might include delaying
loan principal repayments, granting partial debt forgiveness, reducing
interest rates on debt, and converting some or all of debt into equity.
Lenders would have to agree to the restructuring.

Under Chapter 7, lenders would not agree with the terms of Chapter 11 because they may think that the firm is worth more to them liquidated than it is as a going concern. The bankruptcy judge would oversee the sale of the firm's assets to satisfy creditors. The firm would be dissolved.

Summary

Short-term financing is required by almost all firms. Such financing provides the slack that firms need to cope with uncertain cash flows, seasonality, and certain financial transactions like imports and exports. While there are many forms of short-term financing, commercial banks are a major supplier of short-term credit. They offer a wide variety of loan arrangements to meet the corporate borrowing needs of large and small customers. Economic pressures on the banking system have become severe in recent years, making bank borrowing more restrictive. For firms to obtain bank financing, they will have to be more attuned to the bank's need for better borrower information to help them lower risk. That means that to obtain a bank loan, borrowers will have to do their homework and be able to demonstrate that they understand their business and have carefully thought through their financial needs and prospects. While the world is moving on many fronts to more cooperation between buyers and sellers, we think the same is now happening in the relationship between banks and their customers.

Self-Test

1. Mr. Wilson borrows $100,000 from his bank for three months. For the first two months, the interest rate quoted for the loan is 9 percent, and for the last month, the rate is 10 percent. Both rates are compounded monthly. Assume the bank uses a 360-day year for computations and that each month has 30 days. How much will Mr. Wilson be expected to pay at the end of the three months? Repeat the problem using daily compounding. How close are the two numbers?

2. Green Medical Supply is seeking a secured loan, using its inventory and accounts receivable as collateral. The bank applies the following percentages to inventory and receivables:

Raw materials	50%
Work in process	5%
Finished goods	70%
Qualifying accounts receivable	80%

At the end of May, Green has total inventory of $400,000, half of which is raw materials with the remainder divided evenly between work in process and finished goods. Green's accounts receivables in May total $500,000, but $30,000 is relatively old and in dispute. How much can Green expect the bank to loan it on June 1?

3. The Crafton Company has a credit line of $300,000 with its bank for which it agrees to keep a 5 percent balance on the line and pay a commitment fee of ¼ percent per annum on the unused portion of the line. The loan interest charges are 12 percent per annum (1 percent per month) for the average loan outstanding during the month. Assume Crafton could earn 12 percent on cash tied up in compensating balances. Crafton's loan schedule is as follows:

Month	Loan outstanding
January	0
February	0
March	$ 50,000
April	$ 70,000
May	$ 70,000
June	$100,000
July	$150,000
August	$150,000
September	$250,000
October	$250,000
November	$150,000
December	$ 50,000

a. What is the effective annual interest rate on this loan?

b. Suppose a different bank offers Crafton a $300,000 credit line to replace the one it has with its current bank. The new bank would charge no commitment fee and require no compensating balances. Its annual borrowing rate, however, is 14 percent. Would this credit line be better or worse for Crafton?

10

Nonbank Sources of Short-Term Financing

Introduction

Midwestern Specialty Steel (MSS) knew it was headed for a temporary slow-down in sales over the next several months. The industry was being badly battered by a stalled economy, and MSS was in the process of upgrading much of its worn-out equipment. The two forces placed MSS in a very bad cash flow position at least for the next six months. With short-term credit lines already used up and additional long-term credit unlikely given the circumstances of the economy, MSS looked for ways to survive a cash crunch. It held a meeting with major suppliers and told them of the problems the firm faced. Since most suppliers had worked with MSS for many years, they were sympathetic to the situation. MSS asked that normal terms be extended to 75 to 90 days for the next 6 months. While the suppliers were not excited to extend terms, they realized that during this time they would have to comply or lose MSS as a long-term customer.

In Chap. 9 we discussed bank sources of short-term financing. In this chapter we discuss accounts payable as a source of short-term financing, as illustrated in the MSS example, and other nonbank sources such as commercial finance companies, receivable factoring, and commercial paper.

Accounts Payable Financing

Accounts payable arise out of the usual course of business when a buyer makes a purchase on credit. It is very common for corporate customers to

161

be extended credit terms of several weeks or months (see Chap. 12). Whereas most forms of short-term financing must be specifically arranged, payables financing arises spontaneously in the course of making purchases. Its volume increases as purchases increase even if credit terms are not changed. In some cases, like the MSS example above, this form of financing is expanded deliberately when the buyer delays payments.

Accounts Payable Decisions

The decision of when to pay an invoice is often a tug-of-war between the seller's credit terms and the buyer's payables terms. Much depends on the relative strengths of the two opponents. Very large, strong tobacco giants, for example, have very strictly enforced credit terms. Smaller buyers must pay on time or run the risk of nonshipment. On the other hand, small suppliers providing services to, say, large telecommunication firms may have to wait long months for payment. The small supplier could never dictate payment terms to the giant but must accept the larger company's terms if the supplier wants the business.

Besides the factors of relative size and strength, importance of the supplier to the customer is a factor. If a supplier provides a key product to the buyer, the buyer may want to make sure that supplier is paid first, within credit terms, regardless of the supplier's relative size. The same buyer may delay payments to another supplier from whom the buyer purchases only an occasional product.

The Cost of Payables Financing.   If your firm has a credit line at your bank and you borrow against the line, the bank charges you interest. In addition, you may have to pay commitment fees and compensating balances. We saw in the last chapter that, although it may be complex, it is possible to compute exactly the cost of credit line borrowing. Unfortunately, it is not so easy to compute the cost of financing through accounts payable. It turns out to be a multistage problem. By that we mean that some payables financing is very inexpensive and some is very expensive. The problem is that you may not be able to tell when the price suddenly goes up.

"Free" Financing—Within Stated Terms.   Suppose you purchase $1000 of goods from one of your suppliers who gives terms of net 30, meaning that the payment is due in 30 days. Essentially the supplier is providing you with $1000 of financing for 30 days. We call it financing because if the supplier made you pay immediately, you would have to go out and find some other source of financing to make the payment. What is the supplier charging you for letting you keep the $1000 for 30 days? Essentially nothing. The supplier has built the cost of financing into the price of the product. Assuming the supplier does not offer you a discount for early payment, you would

have to pay $1000 whether you paid on day 5, day 15, or day 30. So for 30 days you are given "free" financing. It would be foolish to pay on day 5 when you could take 25 more days to pay.

Moderate Stretching.   Delaying payment beyond stated credit terms, in this example day 30, is called *stretching*. Suppose you decide to pay on day 31. What is the cost of an extra day's worth of accounts payable financing? In most cases, the cost is very little, if any. Occasional stretching for short periods is quite common. In fact, because of mail and check processing time delays, it is difficult to even define the payment date. Is it the postmark date, the check receipt date, the available funds date? Because of these ambiguities, most firms allow grace periods. A payment received any time between 30 and 35 days would likely be considered a timely payment and there would be no visible consequences to the buyer.

Severe Stretching.   What would be the cost if you made the $1000 payment on day 40? day 60? day 120? Likely there would be adverse economic consequences for severe stretching. But what is "severe"? How far could you stretch before these adverse consequences would be imposed? That is the problem with computing the costs of payables financing. There are no easy formulas to apply to payables costs like the ones for credit line financing. We can enumerate some of the possible costs, but we don't generally have a way to apply these to specific suppliers for specific time delays. Here are some of the potential costs of severe stretching:

1. *Psychological costs.*   You and others in your firm may consider intentional stretching to be unethical. Therefore stretching would impose a high psychological cost on you or others.

2. *Reputational costs.*   You may not want to be known as one who does not pay bills on time. Stretching would blemish your reputation as a fair-dealing firm. In addition, suppliers may give information about delayed payments to credit reporting organizations like Dun and Bradstreet. An adverse credit record may affect future relations with other suppliers and financial institutions.

3. *Strained supplier relations.*   Stretching could damage relations with your suppliers on whom you depend for products and services. Your own purchasing and payables departments would especially feel this strain as they have to fend off phone calls from anxious suppliers.

4. *Interest penalties.*   Some suppliers may charge specific interest penalties for late payments. A common practice in some industries is to charge a 1.5 percent interest penalty for each month a payment is overdue. One way some suppliers may choose to impose interest is to convert delinquent accounts payable into a promissory note that contains a provision for interest payments. A promissory note also formalizes the obligation to pay and may put the supplier in a better position in the event of bankruptcy.

5. *Direct financial penalties.* For some types of payments, such as taxes and insurance or license fees, delayed payment could carry severe consequences such as tax penalties, loss of insurance coverage, and loss of license to practice. Such consequences, of course, would far exceed any possible financing gains from stretching.

6. *Stopped shipments.* Stretching could cause the supplier to stop or delay shipments to you. This could have severe indirect consequences. You may have to shut down an assembly line, delay shipments to your own customers, find another supplier, etc.

7. *Legal recourse.* Your supplier may impose one of several legal sanctions available, such as placing a lien on materials you purchased, seizing inventory, or taking you to court where you might have to seek bankruptcy protection.

Most of these cost factors are difficult to quantify in terms of both dollar amount and timing. Therefore it is impossible to put exact numbers on the axes of Fig. 10-1 showing the approximate relationship between payment delay and cost.

Costs When Discounts Are Offered. The decision of when to pay can be more precisely quantified when cash discount terms are offered. Since we covered this topic in Chap. 7, we will only briefly review the calculation of the interest cost of missing discounts. Suppose the supplier above offers you

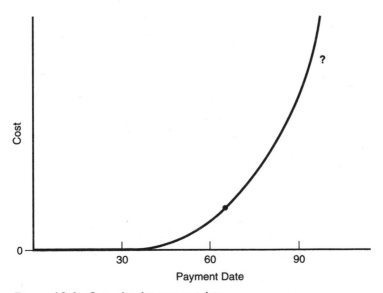

Figure 10-1. Cost related to payment date.

a 2 percent discount on the $1000 invoice if the payment is made by day 10. The full amount is due on day 30 as before. Now we have a choice to make. During the first 10-day period, the supplier is willing to let us pay $980. During the last 20-day period, we would have to pay $1000. We can consider the extra $20 to be interest on the $980. Essentially the supplier is charging us $20 interest if we want to delay payment for 20 days.

We might be tempted to think that 2 percent interest is a very good rate—but that would be a serious mistake. An annualized 2 percent interest is, of course, a very nice rate at which to borrow, but this 2 percent applies only over a 20-day period. We first have to annualize the rate before we can compare it with other financing alternatives. To annualize this rate we remember that the $20 is like interest on $980, divide by 20 (the borrowing period) to get a daily rate, and then multiply by 365 to get an annual rate:

$$\text{Effective annual rate of not taking discount} = \frac{\$20}{\$980} \times \frac{365}{20} = 37.2\%$$

In other words, the supplier is charging us an annualized rate of 37.2 percent to borrow over that 20-day period. This is very expensive financing since we could probably borrow from our banker at a much lower rate. Given the choice of paying $980 on day 10 or $1000 on day 30, we would choose $980 on day 10.

In the example with Midwestern Specialty Steel, suppose the suppliers generally offered discounts of 2 percent for early payment (day 10) and now MSS has asked them to agree to an average payment date of 80 days. What does this cost MSS in terms of missed discounts? MSS would be paying 70 days after the discount period, so we can compute the effective annual rate as

$$(0.02/0.98) \times (365/70) = 10.6\%$$

If MSS can get suppliers to agree to its terms, MSS is receiving financing at a rate equivalent to 10.6 percent—which may be a much better rate than it could obtain from its banks under its strained financial circumstances.

Financing through Commercial Finance Companies

Commercial finance companies are like banks in some ways. For example, they make commercial loans. But unlike banks, they do not take demand deposits, nor do they offer the payment and investment services available through most banks. While banks obtain a significant portion of their financing through relatively inexpensive demand and savings deposits, commercial finance companies obtain their financing through common stock, commercial paper, longer-term notes, and bank loans. They are not bound by the same regulations that govern commercial banks. They also do not loan to consumers, and so they avoid the restrictions that govern consumer finance companies. Of course, some larger commercial finance companies do have divisions that target consumers.

Who Borrows from Commercial Finance Companies?

Commercial finance companies usually make loans that are considered too risky for commercial banks. They often make asset-based loans like inventory and receivable loans. Of course, some banks also have asset-based lending departments or subsidiaries that compete with finance companies for this segment of the loan market. Because of the higher levels of risk that commercial finance companies take, they generally charge higher interest rates than those charged by commercial banks. Finance companies accept a wide variety of collateral assets such as the "franchise value" of a borrower. For example, they may loan to a proprietor who owns the McDonald's franchise for a small town even though the proprietor is not financially strong. The franchise itself is a valuable asset.

Compensation for Commercial Finance Loans

As in the case of commercial bank loans, commercial finance loans carry variable rates tied to a reference rate, such as the prime rate of a money center bank. The increment is usually fairly steep such as prime plus six. While this may seem expensive, there are usually no other fees and never any compensating balance requirements.

Types of Financing

Asset-Based Loans.   Many loans are asset-based loans that are very similar to those of commercial banks discussed in Chap. 9. They can be in the form of credit lines where the amount borrowed is tied to the value of the underlying assets. Often accounts receivable are used. As with commercial banks, commercial finance companies compute qualifying receivables by deleting those receivables that are too old or are from unacceptable credit risks. Then a percentage is applied (usually 70 to 85 percent) to the qualifying receivables. Accounts receivable are usually pledged as collateral, but the borrower is still responsible for collecting the accounts. If problems develop, the finance company can seize the receivables and either collect them or sell them to a collection agency. The borrower is responsible for sending detailed receivable data to the finance company on a weekly or monthly basis.

Inventory is also used as the lending base. Sometimes the inventory is required to be separated from nonbase inventory or to be stored in a third-party warehouse to ensure control. Because commercial finance companies sometimes specialize in certain types of inventory, they may be willing to make higher-percentage loans than commercial banks. For example, a commercial finance company that specializes in the medical instrumentation industry may be willing to loan 70 percent of the stated value of finished goods inventory, while a commercial bank might be willing to loan only 50 percent.

Factoring. Some commercial finance companies provide receivables financing by the outright purchase of receivables. We discuss this topic below in more detail.

Leases. Many commercial finance companies are engaged in equipment and property leasing. They purchase the equipment, buildings, or property for the buyer and hold title until the lease obligations are fulfilled. The lessee signs an agreement to be responsible for lease payments for the life of the lease, for insurance payments on the asset, for maintenance, etc. Most of these leases are long-term and so do not fall conveniently under our scope of short-term financing.

Receivables Factoring

Receivables factoring, or simply factoring, is the sale of accounts receivable to another party (called the *factor*) who becomes responsible for collecting payments from the customer. This is usually done on a nonrecourse basis, meaning that if the factor cannot collect from the customer, that is the factor's problem and not the seller's problem. Factoring is sometimes done by commercial finance companies and sometimes by bank subsidiaries. Factoring is very important in certain specialty industries such as apparel and textiles. New York City's garment industry, for example, finances a significant portion of its sales through factoring.

Although you may not have thought of it in this light before, the most common form of receivables factoring is the credit card. The merchant accepts a credit card for a purchase instead of accepting a receivable directly from the customer. The credit card voucher (receivable) is sold to the merchant's bank at a discount. The banking/credit card issuer system purchases the receivables without recourse to the merchant and later collects payment from the consumer. In effect, credit cards have replaced an older system of making purchases at a department store on credit. Now the department store accepts credit cards and can do away with the entire credit department and associated overhead.

Roles of the Factor

The factor performs several roles. First, the factor plays a financial role by advancing funds to the seller. To provide funding to support this advance purchase, some factors sell receivables-backed commercial paper. When the receivables are collected, the commercial paper is redeemed. When the factor advances funds to the seller, the factor discounts the receivables to cover interest payments the factor must pay.

Second, factors play the role of credit analyst. If many small suppliers sell to numerous buyers, it does not make economic sense for each supplier to have a full credit department to analyze the creditworthiness of all possible buyers. There is much less duplication of effort if just one (or a few) credit department performs the credit function for all. That is a role the factor can play. If a customer wants to purchase a product from one of the suppliers in the factoring network, the customer must be approved for credit by the factor.

Third, the factor absorbs risk for a large number of sellers. It can absorb this risk more economically than the group of sellers because the factor does the credit checking and can more easily spot nonperformers. The factor also diversifies nonpayment risk across a number of suppliers.

Fourth, the factor performs a billing and payment collection service. All invoices are administered by the factor, and payments are collected by the factor. Dunning notices, follow-up phone calls for late payments, management of the receivables information system, etc., are all performed by the factor. With economies of scale, the factor can accomplish these services at a lower cost than the sum of the individual suppliers.

Types of Factoring

While the arrangement you make with a particular factor may utilize the four roles in any combination, two forms of factoring are most widely used: maturity factoring and conventional factoring.

Maturity Factoring. In maturity factoring, the factor buys the receivable but does not advance funds. Hence, it is performing only roles 2, 3, and 4. Cash is sent to the supplier's account at an agreed-upon maturity date corresponding approximately to normal payment terms in the industry. A commission of 0.75 to 1.5 percent is charged for the factor's services.

Conventional Factoring. In conventional factoring the factor performs all four functions, including advance remittance of payments to the seller. Charges for this kind of factoring are, of course, higher because of the interest charges on the advance payment. In addition to factoring fees, which would be on the same scale as those assessed for maturity factoring, the supplier would pay an annualized interest rate of, for example, prime plus 3 percent. The time period is based on the average payment terms.

Example of Factoring Costs. Suppose MSS, in order to generate much needed cash during its period of illiquidity, decides to factor some of its receivables. It works with a commercial finance company with which it negotiates a conventional factoring arrangement. The factor will charge a 1.5 percent fee and an interest rate of 11 percent on cash advances. The factor determines that MSS customers will likely pay in 60 days. During April, MSS factors receivables totaling $200,000. What proceeds will it receive from the factor, and what effective interest rate will MSS pay for this financing?

The factor will pay MSS the present value of $200,000 (discounted at 11 percent) minus the 1.5 percent factoring fee:

$$200,000/[1 + 60(0.11)/360] - 0.015 \times 200,000 = \$193,399$$

The effective borrowing rate charged by the factor is computed by taking the total amount paid ($200,000 - $193,399) divided by the proceeds of the factor's loan and then annualizing:

$$\frac{200,000 - 193,399}{193,399} \times \frac{365}{60} = 20.76\%$$

This may seem like a high interest rate, but remember that the cost of factoring is not simply the cost of financing. Factoring can help the firm offset the costs of its credit department and also reduce bad debts. Hence, these benefits must be taken into account in comparing factoring costs with other forms of financing.

Financing through Captive Finance Companies

If you buy from some very large corporations, they provide you with financing to help purchase their products and services. Major equipment manufacturers, automotive companies, and consumer goods manufacturers often own subsidiaries called *captive finance companies*. The task of these finance companies is to help dealers, distributors, and ultimate consumers purchase the parent company's products. Some captive finance companies have become more generic commercial finance companies, too, and will finance even competitors' sales.

An example is General Motors Acceptance Corporation (GMAC). GMAC loans cash to dealers for the purchase of GM vehicles for their showrooms. When a GM vehicle is sold to a customer, GMAC often lends cash to the customer to make the purchase. This helps the dealer both finance inventory and finance the receivable created by the consumer purchase.

Commercial Paper

Commercial paper represents another form of financing available to corporations. Usually only very large corporations can use this form of financing, but the ability to issue commercial paper is becoming more and more available to medium-sized firms. Commercial paper used as a financing vehicle represents an unsecured loan to an organization. A promissory note evidences the transaction. Commercial paper is usually sold at a discount, with the principal amount being paid back to the purchaser at a fixed maturity date. The maturity date may be set to be as few as 1 day or as many as 270 days. One-month or shorter-maturity commercial paper is common.

Why Issue Commercial Paper?

Selling commercial paper to meet your short-term financial needs allows you to bypass banks. Depending on the circumstances, you may be able to borrow in the commercial paper market at a lower effective rate. There is quite an active primary market for commercial paper. However, there is very little secondary market, especially for smaller firms. That means that once someone buys commercial paper, that buyer has to wait until maturity to get the money back. A buyer rarely goes to the issuer and asks to redeem the paper before maturity.

How Is Commercial Paper Issued?

Very large corporations like General Electric Capital Corporation or General Motors Acceptance Corporation directly issue commercial paper on a daily basis from their own offices. Potential investors call to determine the day's rate and maturity. Most corporate issuers, however, go through investment bankers. A corporation might even use more than one issuer to make sure the best rates are obtained in the marketplace. A bank can help an issuer place commercial paper and might even purchase commercial paper through its trust department (see "Master Notes" in Chap. 9). If you are interested in the prospects of issuing commercial paper, you will want to discuss the matter with an investment banker who understands the commercial paper market well.

Commercial paper may be issued in any denomination from $25,000 and up. The majority is in denominations of $100,000 or more.

Rating Commercial Paper

To be able to sell commercial paper it is almost mandatory to receive a high rating from one of a number of companies that specialize in rating commercial paper. A strong rating is particularly useful when the market for commercial paper is soft. Firms that specialize in rating commercial paper are Standard & Poor's, Moody's, Fitch, and Duff and Phelps. Table 10-1 shows the various rating categories from high to low.

It would be very unusual for a firm to be rated P-1 by Moody's and D-2 by Duff and Phelps. Although each rating company is independent, each has access to the same data and draws similar conclusions about the financial strengths of the companies it rates. If you sell commercial paper, you will be asked to keep the rating companies well-informed about your financial circumstances and changes thereto. A low rating means you may not be able to sell commercial paper. Buyers watch the ratings closely and may be restricted by corporate investment guidelines from buying any commercial paper not in the highest category.

Ratings are based on many factors.

1. Management strength.

2. Financial strength based on the ability of the company to be able to redeem the paper when it comes due. Financial ratios play an important role here. The debt-to-total-asset ratio is key, and cash flow is very important.

3. Competitive pressures on the company.

4. Existence of backup credit lines or letters of credit from solid financial institutions.

5. Longer-term prospects for the firm (since most commercial paper is rolled over at maturity).

Table 10-1. Commercial Paper Ratings

Rating company	Designations used (high-low)
Standard & Poor's	A-1 to A-3, B, C, and D
Moody's	P-1 to P-3
Fitch	F-1 to F-4
Duff and Phelps	D-1 to D-3

Costs of Commercial Paper

Interest rates on commercial paper are determined by the commercial paper market and prevailing rates on other short-term investments. Typically the commercial paper rate is higher than rates for government short-term securities, higher than rates for large bank CDs, and, yet, usually lower than bank lending rates. More risky issuers of commercial paper will have to pay a higher rate than very large, creditworthy customers.

When computing commercial paper rates, however, remember that several cost factors are involved that are not present with bank credit lines. Dealers charge a "spread," meaning that they sell for one price but give the issuer another. The difference is the dealer's profit on the transaction. In addition, the dealer may charge an overhead fee. Since highly rated commercial paper usually has a standby credit line, you must include the costs of the credit line in the cost of the commercial paper.

Effective Interest Rate.   As we have done with other types of borrowing, we calculate the effective interest rate by determining total charges, dividing net proceeds, and annualizing. Suppose that MSS is able to issue $1 million of commercial paper through a dealer. The market rate for an issuer in MSS's risk class is 9 percent, and the paper is to be issued for 60 days. The dealer charges a spread of 24 basis points, and MSS backs up its commercial paper with a $2 million credit line for which it pays a ½ percent annual commitment fee. MSS plans on rolling over its commercial paper after this issue, but we will just look at the effective rate for this 60-day period. Table 10-2 shows the computations used to determine the effective rate for MSS. The effective rate is considerably higher than the 9 percent "nominal" (quoted) rate. This is due to several factors. First, that rate is a discount rate. We are converting it to a yield rate using a 365-day year. The amount of discount is based on a 360-day year. Why? That's just the way the financial world does it! Second, we must include the dealer's spread of $400. Third, MSS has a backup credit line just for this type of financing. We must include 60 days' worth of the cost of the line in our computations.

Summary

We have discussed here various nonbank-related sources of short-term financing. Even very small companies can access one of them: accounts payable. This is a very flexible, sometimes low-cost form of financing. Usually there is no cost to using payables to finance your operations unless you abuse the payment terms of your suppliers too severely or repeatedly.

Another avenue for finding short-term debt is to work with commercial finance corporations. They often make loans where banks would not—especially asset-based loans. While commercial finance companies usually

Table 10-2. Computing the Effective Interest Rate
for Commercial Paper
(Midwestern Specialty Steel)

Market discount rate	9.00%
Dealer spread	24 basis points
Maturity	60 days
Face amount	$1,000,000
Backup credit line	$2,000,000 with ½% fee

Proceeds on day of sale through dealer:

Face value of paper issued	$1,000,000
Market discount of 9% [1,000,000 × 0.09(60/360)]	−15,000
Dealer spread, 24 basis points [1,000,000 × 0.0024(60/360)]	− 400
Net proceeds to issuer	$ 984,600

Financing costs:

Interest costs (1,000,000 − 984,600)	$ 15,400
Commitment fee on credit line [2,000,000 × 0.005 (60/360)]	1,667
Total financing costs	$ 17,067

Effective annual interest rate (I):

$$I = \frac{17,067}{984,600} \times \frac{365}{60} = 10.54\%$$

charge more than banks, loans from them may be cost-effective for certain kinds of assets that would be impossible to fund otherwise.

Factoring is a vehicle to borrow against (actually sell) accounts receivable. In certain specialty industries, factoring is commonplace, but it is becoming more widely available for nonspecialty industries as well. Besides providing a financing vehicle, factors can also perform the bulk of the firm's credit administration, thereby absorbing the costs of a relatively expensive overhead activity.

When a buyer makes a purchase from some large firms, the seller may have a captive finance company to provide financing for inventory and receivables.

Commercial paper, while primarily used by large corporations, is becoming available to medium-sized firms as well. This flexible source of financing bypasses the banking system and borrows directly from short-term investors.

Selecting among short-term financing sources can be a complex task involving many options. There is a rich variety of short-term credit alternatives having a spectrum of features in terms of maturity, size, interest rate, accompanying services, risk levels, and overall cost. There are sources and combinations of sources to fit the needs of virtually every organization.

Self-Test

1. Compute the effective cost of missing a cash discount under the following credit terms. Indicate whether the buyer should take the discount or not, given the buyer's opportunity cost is 12 percent.
   a. 2/10, n/30
   b. 1/10, n/30
   c. ½/10, n/30
   d. 2/10, n/60

2. Gregory Housewares misses virtually all cash discounts and pays on the net date. Most of its suppliers offer terms of 2/10, n/30. If Gregory Housewares purchases a total of $2 million during the year, how much money does the firm gain or lose if its cost of funds averages 12 percent?

3. Wilson Furniture is considering a factoring plan to help it finance its receivables. Sales are currently $1 million/month, and collections average 60 days. Wilson would be paid immediately using the factoring arrangement. The factor would charge a fee of 1.5 percent plus an annualized interest rate of 12 percent for funds advanced. Wilson's opportunity costs are 11 percent per annum.
   a. Compute the effective rate of financing.
   b. Now compute the annual costs of using the factor if Wilson can save $100,000 in overhead by closing down its credit department. Is the factor arrangement worth it?

11

Forecasting Cash Flows

Introduction

Southern Wholesale Building Supply was having an excellent year. Home construction was booming in the county, and sales to contractors were brisk. Jeff Mason, president of the firm, was quite confident in the future and felt he would finally be free of the need to borrow from his bank to meet cash flow needs. As the year progressed, sales continued above expected levels, but Mr. Mason found his cash flow becoming tighter and tighter. He finally sat down and tried to do a cash flow forecast. He was horrified to learn that even if his profits continued to be strong through September, he was going to run out of cash by July and require a much larger loan from the bank than his credit line permitted.

"How can this be?" he thought. "Profits have never been better, and yet I need to borrow more than ever." Mr. Mason was discovering the paradoxical reality of financial management. Profits do not necessarily (and seldom do) equal cash flows. While it is important to know about profits when managing a business, it is also critical to focus on cash flows. In fact, it is possible for a firm to be very profitable and yet have severe cash flow problems.

This chapter discusses the need and the techniques for forecasting short-term cash flows. We focus primarily on medium-term (monthly and quarterly) cash flow forecasts and also discuss how one would go about forecasting daily cash flows.

Why Profits Are Not Cash Flow

Accounting reports are oriented toward profits. Profits are carefully defined to attempt to reflect economic, legal, and auditable events. For example, one important accounting concept used to determine profits is the idea of matching revenues with the expenses that generated them. The matching concept requires that dollars used to purchase inventory be "stored up" until a matching revenue occurs, at which time an "expense" is realized. And yet "revenue" may be counted even if no cash flow is received at the time, say, when a customer purchases goods on credit and pays 60 days later. By applying such concepts as matching, and other rules contained in the generally accepted accounting principles (GAAP), a number is produced called "earnings." It should be clear now that this number is not very closely related to the cash flow the firm experiences. In fact, the only thing you can do with earnings is report them!

Can we relate earnings to cash flows? Yes, if we make enough adjustments to the earnings number to back out the effects of matching and other conventions, we can get a clearer picture of cash flows. That's what we'll spend the remainder of this chapter trying to accomplish.

Why Do Cash Forecasting?

Cash forecasting is done for various purposes. Each purpose has its own time horizon. Long-range forecasts go out several years into the future. A five-year forecast, for example, would be needed to determine the viability of the firm's long-range financing and operating policies. How much cash do we need to raise by selling stocks or bonds? Will we be able to afford a major expansion in three years by cash generated from our operations? When will we be able to start paying dividends to our shareholders? How large a term loan do we need from our bank? How much will we need if we want to acquire another firm in two years?

Medium-range forecasts project cash flows over the next 12 months. A cash manager may, for example, forecast weekly cash flows over the next three months and then monthly cash flows over the remainder of the year. This might be updated monthly. The purpose of medium-range forecasts of cash flows is to determine the firm's need for short-term cash that might be supplied through bank loans (e.g., credit lines), sale of commercial paper, or changes in credit or payables policies. If the cash manager forecasts large cash outflows for a two-month period, for example, this information may help determine the amount to borrow from the bank. It might also lead the firm to slow payments to suppliers and/or redouble efforts to collect cash from customers during that two-month period. A forecast of cash flows may also help the firm set its short-term investment policy. During times of forecasted cash inflows, for example, investments can safely be made in longer-term securities.

Daily cash forecasting implies a much closer horizon. It attempts to project cash inflows and outflows on a daily basis for several days or weeks into the future. Most firms have problems with daily forecasts, especially when projecting more than a week or so into the future. Nevertheless, a daily cash forecast may help a cash manager more effectively control deposits from outlying offices, concentrate cash into a central cash pool, cover disbursement accounts, and make more profitable short-term investing and borrowing decisions.

Since cash managers in small and medium-sized firms spend most of their forecasting time on medium-range forecasts, we devote the majority of the chapter to this task. At the end of the chapter we also investigate some of the approaches to daily cash forecasting. Since long-range forecasting extends over multiple years, cash managers are usually not involved in this task. Hence, we will not treat the subject in this book.

Medium-Range Cash Forecasting

Forecasting Accounting Statements

To forecast cash flow over the next year, we must begin by forecasting accounting statements, namely, balance sheets, income statements, and, ultimately, cash flow statements. In the following discussion, we assume that you are familiar with these statements and the definitions of terms used in them. You need not be an accounting guru, but a basic understanding of accounting principles is essential. If you do not have such an understanding, you will want to review an introductory accounting text (such as *The McGraw-Hill 36-Hour Accounting Course*, 3d Ed., by Dixon and Arnett).

Types of Accounting Variables.   In forecasting accounting statements, we must determine our estimate of the value of each specific number in these closely related statements. We will call each item in the income statement or balance sheet (such as sales, inventory, taxes) variables. Each variable can be classified into one of four types of variables, depending on how its value is computed.

1. *Driving variable (independent variable).*   Sales is an example of a driving variable. The values of other variables are determined to a large extent by the driving variable. Once sales are known, then we have a better idea of what level of inventory must be maintained, what cost of goods sold could be, etc. While sales may be the driving variable for most

firms, other variables are possible. For some heavily advertised consumer goods, the driving variable may be advertising dollars. Once the ad budget is set, then sales are determined.

2. *Technological variables.* Many other variables are determined by their technological relationship to another variable. For example, work-in-process inventory may be fixed by technological processes. To support a given level of sales, the work-in-process inventory is more or less determined by the nature of the firm's equipment, physical plant, and manufacturing processes.

3. *Policy variables.* Some variables are set by company policy. For example, the firm may have a policy of paying 35 days after receiving an invoice. Once the amount of purchases is determined, the cash manager can project a schedule of when payment will be made. The accounts payable level could then be computed.

4. *Variables involving accounting rules and definitions.* Many numbers in accounting statements are set by accounting rules and definitions. Once capital goods are computed, then the cash manager can use depreciation rules to compute the amount of depreciation for the income statement. Gross margin is computed simply by its definition of revenues minus cost of goods sold. As another example, taxes may be considered an accounting definition variable because once pretax income is determined, there are IRS and state tax rules for establishing the amount of taxes that must be paid.

The reason we categorize variables into categories is that we forecast each one differently. Driving variables are perhaps the most difficult to forecast for most firms. To do so, we may have to consult salespeople and actual and potential customers, and may also have to look at forces in the economy, competitive firms and their actions, the weather, foreign policies, etc. But once the driving variable is determined, many of the other variables become easier to compute.

Technological variables require an understanding of the firm's manufacturing, sales, and delivery processes. These variables may be under management control in the long run but may be impossible to affect given the firm's existing technology base. Policy variables, on the other hand, are generally quite controllable by management. It would be possible, for example, to decide to pay vendors earlier or later. Variables related to accounting rules and definitions are essentially outside management control (except for choosing among alternative accounting rules when an option is given— for example, LIFO to FIFO inventory valuation). When projecting cash flows, it is helpful to remember which variables management can control and which it can't. Although most variables are a mixture of these various types, it is helpful to note to which class a given variable primarily belongs.

Scenarios.   Since, for most firms, estimating all the variables we need is a highly uncertain task, it may be helpful to estimate them under different sets of assumptions. Scenario development is a very useful tool for the cash manager. It enables the cash manager to see how changing environments change cash flows. A scenario is a set of assumptions about a particular state of the world. For example, one scenario may be "recession ends, normal growth restored." You would define what you mean by normal growth and perform cash flow projections based on that set of assumptions. You might want to see what would happen with "recession continues, sales decline" and perform similar projections based on that set of assumptions. Since we don't know for sure which set of assumptions will become reality, we can help our firm prepare for several possible situations.

As you can imagine, you could construct an endless number of scenarios of the future, each with its unique combination of numbers and resulting financial statements. For management purposes, it is useful to limit your inquiries to just a handful of likely scenarios. Scenarios in which the firm faces cash flow problems should be particularly useful to the cash manager. They give you the opportunity to determine what your firm would do to survive if cash flows became tight.

Spreadsheets for Forecasting.   In cash flow forecasting it is very useful—if not mandatory—to use a spreadsheet program. Spreadsheets (such as Lotus 1-2-3, Excel, and Quattro Pro) permit you to keep track of many different variables and specify exactly how they relate to each other. Spreadsheets make it easy to generate a series of variables (such as sales levels by month for the next 12 months) by saying how the series grows (or shrinks) from one month to the next. The very useful feature of spreadsheets is that they let you easily modify one or more of your assumptions and observe the impact of this modification on all other variables. Of course, you can do all the computations by hand if you desire, but we strongly recommend that as a cash manager you learn to use a spreadsheet. Usually a couple of evenings' work will give you the essentials you need to do cash flow forecasting. The problems at the end of this chapter can be structured in a spreadsheet format.

Medium-Term Forecast Illustrated

Let's take the example of Southern Wholesale Building Supply we used to start this chapter. This is a firm that is experiencing a strong sales year and yet finds itself in cash flow problems. A cash forecast should tell us why Southern is having trouble and serve to illustrate the procedures we can use for cash forecasting in general. Southern's income statement and balance sheet for the six-month period ending in March are given in Table 11-1.

Southern management needs to determine how much cash will be needed (or generated) each month over the next half year ending in September. Mr. Mason, president of Southern, is worried that the $350,000 credit line he has negotiated with the bank may not be sufficient to meet the firm's needs.

Mr. Mason wants to project these financial statements over the next six months. Projected financial statements are sometimes called *pro forma* statements. As it turns out, by projecting just the balance sheet and the income statement, we can determine what cash flows Mr. Mason faces. Let's take the projections one step at a time. This will provide a general pattern when you want to project your own financial statements. However, be aware that we have simplified these statements so we won't get lost in the numbers. You will likely have many more variables to contend with, but the approach is basically the same whether you deal with thousands of variables or just a few.

Step 1: Forecast the Driving Variable. In Southern's case, as with most firms, the driving variable is sales. While sales may be difficult to estimate,

Table 11-1. Financial Data for Southern Wholesale
Building Supply
(Data in $1000s)

	Six-month period ending March
INCOME STATEMENT	
Sales	1000.0
Cost of Goods Sold (70%)	700.0
Gross Margin	300.0
General Administrative Expenses	150.0
Interest	3.0
Depreciation	24.0
Pretax Profit	123.0
Taxes (40%)	49.0
Net Income after Tax	74.0
BALANCE SHEET	
ASSETS	
Cash	50.0
Accounts Receivable	250.0
Inventory	300.0
Net Fixed Assets	400.0
Total Assets	1000.0
LIABILITIES AND EQUITY	
Accounts Payable	150.0
Short-Term Bank Loan	220.0
Paid-in Capital	540.0
Retained Earnings	90.0
Total Liabilities/Equity	1000.0

Mr. Mason probably has a good feel for the way sales have already gone this year and knows the seasonal sales pattern from the last several years. He also knows that, because of the expanded building market and early sales results through March, it is quite reasonable to expect a 10 percent increase in sales over last year. Last year, sales by month for April through September followed the following pattern (in thousands of dollars):

	Apr.	May	June	July	Aug.	Sept.	Semiannual Total
	198	220	250	187	133	112	1100
% of 1100:	18%	20%	23%	17%	12%	10%	100%

Based on these percentages from last year and Mr. Mason's estimate that total sales should be $2,200,000 during this year ($1 million of which has already occurred through March), he projects sales for the same period April through September:

Apr.	May	June	July	Aug.	Sept.	Semiannual Total
220	245	270	200	150	115	1200

Step 2: Project the Income Statement. Once the driving variable is forecast, the income statement can be forecast. Cost of goods sold is a technological variable often estimated as a percentage of sales. In the past, cost of goods sold was 70 percent for Southern. Unless Mr. Mason has good reason to believe this percentage is likely to change, 70 percent is a reasonable estimate for cost of goods sold over the next six months. Gross profit is now easy to compute because it is an accounting-defined variable: sales minus cost of goods sold. See Table 11-2 as we compute each variable.

General administrative expenses represent the overhead expenses not directly covered in other categories. Included would be the management salary, lease payments, secretarial and other administrative support, and sales staff expenses. Often these expenses are relatively fixed over the time horizon of a medium-term forecast. Mr. Mason estimates these expenses to be $25,000 per month.

Interest expense is a technological variable determined by the interest rate and the amount borrowed. Interest expense is much more difficult to compute since it depends on the amount Southern will need to borrow. Problem: We don't know how much Southern needs to borrow at this stage. For now, let's suppose that we can project interest expense as the monthly interest payment up to this point. Since $3000 was paid for the first six months, we could use $500 per month for the rest of the year. We will see that we may need to change this after we complete our first pass at the balance sheet.

Depreciation is defined by accounting and IRS rules. We won't go into the details here, but your accountant can tell you far in advance what your firm's depreciation schedule is. Let's suppose Mr. Mason's accountant tells him that depreciation is $8000 per month.

Pretax profit is another accounting-defined variable: gross margin minus overhead expenses. Taxes represent another fairly complex variable. Again, your accountant can help you know in advance what your taxes will be. Corporate taxes are around 34 percent, but you must also pay state income taxes and a host of other state taxes. To get an idea of your approximate tax rate, look at past income statements. Mr. Mason has done this and thinks that total taxes will approximate 40 percent of pretax profits. This gives net income after tax. Southern Wholesale Building Supply is doing quite well measured by profits. Profits for the year should total $169,200, which represents a very significant increase in retained earnings over the year.

Step 3: Compute Retained Earnings in the Balance Sheet.   This may seem like a backward way to start, but retained earnings represent the bridge between the income statement and the balance sheet. Retained earnings are a summary of the firm's total past earnings minus dividends paid out. Southern does not pay dividends—a common practice for small firms. So this month's retained earnings number will just be last month's retained earnings plus this month's net income after tax. We would subtract dividends were any paid. Retained earnings is an accounting-defined variable—you can't do anything to change it unless you change the income statement.

Step 4: Forecast Assets in the Balance Sheet.   Cash is usually a policy variable. Mr. Mason believes his cash balance has been relatively low at $50,000, and he would like to maintain a higher level, say, $80,000. This number represents what the firm records in its checkbook and not what is actually in its bank account.

Accounts receivable can also be classified in large part as a policy variable that depends on the firm's credit and collection policies. Lengthening credit terms would make accounts receivable go up, and tightening credit collection efforts would send accounts receivable down. Accounts receivable also depend on the level of sales. Higher sales mean higher accounts receivable—assuming credit terms stay the same. In this example, Southern has credit terms of net 30 days, but customers don't always pay promptly. Mr. Mason notes that, in the past, accounts receivable for a given month has been approximated by that month's sales plus about 50 percent of last month's sales. In March, for example, sales were $150,000. Hence, April's accounts receivable should be 50 percent × $150,000 plus April's sales of $220,000, making a total of $295,000. In actuality, your firm could follow a more complex pattern than this, but we hope you get the idea.

Inventory is a combination of a policy variable, technology variable, and accounting-defined variable! In other words, it is often very difficult to compute. In Southern's case, Mr. Mason has a schedule of purchases he thinks is needed to support projected sales:

	Apr.	May	June	July	Aug.	Sept.	Semiannual Total
Planned purchases	250	200	150	130	60	10	800

When goods are purchased, they do not count as an expense under the rules of accrual accounting. The purchase price is stored in inventory. When the goods are sold, they then go into an expense in the form of cost of goods sold. If labor were applied to add value to the goods, the cost of the labor would be stored as part of inventory, too. In this case, Southern just purchases goods and sells them without adding direct labor. Hence, inventory may be computed from the accounting definition

$$\begin{matrix} \text{Inventory} \\ \text{this month} \end{matrix} = \begin{matrix} \text{inventory} \\ \text{last month} \end{matrix} + \begin{matrix} \text{purchases} \\ \text{this month} \end{matrix} - \begin{matrix} \text{cost of goods sold} \\ \text{this month} \end{matrix}$$

Net fixed assets are an accounting-defined variable but are set by the firm's current investment in fixed assets. They are adjusted by capital investments and sales of capital equipment and depreciation. The "net" refers to the fact that depreciation has been subtracted. Alternatively, the balance sheet could report gross fixed assets and then have a separate account for depreciation. We'll simplify and report just one account. Net fixed assets this month equal last month's fixed assets minus depreciation, plus new fixed assets minus sale of fixed assets. In this example, we know that depreciation is $8000 per month. Mr. Mason plans to purchase new equipment for $60,000 in May. (Assume the depreciation amount has already taken this into account.)

Step 5: Forecast Liabilities in the Balance Sheet.   We have already forecast one variable on the liability side: retained earnings. We next have to forecast the remaining variables. One of those variables, accounts payable, is a policy variable that depends in large part on the firm's payables policy. Mr. Mason notes that, in the past, accounts payable are generally one month's purchases since the terms he receives from his suppliers is net 30. He pays bills promptly in 30 days to ensure good relationships with suppliers.

For the time being, we will leave the short-term bank loan at its current level of $220,000. We will come back to this variable later and make adjustments when we determine how much cash Southern will need.

Paid-in capital represents the amount shareholders paid into the firm in the past. Southern plans no new stock offerings or stock repurchases during the next six months, and so this variable is constant.

Step 6: Compute the Additional Financing Required. We add a new variable to the balance sheet: additional financing. Accounting rules require that the balance sheet balance. That means that in order to get the assets to balance with the liability/equity accounts, there is only one number possible for the additional financing variable in any given month. It turns out that this number represents precisely the negative cash flow Southern will experience.

Table 11-2 shows the result of applying these six steps to the next six months of Southern's accounting statements. Note that the additional financing (cash outflow) required goes from zero in March to a peak of $222,000 in June. Then the additional financing goes down to zero again in September. In fact, it would be negative $13,400 in September, but we simply reduced the bank loan by that amount. If Mr. Mason expects to have the short-term bank loan provide needed financing, he will need to renegotiate the credit line. He has currently a credit line of only $350,000 with the bank. But the additional financing plus the existing credit line borrowing totals $442,000. Mr. Mason would need $92,000 extra.

The additional financing information is valuable to Mr. Mason. It may help him to figure out some way to bridge the cash flow gap in May and June. One possibility he might consider is:

Borrow against credit line	$130,000
Reduce May/June cash	$ 50,000
Slow payables in May/June	$ 40,000
Total financing provided	$220,000

This would be enough to survive May and June without additional financing. It has problems, however. Cash may be too low for comfort, and suppliers may be reluctant to get paid later. These are policy decisions that Mr. Mason will have to face. Other alternatives are increase the credit line to $450,000 or find additional sources of equity financing such as selling new stock. The latter is probably not a good idea because the cash flow need appears to be only seasonal. Equity is generally used to supply permanent financing.

Step 7: Adjust Interest Expenses and Other Accounts. We don't quite have a consistent set of financial statements yet. Suppose Mr. Mason were successful in convincing the bank to loan him the entire $442,000 in June. Unfortunately, we have used only $500 per month for our interest expense variable in the income statement. If the bank charges, say, 10 percent interest per annum, then the interest in June alone would be approximately $442,000 × 0.10/12 = $3680. Unfortunately, we can't change only the interest expense and solve the problem. Note that if the interest expense goes up, then net income has to go down. This in turn effects a change in

Table 11-2. Pro Forma Statements for Southern Wholesale
Building Supply
(in $1000s)

	Oct.–Mar.	Apr.	May	June	July	Aug.	Sept.	Total
INCOME STATEMENT								
Sales	1000	220.0	245.0	270.0	200.0	150.0	115.0	2200.0
Cost of Goods Sold (70%)	700	154.0	171.5	189.0	140.0	105.0	80.5	1540.0
Gross Margin	300	66.0	73.5	81.0	60.0	45.0	34.5	660.0
General Administrative Expenses	150	25.0	25.0	25.0	25.0	25.0	25.0	300.0
Interest	3	0.5	0.5	0.5	0.5	0.5	0.5	6.0
Depreciation	24	8.0	8.0	8.0	8.0	8.0	8.0	72.0
Pretax Profit	123	32.5	40.0	47.5	26.5	11.5	1.0	282.0
Taxes 40%	49	13.0	16.0	19.0	10.6	4.6	0.4	112.8
Net Income after Tax	74	19.5	24.0	28.5	15.9	6.9	0.6	169.2
BALANCE SHEET								
ASSETS								
Cash	50	80.0	80.0	80.0	80.0	80.0	80.0	
Accounts Receivable	250	295.0	355.0	392.5	335.0	250.0	190.0	
Inventory	300	396.0	424.5	385.5	375.5	330.5	260.0	
Net Fixed Assets	400	392.0	444.0	436.0	428.0	420.0	412.0	
Total Assets	1000	1163	1304	1294	1219	1081	942	
LIABILITIES AND EQUITY								
Accounts Payable	150	250.0	200.0	150.0	130.0	60.0	10.0	
Short-Term Bank Loan	220	220.0	220.0	220.0	220.0	220.0	206.6	
Additional Financing	—	43.5	210.0	222.0	150.6	75.7	-0-	
Paid-in Capital	540	540.0	540.0	540.0	540.0	540.0	540.0	
Retained Earnings	90	109.5	133.5	162.0	177.9	184.8	185.4	
Total Liabilities/Equity	1000	1163	1304	1294	1219	1081	942	

retained earnings, sending it down. This forces additional financing to be higher in order to balance total assets. But an increase in additional financing increases interest expense, which further reduces net income, etc. We find ourselves in a constant series of circles. Fortunately, some spreadsheets handle the problem for us, or if we have to do it manually, we usually only have to go through the process once or twice and the interest number becomes consistent with the total financing.

In many cases, it will make a significant difference in cash flows. In the Southern case we originally based our interest expense on the six months of the year when sales were relatively low compared with the summer months. Our interest expense was far below what we end up paying for actual borrowing amounts. In many other cases, adjusting the interest expense may not make much difference. Table 11-3 shows the result of making the interest expense consistent with a bank loan of 10 percent. Net profits are down by $8400 because of the higher interest, and peak borrowing is higher than we anticipated. This is because we reduce cash flows by the amount of the interest expense (minus tax savings).

Is Cash Flow Really the Same as "Additional Financing"?

Yes. But to the skeptic, let's approach the problem of cash flow the way many financial managers see the issue. They start with net profits after tax and then make non-cash flow adjustments to determine a cash flow number. People probably use this approach because they like to focus on earnings.

Table 11-3. Southern Wholesale Building Supply Pro Forma Statements Adjusted for Interest Expense (in $1000s)

	Oct.–Mar.	Apr.	May	June	July	Aug.	Sept.	Total
INCOME STATEMENT								
Sales	1000	220.0	245.0	270.0	200.0	150.0	115.0	2200.0
Cost of Goods								
Sold (70%)	700	154.0	171.5	189.0	140.0	105.0	80.5	1540.0
Gross Margin	300	66.0	73.5	81.0	60.0	45.0	34.5	660.0
General Admini-								
strative Expenses	150	25.0	25.0	25.0	25.0	25.0	25.0	300.0
Interest 10%	3	2.2	3.6	3.7	3.1	2.5	1.8	20.0
Depreciation	24	8.0	8.0	8.0	8.0	8.0	8.0	72.0
Pretax Profit	123	30.8	36.9	44.3	23.9	9.5	−0.3	268.0
Taxes 40%	49	12.3	14.8	17.7	9.5	3.8	−0.1	107.2
Net Income	74	18.5	22.1	26.6	14.3	5.7	−0.2	160.8
BALANCE SHEET								
ASSETS								
Cash	50	80.0	80.0	80.0	80.0	80.0	80.0	
Accounts								
Receivable	250	295.0	355.0	392.5	335.0	250.0	190.0	
Inventory	300	396.0	424.5	385.5	375.5	330.5	260.0	
Net Fixed Assets	400	392.0	444.0	436.0	428.0	420.0	412.0	
Total Assets	100	1163.0	1303.5	1294.0	1218.5	1080.5	942.0	
LIABILITIES AND EQUITY								
Accounts Payable	150	250.0	200.0	150.0	130.0	60.0	10.0	
Short-Term								
Bank Loan	220	264.5	432.9	446.8	377.0	303.3	215.0	
Paid-in Capital	540	540.0	540.0	540.0	540.0	540.0	540.0	
Retained Earnings	90	108.5	130.6	157.2	171.5	177.2	177.0	
Total Liabilities/								
Equity	1000	1163.0	1303.5	1294.0	1218.5	1080.5	942.0	

Depreciation.   What variables have we used that do not really represent cash flows? Many! Depreciation is the one that most readily comes to mind. We paid for the equipment perhaps years ago but are counting depreciation as an expense only now because of accounting rules. But it is not a current cash flow. So we add back depreciation to the net profit after-tax number. But the adjustments are only beginning.

Balance Sheet Adjustments.   We counted sales in our net profit number, but sales is really not a cash flow. Customers don't pay in the month of sale but wait a month or two to write us checks. Therefore we have to adjust for this by subtracting the increase in accounts receivable.

Many other changes occur in the balance sheet. For example, we purchased goods, but they are stored in inventory and do not count against cost of goods sold until a later time. An increase in inventory is therefore like a cash outflow. Likewise, an increase in accounts payable is like a cash inflow—it's an adjustment to cost of goods sold because we haven't paid for some of the things we purchased on credit.

These adjustments can be summarized in Table 11-4. The table is set up to tell you what to do with *increases* in variables. It says that an increase in receivables is subtracted as a cash outflow. Of course, if there is a *decrease* in receivables, the amount of decrease would be considered equivalent to a cash *inflow*. The same logic goes for other variables that do the opposite of what we list in the table.

Applying the interest-adjusted pro forma statements in Table 11-3, we construct a cash flow statement shown in Table 11-5.

Take April, for example. Starting with a net profit after tax of $18,500 and making adjustments for noncash expenses and balance sheet changes, instead of a positive cash flow, the result is a negative cash flow of $44,500. Note that this is *exactly* the same as the increase in bank loan required to make the balance sheet balance in Table 11-3. In May, the cash flow state-

Table 11-4. From Net Profit to Cash Flow

Net Profit after Tax
Plus
   Depreciation and other noncash expenses
   Increase in accounts payable
   Increase in financing
   Increase in paid-in capital
Minus
   Dividends paid
   Increase in cash and marketable securities
   Increase in accounts receivable
   Increase in inventory
   Increase in new fixed assets
Equals net cash flow

Table 11-5. Determining Net Cash Flows Starting with
Net Profit after Tax (Southern Wholesale Supply Building Company)

	Apr.	May	June	July	Aug.	Sept.
Net profit after tax	18.5	22.1	26.6	14.3	5.7	−0.2
Plus						
Depreciation	8.0	8.0	8.0	8.0	8.0	8.0
Increase in accounts						
payable	100.0	−50.0	−50.0	−20.0	−70.0	−50.0
Minus						
Increase in cash	30.0	0.0	0.0	0.0	0.0	0.0
Increase in accounts						
receivable	45.0	60.0	37.5	−57.5	−85.0	−60.0
Increase in inventory	96.0	28.5	−39.0	−10.0	−45.0	−70.5
Increase in new assets		60.0				
Net cash flow	−44.5	−168.4	−13.9	69.8	73.7	88.3
Cumulative	−44.5	−212.9	−226.8	−157.0	−83.3	5.0

ment shows we need an additional $168,400. This amount is exactly the
same as the increase in the short-term loan from April to May.

What do we conclude from this? That we don't have to forecast cash flows
separately. It is sufficient to forecast just an income statement and a balance
sheet. Cash flows can be determined simply by looking at the *change* in new
financing required to make the balance sheet balance.

When Cash Flows Are Positive.   In the Southern Wholesale Building
Supply example, we found that the firm needs cash over the next few
months. What would happen if a firm is generating extra cash? If you projected balance sheets and income statements for such a firm, you would
find that needed financing was a negative number. This means that the firm
is generating cash and you could use the cash to pay off existing loans.
What happens when loans go to zero and you still have extra cash? You
would create an account on the asset side of the balance sheet called
"Excess Cash" or just build up the cash account.

Variations in Computing Variables

We have illustrated cash flow forecasting with fairly simple relationships.
Your situation may be different, and relationships among variables may be
much more complex than we have shown here. Nevertheless, the approach
would be the same. In other cases, you may not need to get as detailed as we
have made this example.

Percent-of-Sales Method.   When analysts need a "quick and dirty" set of
pro forma statements, they often make some additional simplifying assump-

tions that permit ready computation. One approach is to assume that most of the variables in the statements are proportional to sales. That's not a bad assumption for many firms. We used this idea for cost of goods sold, but it could also apply to some of the other variables. Based on past accounting statements, historical proportionalities are computed and then extended into the future. Variables such as accounts receivable, accounts payable, inventory, and overhead expenses are often treated this way. This approach is sometimes called the *percent-of-sales method*. Variables are computed by the following relationship:

$$
\begin{array}{c}
\text{Forecasted value} \\
\text{of variable} \\
\text{(next month)}
\end{array}
=
\begin{array}{c}
\text{past ratio} \\
\text{of this variable} \\
\text{to sales}
\end{array}
\times
\begin{array}{c}
\text{Forecasted sales} \\
\text{level (next month)}
\end{array}
$$

For example, we see in the Southern Wholesale Building Supply example that inventory in March was 1.8 times the average monthly sales for the six-month period [300/(1000/6) = 1.8]. So we could apply this ratio to April inventory. We estimate April sales to be $220,000. Multiplying by 1.8, we estimate April inventory to be $396,000, which happens to be exactly the same number we estimate using the more complex method we used in Table 11-2. For May, however, the estimate is 1.8 × $245,000 = $441,000. This compares with the $424,500 we estimated from our more exact approach.

Relating Variables to Timing. For some variables like inventory or accounts receivable, it is helpful to bring in an element of time. For example, accounts receivable can be associated with a *days sales outstanding* (*DSO*) number that gives the analyst a feeling for how long it takes customers to pay the firm. Inventory days tell the analyst about how many days' worth of inventory the firm has. DSO is found by dividing accounts receivable by sales per day, where the number of days is represented by N. For annual sales, the number to use for N is 365 (some use 360). For semiannual data, N is 182, etc.

$$
\text{DSO} = \frac{\text{accounts receivable}}{\text{sales}/N}
$$

For example, the number of days Southern has in receivables at the end of March is

$$
\text{DSO} = \frac{250{,}000}{1{,}000{,}000/182} = 45.5 \text{ days}
$$

This means that, on average, customers are paying Southern in about 45.5 days. By rearranging the equation, the value of accounts receivable may be computed for a different DSO level:

$$
\text{Accounts receivable (forecast)} = \text{DSO} \times (\text{sales}/N)
$$

Suppose, for example, that Southern focused more attention on receivables and enforced credit terms more aggressively. Suppose this effort results in a collection period of 35 days. Then the April level of accounts receivable would be forecast as

Accounts receivable (Apr.) = (220,000/30) × 35 days = $256,667

Ten days' reduction in collection time reduces receivables by about $38,333 below what we have forecast in Table 11-3.

Inventory is another variable that can be treated in this same manner. Instead of using sales, however, most analysts use cost of goods sold in the denominator. For March, Southern has approximately 78 days' worth of inventory.

$$\text{Days inventory} = \frac{\text{inventory}}{\text{cost of goods sold}/182} = \frac{300,000}{700,000/182} = 78 \text{ days}$$

This equation, too, can be rearranged to use it in a forecasting mode.

$$\text{Inventory} = (\text{cost of goods sold}/N) \times \text{days inventory}$$

For example, if Southern kept only 60 days' inventory instead of 78 days', then the inventory in March would have been

Inventory in March = (700,000/182) × 60 days = $230,800

Accounts payable may be also associated with a days payable outstanding. Instead of using sales in the denominator, cost of goods sold is used (or, better, total purchases if that number is available). For Southern, this number is estimated for the semiannual period:

$$\text{Days payable outstanding} = \frac{\text{accounts payable}}{\text{cost of goods sold}/182}$$

$$= \frac{150,000}{700,000/182} = 39 \text{ days}$$

It appears that Southern is not too far off its target payment terms of 30 days.

You should realize that this method of forecasting is quite approximate and works best when sales or cost of goods sold is not seasonal. Strong seasonality causes significant forecast errors, but these tend to balance out over time.

Daily Cash Forecasting

For small and medium-sized firms, daily cash forecasting is not used as much as medium-range forecasting. In most cases, larger firms have more to gain from daily cash forecasts than smaller firms do. Nevertheless, there may be instances in which it would pay you to forecast daily cash flows. There are several possible benefits from daily cash forecasting.

Better Cash Flow Control

Suppose your firm operates three stores in different cities. Based on past deposit patterns, you have developed a forecast of cash deposits for each of the three deposit accounts associated with the three stores. Suppose you forecast that $15,000 should be deposited into store 1 on Monday morning. You find out from your balance reporting system (see Chap. 5) that only $5000 was deposited on Monday. This large discrepancy may signal some problem at store 1. (It might, however, just signal that your forecast isn't very good.)

More Profitable Short-Term Investments

If you have no idea of the amount that may clear your disbursement accounts over the next five days, you will probably keep enough cash in the account (earning no interest) to cover the highest possible amount that might clear. On the other hand, if you have a fairly accurate forecast of what will clear over the next five days, you may be able to keep much of the anticipated clearing amount invested in short-term securities.

The result of investing primarily in overnight securities is that the rate of return is low relative to longer-term investments. Such investing practices also result in excessive transactions costs when securities have to be sold before maturity. Administrative costs may also be high because of the daily management attention required by such a policy. Generally, longer-term investments give higher interest rates than shorter-term investments.

Less Costly Borrowing

Most borrowing arrangements require you to act in advance (usually a day or so) of when you need the cash. If you have no forecast—or an inaccurate forecast—of when you will need to move cash into your accounts, you will likely borrow before you actually need the cash. With an accurate daily cash forecast, you will be able to hold off borrowing until just the right time. This could save you interest expense.

How to Approach Daily Cash Forecasting

There are two basic approaches to daily cash flow forecasting: looking at historical patterns and scheduling. The *historical-pattern approach* works best with cash flows that consist of lots of small transactions. Some firms get very sophisticated and use computerized statistical programs to help them search for historical patterns. You may find that you can use a very simple approach that averages daily cash flows from previous time periods. For example, based on past observations, you may be able to determine that 30 percent of total weekly deposits are received on Monday, 20 percent on Tuesday, etc. This pattern could be used to forecast deposits in some future week. You would have to estimate the total week's sales and then use the percentages to allocate the total over days of the week.

The *scheduling approach* works well with large payments that can be forecast individually. Examples are tax payments, dividend payments, bond redemptions, and lease payments. For example, you can often know far in advance when you have to write a check to make your quarterly tax payment. The date and amount can be determined by asking your tax accountant. Based on past experience with tax payments, you can determine when the payment will be taken out of your tax account at the bank. You can also determine in advance when an upcoming lease payment must be made and how much the payment will be.

With these approaches in mind, you can follow these steps for cash forecasting:

Step 1: Separate Cash Flows into Major and Nonmajor Cash Flows. This means examine the types of payments you make and deposits you receive and classify them into large, lumpy cash flows (such as tax payments, lease payments, contract payments) or small, numerous cash flows (such as receipts from customers, payments to vendors).

Step 2: Forecast Large Payments and Receipts Individually. For each large, lumpy payment or receipt, use information sources you have to determine the timing and amount. For check payments, estimate how many days on average it has taken in the past for that particular type of payment to clear. You will have to look at historical data to help you here. For a past building lease payment, for example, determine when checks were mailed. Then look at bank statements to see when lease payment checks cleared. This will let you compute the average number of days in check clearing for that type of payment. Use this average and apply it to known future lease payment dates. Using a spreadsheet, construct a matrix showing when each payment is expected to clear. For large, lumpy cash inflows, attempt to do the same. Of course, estimating timing of inflows is much harder since you do not have control over them. For repeating cash inflows, examine past bank statements and determine when large payments were deposited into your account and when such payments became available. Enter these deposits into your spreadsheet. Table 11-6 shows what such a matrix would look like. Inflows and outflows are in separate matrices but are combined to form net major cash flows at the end of the table.

Table 11-6. Scheduling Approach Cash Flow Matrices
for Large Payment and Deposits

Outflows	Business day that payment clears										
	...20	21	22	23	24	25	26	27	28	29	30...
Type of payment											
Withholding payment	■			$3500							
Sales tax payment			■				$5400				
State income tax								■		$23,000	
Building lease					■			$4200			
Dividend payment								■			$9000
Loan interest payment				■				$2800			
Total outflows (000s)	0	0	0	3.5	0	0	5.4	7.0	0	23.0	9.0...

Inflows	Business day that payment becomes available										
	...20	21	22	23	24	25	26	27	28	29	30...
Type of payment											
Progress payment		$10,300									
Contract payment 1					$5600						
Contract payment 2								$8200			
Sale of equipment								$4500			
Royalty payment					$2700						
Total inflows (000s)	0	10.3	0	0	8.3	0	0	12.7	0	0	0
Net major cash flows ...	0	10.3	0	–3.5	8.3	0	–5.4	5.7	0	–23.0	–9.0...

■ = Date payment is mailed.

Step 3: Determine Patterns for Nonmajor Cash Flows. Divide non-major cash flows into homogeneous categories. For example, payroll checks represent such a category. Your firm may write numerous payroll checks, and likely these are cashed in some pattern. You may have a pretty good idea of the total payroll for a given week, but when will individual payroll checks be cashed? By looking at past data from the payroll account, it should be possible to determine what percentage of the total payroll clears N days after payday. For example, suppose, based on historical patterns, you observe that payroll checks, issued every other Thursday, clear as follows:

Day of week	Percentage clearing
Thursday	20%
Friday	45%
Monday	20%
Tuesday	10%
Wednesday	5%
Total	100%

Rather than attempting to estimate when each check might clear, we can apply these percentages to the entire payroll. If, for example, total payroll for a particular Thursday is $100,000, then daily cash flow estimates are:

Thursday	$= 0.20 \times 100,000 =$	$ 20,000
Friday	$= 0.45 \times 100,000 =$	45,000
Monday	$= 0.20 \times 100,000 =$	20,000
Tuesday	$= 0.10 \times 100,000 =$	10,000
Wednesday	$= 0.05 \times 100,000 =$	5,000
Total		$100,000

Note that we are really doing two estimates here. First we estimate the historical pattern, and then we apply the pattern to our estimate of the total payroll amount. This approach could be applied to other homogeneous groups of cash inflows and outflows. For example, suppose you have a weekly billing cycle and payments are due 30 days from date of invoice. As with the payroll, you could determine the cash inflow pattern for payments arising from each billing cycle. You could then obtain historical percentages to apply to future billing cycles.

Simple averaging of past data may be sufficient to determine the percentages, or you may, if you want to get more sophistication, use regression or time series analysis to assist you.

Step 4: Apply Historical Patterns to Nonmajor Cash Flows. Table 11-7 illustrates how the historical-pattern approach can be applied to three types of cash flows: payroll, vendor payments (outflows), and customer receipts (inflows). The patterns were computed from observation of past patterns. The percentages tell how much is expected to clear the bank or become available at the bank n days after the initiating event. Payroll day is one example of an initiating event. For vendor payments, the initiating event may be the date on the batch of invoices received from vendors. For customer payments, the initiating event is the date on invoices mailed to customers. Other initiating events are possible, such as the date we mail a check to a vendor. That approach would be more accurate but doesn't give us a very long forecast horizon.

We measure time in terms of business days, not calendar days. This is because checks don't clear or become available on weekends. When you forecast using calendar days, remember to skip over weekends and holidays when banks do not process.

To use the historical-pattern approach, determine the dollar amount of the total payroll and the date it is issued. Then multiply the expected clearing percentage by the amount and write the result under the appropriate business day. Do the same for batches of vendor payments and for customer receipts. You will want to have a more complete matrix than that given in

Table 11-7. Forecasting Cash Flows Using Historical Patterns

	Business days after initiating event											
	0	1	2	3	4	...	20	21	22	23	24	25
Payroll	0.20	0.45	0.20	0.10	0.05							
Vendor payments (from invoice date)							0.20	0.20	0.30	0.20	0.10	
Customer receipts (from invoice date)							0.25	0.35	0.10	0.10	0.15	0.05

	Business day that payment clears (or becomes available)										
(in $1000s) Type of payment	...20	21	22	23	24	25	26	27	28	29	30...
Payroll ($100, day 23)				20	45	20	10	5			
Vendor payments ($200, day 2)			40	40	60	40	20				
Vendor payments ($100, day 7)								20	20	30	20 ...
Customer receipts ($200, day 2)			50	70	20	20	30	10			
Customer receipts ($300, day 7)								75	105	30	30 ...
Net cash flow			10	10	−85	−40	0	60	85	0	10 ...

Notes: The payroll is issued on day 23, and so 20% clears the same day. One set of vendor payments is tied to $200,000 of invoices dated on day 2. According to the pattern, the first group of payments will clear 20 business days later, or on day 22. The next set of invoices is for $100,000 and is dated business day 7. Hence the first group of checks is forecast to clear on day 27. There are also two sets of customer payments. The first set is for invoices for $200,000 and dated business day 2. According to the historical pattern, these payments should become available 20 business days later, on day 22. The net cash flow is determined by adding inflows and outflows.

the table, which only shows a portion of the matrix covering a few weeks. To determine total cash flows, simply add inflows and subtract outflows.

Step 5: Add Daily Cash Inflows and Outflows from All Sources. Once you have cash flow estimates from major cash flows and nonmajor cash flows, these can be combined to give an estimate for total cash flow on a given day. The numbers in the example below have been rounded for clarity.

Business day	...21	22	23	24	25	26	27	28	29	30 ...
Major cash flow	10	1	−4	8	0	−5	6	0	−23	−9 ...
Nonmajor cash flow	0	10	10	−85	−40	0	60	85	0	10 ...
Net cash flow	10	10	6	−77	−40	−5	54	85	−23	1 ...

Summary

Cash forecasting is an important task for the cash manager. It helps management understand the nature of the business and the consequences of various decisions and external factors on the firm's operations. Medium-range forecasting can help you prepare for cash excesses and cash crunches and point out areas of vulnerability. If you want to impress your banker, shareholders, or other financial providers with your knowledge of your business, you must be able to understand your firm's cash flows and project them into the future under different scenarios.

Daily cash forecasting is more difficult to perform very accurately—especially cash inflows over which you have little control. Nevertheless, daily cash forecasting can help you reduce interest expenses, ensure better control, and increase returns on your short-term investment portfolio.

There is no easy method for forecasting. In fact, good forecasting is more an art than a science. While the nature of your particular cash flows may not permit you to forecast very accurately, the very process of cash flow forecasting will help you obtain a more thorough understanding of how your business works and what dangers you face that could dry up your cash flows and force you into a very uncomfortable position.

Self-Test

1. Davis Electric is attempting to project its cash flows over the next 12 months. The December income statement and balance sheet are given below with numbers in $1000s.

12-month period ending December				
Income Statement		**Balance Sheet**	December	
Sales	1500.0	Assets		
Cost of Goods Sold	1000.0	Cash	25.0	
Gross Margin	500.0	Accounts Receivable	250.0	
General Administrative		Inventory	200.0	
Expense	350.0	Net Fixed Assets	475.0	
Interest Expense	20.0	Total Assets	950.0	
Depreciation	50.0			
Pretax Profit	80.0	Liabilities and Equity		
Taxes (40%)	32.0	Accounts Payable	150.0	
Net Income after Tax	48.0	Short-term Bank Loan	200.0	
		Paid-in Capital	320.0	
		Retained Earnings	280.0	
		Total Liabilities/Equity	950.0	

Ms. Davis would like to project the income statement and balance sheet for next December. She estimates that sales will increase by 10 percent. General administrative expenses will go to $370 (all dollar amounts are in thousands), and interest expense should be about 10 percent of the short-term bank loan. Depreciation for the year will total $60. The increase is due in part to the purchase of new capital equipment for $40 during the year. Taxes should remain at about 40 percent of pretax profit. Ms. Davis thinks that cash should be increased to $70 by the end of the year. The firm has plans to reduce DSO next year to 40 days. Credit collections have been poorly managed in the past. Inventory should remain in about the same proportion to sales as this year. Suppliers are not happy with Davis's payment policies and are clamoring for faster payments. Ms. Davis has promised to bring payables down to 35 days. A new stock issue is planned to bring in $50 during the year.

  a. Project the income statement for Davis Electric for the next year ending in December.

  b. Project next December's balance sheet. Use the bank loan or cash as the balancing variable. Be sure you adjust interest expense to reflect the loan amount you compute.

  c. What size bank loan does Davis need by the end of next December?

  d. Starting with next December's profit after tax, show how cash flow for the year can be computed. Does this number match the increase (decrease) in the short-term bank loan?

  e. If the amount Davis needs is larger than the credit line at the bank, where else could Davis obtain needed cash? If the required loan is less than zero, where should Davis put its extra cash?

2. Ms. Davis would like to project cash flows over the same year but now on a month-by-month basis. Besides the information given in the first problem, she has refined her information as follows. Sales are projected for the next 12 months:

Jan.	Feb.	Mar.	Apr.	May	June	July	Aug.	Sept.	Oct.	Nov.	Dec.	Total
50	80	120	125	130	200	220	220	200	130	95	80	1650

General administrative expenses will be about $30.8/month. Depreciation for the year will be $5/month. New capital equipment will be $40 payable in June. Ms. Davis thinks that cash should be increased to $50 in January and then to $70 in June. Accounts receivable should average this month's sales plus one-third of last month's sales. Inventory in a given month should be about 2.5 times sales in that month. To satisfy suppliers, Ms. Davis promises to bring payables down to the current month's cost of goods sold plus one-sixth of last month's cost of goods sold. The new stock issue is planned to bring in $50 during August. You'll want to use a spreadsheet program to perform the required computations.

  a. Project the income statement for Davis Electric for the next 12 months ending in December.

    b. Project Davis Electric's balance sheet for the next 12 months. Use the bank loan or cash as the balancing variable and be sure to have your interest expense number agree with your loan amounts.

    c. What size bank loan does Davis need during the peak borrowing month? How does that amount compare with the loan you computed in Prob. 1 for the end of next December? Explain the difference.

    d. Starting with each month's profit after tax, show how cash flow by month can be computed. Does this number match the month-to-month increase (decrease) in the short-term bank loan?

3. The following data have been collected regarding invoice payments received from Ying Technology customers. Using the invoice data as day zero, Ying examines how many days it takes for customers' checks to become available in Ying's collection bank. Invoices are batched and sent out on a weekly basis. These data are from a three-week period. Days are in terms of business days, not calendar days.

Invoice amount (000s)	Cash flow into deposit account Business days after invoice date										
	21	22	23	24	25	26	27	28	29	30	31
550	11	25	35	43	36	81	120	152	23	18	6
675	13	32	36	68	41	90	151	183	27	25	9
380	8	17	22	35	28	68	77	94	12	12	7

    a. From this information, compute the average percentage that should become available each day *N* days after the invoice date. (*Note:* It is best not to average averages. Add up the total of all three deposits and then compute the total cash flow percentage for each day.)

    b. October 4, 1993, is a Monday. Suppose Ying Technology sends three batches of invoices to its customers on each of three Mondays starting with October 4, 1993. Total invoices are as follows:

October 4	$425,000
October 11	$693,000
October 18	$487,000

Using the percentages you computed in part *a,* forecast the total cash flow into Ying's deposit account by *calendar days* (remember that the above days are measured in business days) from customer payments. You will want to forecast each of the three streams separately and then add up the columns.

12
Credit and Collections

Introduction

The Green Lumber Company currently operates as a cash-and-carry supplier of building materials, primarily to the retail market. All sales are paid for in cash, by major credit card, or by check. The sales manager feels the company has saturated the retail market. She has proposed expanding the penetration into the contractor market by offering credit to contractors. The proposal is to allow contractors to "run a tab" for purchases during a month. They will be billed once each month for all purchases during the prior month. The rest of the management team are unsure of the advisability of this proposal, and have turned to the financial manager for his assessment of the financial impact of the sales manager's proposal.

Establishing Credit Policy

An emerging firm, or a firm such as Green Lumber which sells only on a cash basis, is in a unique position. It has the opportunity to establish a credit policy from scratch. As such, it has the chance to clearly define all the elements of the policy in a way that everyone concerned will understand the strategic focus of the policy and how it should be implemented. Most firms have an existing credit policy. Some elements of the policy may be more clearly stated and understood than others. In some companies the details of the policy may exist only in the memory of the old-timers. Attempts to adopt new credit policy elements involve changing existing policy. Therefore, most decisions involve comparing a potential situation to the current situation, rather than attempting to design the "best" policy.

Credit policy is a critical operating aspect that affects many parts of the firm. Marketing, production, purchasing, and cash management are all affected by the credit policy and its application. This chapter examines the elements in a credit policy, presents a framework for the analysis of policy changes, and discusses the issues addressed in deciding whether to accept a credit applicant. The next chapter examines a system for monitoring the credit policy and for expediting collections.

Importance of Credit Policy

Financial versus Marketing Focus.   If the financial people had total control of credit policy, credit would be granted on very restrictive terms only to the very highest quality customers. Accounts receivable would be low. Little effort would need to be expended monitoring and collecting accounts. However, sales would likely be low.

If the marketing people had total control of credit policy, credit would be granted on very liberal terms to any customer who had even the slightest prospect of paying. Sales would be high. Accounts receivable would be high. Costs of monitoring and collecting delinquent accounts would be substantial.

These two exaggerated, contrasting views of credit policy serve to illustrate the trade-off involved. Credit policy has both marketing and financial consequences, and the analysis of credit policy alternatives must incorporate both views. The trade-off can be best analyzed by looking at the impact on the value of the firm. The most straightforward way to investigate the impact on value is to examine the incremental profit expected to result from alternative policies. The profit is calculated net of all costs for administering the credit function, carrying accounts receivable, collecting slow-paying accounts, and writing off nonpayers. Unfortunately some of these costs are difficult to determine. In addition, both short-term and long-term consequences exist, and the short-term consequences are easier to estimate than the long-term ones. A particularly troublesome long-term issue is the profitability of future sales generated by granting credit to a customer today. Perhaps even harder to estimate is the potential sales and profits lost from denying credit to a potential customer.

Before attempting to develop a framework for analysis of alternative credit policies, we examine two other aspects of credit policy. The first is a more in-depth look at why credit sales exist. The second is a specification of the elements that make up an effective credit policy.

Reasons for Selling on Credit.   Selling on credit results in additional costs and efforts. It is costly to collect and evaluate information to determine if a credit sale should be made. There is a time value cost from waiting until the due date for the collection of cash for the sales. In addition, not all customers pay at the agreed time. And efforts to identify and collect from late-paying customers are not without cost. Even with all these costs, though, most sales in the United States, particularly commercial sales between trading partners, are made on credit. There must be some overriding advantage to credit sales. In very simple terms the advantage is *increased sales*. What would happen if credit sales for all firms could be converted to cash sales tomorrow without any impact on current or future sales? Cashier lines in retail stores would move much more quickly. Post office volume would drop. Wallets would return to being billfolds instead of credit card carriers. Unemployment claims would increase from all the laid-off credit department workers. In sum, credit sales would virtually disappear. There are several reasons why sales may be higher if credit is offered.

Price Reduction for Credit Customers. A key benefit to a credit purchaser is the time delay allowed for payment. The opportunity cost of funds makes the ability to delay a payment equivalent to a price reduction. Of course, the advantage of a price reduction to the buyer is a disadvantage to the seller. The value of the revenue will be higher with credit sales only if the increase in unit sales is sufficient to offset the opportunity cost of delayed collections. To the extent the selling firm can be selective in granting credit, it can offer a slightly lower price to some customers. However, care must be taken to ensure the credit offering is cost-justified and nondiscriminatory.

Customer Loyalty. Credit may help to solidify a customer relationship. The hope is that a customer will be more inclined to purchase from a supplier offering credit. We see this philosophy in retail credit. The ABC Department Store hopes customers who see the ABC credit card when they open their wallets will go to ABC for a shopping trip. In addition, the monthly bill provides an opportunity for targeted direct-mail advertising.

Inspection Period. A firm offering a deferred payment date offers an implicit warranty on the quality of the goods. Payment is not required until the purchaser has a chance to inspect the goods. It is easier for the customer to return unsatisfactory goods if payment has not occurred. We are all familiar with the opposite of this situation, where mail-order goods of questionable quality or usefulness are shipped only after sufficient time has passed to ensure the check has cleared.

Expanding Market Share versus Market Demand. In examining the marketing impact of credit sales we need to distinguish between only increasing market share and expanding total market demand. Credit policy changes that only affect market share are likely to be a zero-sum game—one firm's gain comes at a loss from a competitor. In a highly competitive market, credit policy changes are matched by competitors. The net result is an increase in costs or a decrease in the value of the revenues for all competitors without a corresponding increase in sales for any of them.

For example, suppose National Screw and Nut, a fastener manufacturer, changes credit terms to retail hardware stores from net 30 days to net 45 days. A hardware store currently ordering from General Fasteners may be more inclined to order from National to take advantage of the longer payment period. Any gain in sales for National is at the expense of lost sales by General. If General Fasteners matches the change in credit terms, the hardware store owner is happier, and perhaps slightly more profitable, but still orders from General Fasteners. Retail customers will not suddenly increase their purchases of fasteners because of the change in credit terms to the hardware store. Thus, the change in credit policy by National Screw and Nut will have the desired result, to increase sales, only if competitors do not also change their credit policies.

Some changes in credit policy may affect total market demand. For this to occur the new credit policy either results in a price reduction or opens the market to customers who otherwise would not have been able to finance the purchase. In the 1980s automobile companies started offering low interest rate financing through their captive finance companies. Most new car purchases are made on installment credit. Paying a lower rate, such as 2.9 percent instead of 9.0 percent, on a 48-month loan for $15,000 reduces the monthly payment from about $373 per month to about $331 per month, or an 11 percent reduction in monthly payment. These actions stimulated an increase in sales for the auto companies, even though they were quickly matched by competitors. Whether these generous credit terms increased long-term demand or just shifted purchase forward in time is debatable. Another example is farm equipment manufacturers establishing credit arrangements that allow dealers and farmers to purchase equipment that financial institutions might not be willing to finance.

Elements of Credit Policy

The first issue in establishing credit policy is one that is frequently overlooked by many firms: do we want to sell on credit? All too often the decision is made by default by adopting industry practices. In a recent discussion with the treasurer of a boat manufacturer the topic of credit policy was raised. The treasurer said the company made the decision to deviate from normal industry practice and sell to dealers only on a cash basis. The company felt, and evidently the dealers agreed, the combination of features, quality, and price of its product was superior to the competition and it did not have to offer credit as an incentive to make the sale.

Own Credit or Third-Party Credit.   Even if a company has decided to sell on credit, it does not have to operate its own credit department. Instead, the company can contract with a third party to conduct all the credit department activities for a fee. The most familiar example is retailers accepting syndicated credit cards—such as Visa, MasterCard, American

Express, or Discover—instead of issuing their own credit cards. For a fee, usually a percentage of the sale, the credit card company handles all the credit activity. Another example is something called *private label financing*. In this third-party arrangement, the customer may not be aware the credit is not being issued by the seller. Credit applications are taken by the seller, and billing appears to come from the seller, even though all activity is conducted by the third party. The seller retains the image and customer loyalty aspects of its own credit policy while paying a financial institution to conduct all the credit activities. The financial institution charges a slightly higher fee for this arrangement than it charges for a "generic" third-party credit arrangement.

Credit Terms.   One of the critical elements of credit policy is the terms under which the sale is made. Many companies make this decision by default by simply adopting industry credit terms. Credit terms consist of a required and, perhaps, two optional portions. The required portion is the due date. One common option is a discount for early payment. A second, but less common, option is a penalty for late payment. Many firms are uncomfortable with a penalty for two reasons. First, it is difficult to collect. Second, it implicitly tells customers that they may pay late and defines the cost of so doing.

We frequently think of credit terms being driven by industry standards. However, many firms have products sold in different industry segments. Thus, they have a wide array of credit terms across their product lines.

If a firm is unwilling to sell on credit, it may quote terms of *cash on delivery (COD)*. Usually the shipper collects the payment and a handling fee. An even more stringent term of sale is *cash in advance*. This is used when the seller does not want to take any risk, including the risk of having to pay for shipping if payment cannot be made at the time of delivery. *Cash terms* usually refers to payment due within a week to 10 days. This allows for mail and a short processing time.

The most common credit terms are net 30 or net 60 days. These are sometimes referred to as *standard terms*. *Discount terms* combine standard and cash terms. The net payment is due on the standard date, but the buyer may take a specified discount if payment is made in cash terms, usually 10 days.

Some companies use *prox terms*, where payment is due the next month. The seller establishes a cutoff date, say the 20th of the month. Payment for all shipments before that date is due the following month. Any shipments after the 20th will be invoiced the following month, and payment will be due the month after that. Frequently prox terms incorporate a discount for payment in the first 10 days of the month with a due date of the end of the month. Some companies having products with highly seasonal sales patterns, such as garden supplies or holiday decorations, use *seasonal dating*. The seller allows the buyer to defer payment until the normal selling season. If buyers order early, the seller can smooth out production and shipping and can reduce the need to carry inventory. The seller gives the buyer an inducement to carry the inventory rather than waiting and placing a rush order. In some industries the producer sells on *consignment*. The producer retains title to the goods, and the "buyer" is not obligated to make payment until the goods are sold to the final consumer. This arrangement is commonly used by artists who sell their works to art galleries. The seller usually requires the buyer to segregate consigned goods and provide periodic inventory accounting. Care should be taken to avoid the illusion that a sale has occurred before the "buyer" has actually sold the goods.

If the amount of the sale is large and the seller is unfamiliar with the buyer, the seller may require the buyer to get a *letter of credit* from his or her bank before a credit sale will be made. The bank supplying the letter of credit agrees to loan the funds to the buyer, if necessary, to make the payment when due.

Changing Credit Terms.   A major cost element in setting credit terms is the opportunity cost of delayed receipt of funds. Since the opportunity cost is a function of the level of interest rates, it would seem reasonable for sellers to change credit terms as interest rates change. However, changes in credit terms are infrequent. Customer payment practices become ingrained in the payables department. A change in credit terms may go unnoticed, particularly if it is a tightening of terms. Because of the difficulty in changing credit terms, it is particularly important to consider the credit terms carefully when establishing the credit policy.

Acceptable Risk Level.   Specification of the risk level the firm is willing to accept is probably the most critical credit policy element. Credit risk affects cash flows on two dimensions: the timing and the amount of the cash flows. The timing is affected because some customers pay later than the specified terms. The seller incurs greater opportunity costs, and perhaps higher collection costs, than anticipated. The result is a lower profit on the sale than planned. The amount of the inflow is uncertain because some customers will never pay, or at least never pay in full.

Establishing an acceptable credit risk involves a trade-off between lower sales from too strict credit standards and higher collection and bad debt costs from too lax standards. Below we will examine how to analyze the trade-off between the costs and benefits of different credit standards.

Credit Limits.   One way to try to control potential losses is to set a credit limit for each account. A credit limit does not necessarily improve the probability a customer will pay; rather it limits the amount of the bad debt loss if payment does not occur. By setting low credit limits on new accounts a seller can accept customers with a slightly higher credit risk. As experience is gained with the account, the credit limit can be raised if payment experience justifies. If credit limits are to be effective, it is necessary to monitor the accounts closely and require credit approval before additional sales are made to the customer.

Collection Practices.   *Collection practices* are the actions a firm takes to improve the timing or the amount of the cash inflow from the credit sale. Many firms initiate collection practices on the due date or shortly thereafter. Actually, collection practices can start before the due date. A midwestern wholesale florist selling primarily to small retail flower shops has an average collection period of about 25 days. Terms of sale are net 30 days. The credit manager calls each new account (defined as an account sold to for less than 3 months) on about the 15th day to see if there are any problems. He also reminds the retailer when the payment is due. The usual response is a check is received within a week. The retailer knows the wholesaler is watching the account and noticing when the payment arrives. Once a pattern of early or on-time payment is established, the credit manager can concentrate on those who are having difficulty and are paying late. Of course, it helps that the wholesaler is a critical supplier to the small retail florist.

The collection practice policy decision includes determining when late-payment notices should be sent, whether the contact should be by phone, fax, or letter, and what steps to follow if payment is not received. The policy should outline a complete sequence of events from a cordial reminder to turning the account over to an attorney or collection agency for action.

Credit risk and collection practices are interrelated. A firm with very stringent credit standards and low credit limits can have kinder and gentler collection practices. Most low-risk credit customers will pay with very little dunning. Late payments are more likely a simple oversight, or a temporary problem, rather than an indication of unwillingness or inability to pay. On the other hand, a firm accepting high-risk customers has to take quick and firm action to keep bad debts under control.

Analysis of Policy Trade-offs

A credit policy involves trade-offs between alternatives that have different costs, benefits, and degrees of uncertainty. Marketing initiatives usually drive the establishment of or changes in credit policy. Proper financial analysis of the policy alternatives determines the best route for the firm to follow. The financial manager can have a major impact on improving business practices both by serving as an integrating force and by properly analyzing the policy change. The level of sales, profitability of the product, opportunity cost of delayed payment, bad debts, and credit administration costs are factors considered in analyzing credit policy.

Most credit proposals involve a change to a new policy from an existing policy. An incremental analysis of all the costs and benefits provides the most straightforward assessment of the value of the proposed change. If the proposed change results in a net benefit, the change is financially worthwhile. If not, the proposed change should not be made unless some overriding nonfinancial consideration dictates the change. Even in this case, the analysis is beneficial because it provides an estimate of how much the change will cost. This analytical approach is most easily understood through a numerical example.

Incremental Sales. The Green Lumber Company, mentioned at the beginning of this chapter, is considering a change in credit policy. Currently sales are made only on a cash-and-carry basis, which includes accepting bank cards and checks. Seventy-five percent of the sales are to individuals carrying out do-it-yourself home repair projects. The other 25 percent of sales are to contractors. The sales manager has proposed the company offer credit sales to the contractors.

Level of Sales. The sales manager believes the new policy will increase sales. To analyze the impact of the new policy, the manager must estimate the level of sales after the change in policy. The sales manager feels sales will increase from the current level of $24 million per year to $30 million per year. She expects all the increase to come from sales to contractors currently not buying from Green Lumber because they do not want to pay cash. A complete analysis should include all future sales, not just the first year's sales. If we can assume the impact will grow over time, the first year's incremental sales will be the smallest. Examining only one year results in a conservative estimate of the change in sales.

Profitability of Sales. Sales volume in itself is worthless unless the sales are profitable. We want to look at the incremental profits to be achieved on the new sales. The starting point is to deduct the variable costs of generating the new sales. Variable costs include materials, labor processing, handling, selling, shipping, and any other costs directly connected with making the additional sales. Using average costs is inadequate for two reasons. First, average costs will correctly assess the fixed costs at the new level of sales only by chance. It may be necessary to add additional yard or office personnel to handle the higher level of sales. A credit department will have to be created to handle approval, billing, collection, and follow-up on slow payers. Additional materials handling equipment might have to be purchased. Perhaps new storage space will have to be constructed. Second, average costs assume a constant product mix. It is unlikely Green Lumber will maintain the same product mix if it moves from 25 percent contractor sales to 40 percent contractor sales. From Table 12-1 we see that the net incremental operating profit from the new sales is expected to be $1 million.

Here is where the financial manager can perform an integrating function in the policy decision. The sales manager, the purchasing agent, the yard manager, the office manager, and the controller all have to provide information for the analysis. In collecting and analyzing the information, the financial manager is in a position to identify inconsistent planning in different parts of the organization.

Bad Debt Costs. The bad debt costs will be a function of the risk level of the approved credit customers, the credit limit, and the collection practices. The bad debt costs essentially represent product that has been sold for which no collection has occurred. This cost is subtracted from the incremental operating profit. Assume the managers of Green Lumber have estimated the bad debt costs will be 3 percent of sales. The estimate of bad debt costs is $180,000.

The next step in the analysis is to subtract income taxes. At a 34 percent tax rate, tax on the incremental profit will be $279,000. This leaves Green Lumber with additional profits after taxes of $541,000, as shown in Table 12-1. The analysis is not yet complete. Additional investment is required to achieve the level of sales that generates these incremental profits. We need to subtract the opportunity cost on the investment to determine if the proposal really generates any value for the firm.

Table 12-1. Incremental Operating Profit on New Credit Sales

Incremental sales		$6,000,000
Variable costs:		
Material costs	$3,760,000	
Shipping and handling	380,000	
Sales commissions	400,000	
Shrinkage	260,000	
Incremental variable costs		4,800,000
Incremental fixed costs		200,000
Net incremental operating profit		1,000,000
Bad debt costs		180,000
Incremental profit before taxes		820,000
Incremental taxes (34%)		279,000
Incremental value before opportunity costs		541,000
Opportunity cost of incremental investment		124,000
Incremental profit after taxes		$ 417,000

Opportunity Costs of Incremental Investment. The most obvious investment is the commitment of funds to support accounts receivables. Under the proposed credit terms, payment will be due 30 days after the billing date. Billing will occur once a month for all purchases made since the last billing date. Assume the contractors will be good customers and pay 35 days after the billing date. The billing date occurs on average 15 days after a sale is made. Thus, accounts receivable are outstanding for an average of 50 days. If sales are uniform over time (unlikely, but it keeps our example simple), the average accounts receivable will be $6,000,000 × 50/360 = $833,333. However, Green Lumber will not have the full $833,333 invested in these receivables. From Table 12-1 we see incremental costs will be approximately 83.3 percent of the sales. Thus, the sales of $833,333 in accounts receivable include 16.7 percent, or approximately $139,000, in profit. The real out-of-pocket investment in the accounts receivable is only $694,000.

Green Lumber will have to carry a larger inventory to support the higher level of sales. For our purposes suppose the increase in inventory is $256,000. Any additional investment in buildings or equipment should also be considered. For simplicity this is zero in this case.

The total incremental investment is $950,000. The dollar opportunity cost of this investment is found by multiplying the opportunity cost rate times the amount of the investment. The opportunity cost rate should include a premium for the risk of the investment. The financial manager for Green Lumber determines that the appropriate risk-adjusted opportunity cost is 13 percent after taxes. The annual dollar opportunity cost of the incremental investment is approximately $124,000. This is subtracted from the incremental operating profit in Table 12-1. The result is net incremental profits after considering the opportunity cost of $417,000. So far the financial analysis indicates this would be a good decision.

Other Considerations. If all estimates had carefully considered all costs and consequences, the decision is easy. Adopt the suggested credit terms for the contractors. However, some additional questions should be asked. What will happen to the contractor sales that currently are being made on a cash basis? If they will be converted to credit sales, the estimate of the investment in accounts receivable will have to be increased. Credit department costs to handle the additional accounts may be higher than estimated. Will the additional credit sales to contractors be to new contractors that currently are not buying from any other lumber company? Since this is not likely to be true, what will be the reaction from the competition? Will they reduce prices to prevent the loss of sales? If so, the profit on the sales has been overestimated. Will it be necessary for Green Lumber to offer more lenient credit terms than the competition? This may raise the estimate of the amount of the investment in accounts receivable. Bad debts may be higher if longer credit terms provide a customer more opportunities to encounter problems before the payment is made. If the incremental net after-tax profit is still positive after these adjustments, the financial analysis still indicates a go decision on the proposed credit policy.

Let's summarize our approach to analyzing a change in credit policy. First, estimate the incremental sales from the proposed change in credit policy. Second, estimate the incremental costs connected with the change in sales. The difference between these two results is the estimated incremental operating profit. Third, subtract the bad debts connected with the incremental sales. Fourth, determine the taxes on the incremental profit to calculate an incremental profit after taxes. Finally, determine the opportunity cost, adjusted for risk, of the incremental investment. Subtract the opportunity cost to determine if the proposal generates a net benefit after considering opportunity costs. In our example, sales increase due to the change in credit policy. Some proposed policy changes will result in a decrease in sales. The analysis would proceed in the same manner. The primary difference is the costs would have to decrease more than the sales for there to be a positive incremental impact on profits.

Credit Policy Implementation

Once the credit policy is established, it is necessary to determine a set of procedures to implement the policies. The most difficult implementation issues are deciding on acceptable credit applicants, monitoring the accounts, and instituting collection practices. The latter two of these are treated in Chap. 13.

One of the elements of credit policy was establishing an acceptable risk level. This can be expressed either as the probability of an account not paying or as bad debts as a percentage of sales. Implementing the risk standard involves examining each credit applicant to determine which meet the standard and should be granted credit. Those not meeting the standard should be sold to only on a cash basis.

There are two types of potential errors in granting credit. First, the seller can accept a credit customer who pays slowly or does not pay. Second, the seller can reject a potential customer who is actually a good credit risk. Either error will prevent the credit policy from having the desired results.

The Five C's of Credit

One approach to the credit applicant decision is to make a qualitative assessment of whether the applicant meets the risk standard. This is sometimes know as assessing the applicant on the *Five C's of credit:* character, capacity, capital, collateral, and cautions.

Character.   The character of the applicant is essentially the most important element. The seller tries to determine the *willingness* of the applicant
to pay bills when due. Some idea of the applicant's character can be gleaned
from the credit history and credit references. People and organizations are
generally creatures of habit. If they have a habit paying their debts and paying on time, they will likely continue to do so. If they have demonstrated a
pattern of late payments and frequent disputes over the amount owed to
other credit sources, they are likely to do the same with you.

Capacity.   Capacity attempts to assess the *ability* of the applicant to pay
according to the agreed terms. Will the applicant have sufficient cash flow
to pay according to our terms? Financial statements, both historical and
projected, serve as a good source for assessing the capacity of an applicant.

Capital.   Capital assesses the applicant's financial strength or financial
reserve. A well-capitalized firm is not overburdened with debt. A sufficient
amount of equity provides a cushion to withstand losses. It also represents
the amount the owners stand to lose in default.

Collateral.   Collateral represents the assets the creditor can secure to
help reduce losses if the client cannot pay. Most trade credit arrangements
are on open account without any specific assets serving as collateral. The
costs and time to perfect assets serving as collateral make this infeasible for
most credit sales. Collateral is not an issue in most trade credit arrangements. Exceptions occur when the sale is for a large-value, uniquely identifiable asset such as a piece of heavy machinery.

Cautions.   Trends in the economy, the buyer's industry, or the buyer's
position in the industry may have an impact on the ability to pay. Key cautions are economic forces that enhance or degrade the buyer's ability to pay.

Quantitative Analysis

Qualitative analysis may be very effective in choosing the right customers. It
is highly dependent on the judgment of the analyst and is not easily transferred to others in the firm. Quantitative analysis strives to develop a more
objective and consistent approach that is less dependent upon the individual analyst.

Financial Statement Analysis.   If the credit applicant is a large purchaser or potentially exposes the seller to significant risk, the seller may
find it worthwhile to conduct a detailed financial statement analysis. This
includes examining balance sheet and income statements as well as projecting cash flows. Key financial ratios are examined and compared with

industry standards. A detailed coverage of this important topic is beyond the scope of this book. Several books have been written on this subject and should be consulted by the cash manager whose job encompasses this topic.

Credit Scoring. A *credit scoring* system identifies factors related to discriminating between good and bad credit risks. These factors may be items such as the total amount of debt, the income, the number of years on the current job, the number of years at the current address, or home ownership for retail customers. Financial statement ratios, earnings growth, or the ratio of debt to total assets may be used for commercial customers. Values for each of these factors are weighted by multiplying by a weight determined from a computer statistical analysis, called multiple discriminate analysis. The computer model uses historical data on these factors and on the customers' payment records.

The model sets a cutoff score that best separates good and bad credit risks. However, no scoring system can perfectly identify good and bad credit risks, and inevitably some applicants will fall into a gray area between good and bad risks. When this happens, a credit analyst scrutinizes these accounts and makes a judgmental decision whether to grant credit.

A credit scoring system is most useful for sellers with a large number of customers who individually buy in relatively small amounts. Care must be taken to reevaluate the credit scoring system as economic conditions change.

Information Sources for Credit Analysis

Credit analysis, whether by qualitative or quantitative means, requires information about prospective customers. The information is used to make an assessment of the likelihood of collecting and to gauge the cost of handling the account. The more data collected, the better should be the credit decision. Unfortunately, information and analysis are neither instantaneous nor free. Sellers must trade off the benefits of better decisions against the information and analysis costs to achieve those decisions. Generally, the amount of information and the depth of the analysis are directly related to the size of the potential loss from nonpayment.

Past Credit History

The most readily available and reliable credit information is that contained in the credit files of the selling company. This information tells how the customer will pay this particular firm, with due recognition to the relative economic power of buyer and seller. However, this information is only available for current or past credit customers. Many large, multidivisional firms have separate credit operations for different divisions. Although an applicant may represent a new customer to division A, it may be a current credit customer of division B. A common database, or at least a system to make inquiries of other divisions, facilitates use of internal company data.

Credit References

Credit references, such as banks and other suppliers, can provide valuable information about a credit applicant. One problem with the use of references is the applicant has the incentive to provide only those names that will supply positive references. A second problem is these references may not have the same importance to the applicant as the seller; thus the experience may be different. The applicant may treat the bank holding the mortgage on the company building differently from a company selling the applicant office supplies.

Financial Statements

Current and past financial statements can show the applicant's position and any trend in the financial condition. Audited statements are much more useful than unaudited statements because of the consistency of accounting treatment. Substantial administrative time may be required to analyze the statements, although templates for spreadsheet computer applications will ease the burden somewhat.

Credit Reporting Agencies

Credit bureaus and other credit reporting agencies maintain information on an applicant's credit history, including payment history, length of time sold, maximum credit amounts, and any judgments or collection actions. The information is provided for a fee and may require a subscription to the agency reports. Increasingly this information is available in electronic form in a very short time. Some credit agencies have their own rating system which purports to give a relative assessment of creditworthiness.

Industry and Trade Associations

Many industry and trade associations maintain credit files, if not on individual customers, at least on the average for the industry. These can provide valuable benchmarks against which to compare the performance of an individual applicant.

Investment Advisory Services

Investment advisory services of brokerage houses and investment bankers offer another potential source of information for publicly traded firms. These assessments are geared to the investment potential of the firm. Nevertheless, they frequently include information about the liquidity position of the firm.

Published News Reports

Local news media and business publications may provide insights to the creditworthiness of credit applicants. News of a drop in sales, a layoff, or a labor dispute may provide an early warning of future problems. Industry trade journals may provide insights to the financial health of an entire industry.

Summary

Credit policy has both marketing and financial aspects. Credit can increase sales. Credit increases funds requirements and costs. In establishing a credit policy, managers consider whether to handle the credit internally, set the credit terms, determine the acceptable level of risk, and decide the collection practices that will be followed for delinquent customers. The financial manager can perform an integrating function in the analysis of credit policy proposals. The most straightforward decision approach is an analysis of the incremental after-tax profits that result from the change in credit policy. This analysis considers the incremental sales, the profit on those sales, the expected bad debts, and the opportunity cost on the out-of-pocket investment necessary to achieve the new policy. Once the policy is established, managers institute procedures for implementing the policy. The process for deciding whether to grant credit to individual applicants is the most important of the implementation procedures. The best implementation gathers information from internal and external sources and combines quantitative and qualitative factors in the credit decision.

Self-Test

1. United Textiles, Inc. (UTI), manufactures sportswear clothing. The current terms of sale are net 30 days. Sales are $500 million/year, inventory is an average of $100 million, and accounts receivable average $50 million. The marketing manager has proposed seasonal dating terms.

Retailers ordering early in the season (January through March for summer clothing) would not have to pay until the end of April. The sales manager estimates that the change in terms would increase sales 10 percent. Out-of-pocket incremental expenses are estimated to be 60 percent of the selling price. Because customers would order earlier, the sales manager estimates inventory could be reduced by $25 million, but accounts receivable would at least triple. Bad debts are expected to increase from 1 percent of sales to 2 percent of sales. The tax rate for UTI is 34 percent, and the after-tax opportunity cost is 15 percent. Estimate the incremental after-tax profits from the proposed seasonal dating terms and recommend whether seasonal dating should be adopted.

13
Managing Accounts Receivable

Introduction

Green Lumber Company, the example used in Chap. 12, initiated the credit policy proposed by the sales manager. A credit limit was established for each account, and procedures were adopted to ensure no sales were made on credit to a customer who was over the credit limit. Sales increases have been greater than estimated, and profits are good. Neither the sales manager nor the financial manager is happy. The sales manager is receiving complaints from customers who say they are denied credit for additional sales even though they have paid the prior bill and are below their credit limit. The financial manager is complaining because accounts receivable are higher than estimated, which means more funds have to be raised. He is concerned the company is too lenient in granting credit and not aggressive enough in collecting overdue accounts. In this chapter we examine how accounts receivable can be monitored to see if the credit policy is being properly implemented and how they can be managed to effectively achieve the credit policy.

Cash Management–
Accounts Receivable Interface

The first question that may occur to a cash manager is why should I be concerned with these issues? Isn't it the responsibility of the sales and credit people to worry about accounts receivable? The cash manager, or at least the systems established by the cash manager, interfaces with the sales and credit functions. Cash management systems process and channel the information necessary for the credit department to function efficiently. Actions taken by the credit department to collect overdue accounts may affect both the functioning of the collection system and the accuracy of cash flow forecasts.

Cash Collection System

In Chap. 6 we saw that the primary focus of collection system design is to transfer value from customers paying their bills to the selling firm. The cash management collection system is the tail end of the entire accounts receivable collection process of the firm. The cash collection system is also the entry point for payment information from customers. The cash manager's primary focus is on the speed of converting the payment to available funds. That is as it should be. However, the cash collection system also processes the information accompanying the payment. The speed with which the payment is collected and processed and the speed with which the information is transferred to the credit department affect how quickly the accounts receivable can be updated. Delays in any part of the system could be contributing to the situation described for Green Lumber Company in the introduction to this chapter. Customers have paid their bills, but the credit has not yet been recorded on their accounts receivable balance. When the credit personnel evaluate a credit sale, they examine the accounts receivable balance. They have no way of knowing if a payment has not been made by the customer, or if the payment has been received by the company but not yet processed and credited to the proper account. A substantial number of customer complaints about slow processing, later found to be valid, will likely result in relaxing the application of credit limits. This could be a recipe for disaster if customers figure out they can simply complain about the seller's processing and receive credit above their limit. Thus, the cash manager needs to work with the credit people to ensure the cash collection system aids rather than impedes the functioning of the full credit and collections system.

Cash Application

Cash application is the process of recording payment information on the company's books. This should be considered an integral part of the cash collection system. The billing process, the type of customer, the payment form accepted, and the responsibility for collection—whether the collection is done internally or by a third party—all affect the cash application process.

The design of the invoice is the first step in the cash application process. If the invoice contains a machine-readable account code and the amount of the bill, it can be quickly scanned. The only manual input required is the actual amount of the payment.

A scannable return document is very common for consumer payments. There are at least two reasons for this. First, the large number of payments handled dictates minimizing manual processes. Second, consumers generally write a single check for a bill and pay the amount owed, or the minimum payment if they are given that option. Disputes are handled outside of the payment/cash application process. Commercial customer invoices less frequently include scannable return documents. Some businesses will not return the physical billing documents with their payment. Many businesses consolidate multiple invoices into one payment. Determining which invoices are being paid, which are being disputed, and which should receive discounts is often a laborious task, not easily automated.

Payment by check is usually done through the mail, and payment information is usually included in the same envelope. Electronic payments, particularly if one of the limited ACH formats is used, may only have a reference number. Payment information, whether in the form of paper documents or EDI transmissions, may arrive by a separate route and must be reconciled with the record of payment. Again, the cash collection system should be designed to allow capture and transmission of information to the accounts receivable area as quickly and efficiently as possible.

If a bank lockbox is used for collecting payments, the bank can capture the information from the physical documents and electronically transmit the information to the company. Because of the volume of their operations, many banks can process the payment information more quickly and at a lower cost than the companies. The key issue is to ensure the information can go directly to cash application without manual intervention.

Information Format

Payment information transferred to accounts receivable should be in a format that can be directly applied to update individual accounts. If the information is either scanned or keyed in by the company collection center, this should be no problem. Information transmitted from a third party, be it a bank or an EDI VAN, may not be in the form that can be used directly by the accounts receivable system.

Information from a bank lockbox can be in a variety of formats. Some banks have a proprietary format that they have developed for their systems. Lockbox clients receive information in the bank format and worry about converting it to their own internal format. Some large companies have their own proprietary format in which they receive the information. The bank must translate the information into the company's format. Clearly, banks will take this step only for large-volume clients from whom they can recover the cost of translating the data. Many banks use a BAI format. This format was developed early in the days of electronic transmissions by the Bank Administration Institute. Although it has been commonly used by active lockbox banks, it is being replaced. The ANSI X12 standards are gaining as the preferred format for EDI activity (see Chap. 5). One of those standards, ANSI X12 823, is the standard for lockbox information transmission. Companies that can automatically convert from the ANSI X12 transmission to their accounts receivable application can simplify the cash application process. The ability to use the same system, regardless of the bank involved, and to handle automatically the payment information coming either directly from the customer or indirectly from a bank in the same way is a real advantage of being able to receive and convert ANSI X12 data transmissions.

Determining the Appropriate Level of Receivables

In many firms there is concern over the total amount of funds tied up in accounts receivable. The question may be raised, "What is the appropriate level of accounts receivable?" This is the wrong focus. The correct question should be, "Do we have a credit policy that increases the value of the firm, and is it being implemented correctly?" We presented a framework for credit policy analysis in Chap. 12. If this framework is consistently applied and if credit policy is frequently reviewed in the philosophy of continued improvement, the credit policy should be generating value for the company. The appropriate level of accounts receivable will be a result of the policies adopted. The level of accounts receivable is not the issue. Rather the issue is whether the policies that generate the level of receivables are value-enhancing policies. Attempts to reduce accounts receivable are based in changes in the specification or implementation of the credit policies. If the policies generating the current level of receivables generate more value than the policies necessary to reduce the level of receivables, the current policies are appropriate. There should not be undue concern over the level of receivables. If policies to reduce receivables generate greater value, they should be adopted. If not, the current policies should be maintained. The reason to change policies is because the new policies are expected to generate greater value, *not* because they will reduce accounts receivable. The reduction of accounts receivable is simply a side benefit of the new policies.

Monitoring Accounts Receivable

A firm's management may think they have adopted the best set of credit policies (if they didn't, they probably would have adopted a different set of policies to begin with). However, conditions change. As conditions change, it may be desirable to change either the policies or the way the policies are implemented. A policy of constant improvement requires a system to monitor the accounts receivable, on both an individual and a total level, to achieve proper collection practices, and to use the results of the monitoring to improve credit policy decisions. A schematic of this process is presented in Fig. 13-1.

Individual Account Monitoring

An accounts receivable monitoring system must be capable of monitoring the activity in each account. We have already discussed the need for the

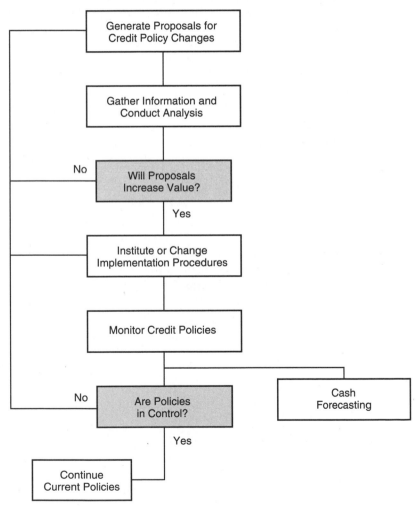

Figure 13-1. A credit policy monitoring and feedback system.

account to be kept up to date for purposes of additional credit orders. Individual accounts are also monitored to determine whether payment is occurring on the agreed terms, when to institute collection practices, and whether the credit limit should be increased.

Aging Schedule.   An aging schedule can be as simple as a listing of the amount owed and the age of the bill for each account. An example of an individual account aging schedule is given in Table 13-1. An aging schedule raises questions that the credit manager can pursue to determine if there is a problem. For example, in Table 13-1 we see that Able Builders is current on most of its outstanding receivables, but has an amount that is at least 60 days past due. The dimensions of the problem and the nature of the action to be taken depend upon the reason the item is past due. Let's look at two different reasons. Suppose Able has been ordering and paying on time each month, with the exception of the $500 item, which was for merchandise that had been damaged in shipment. The action would be to attempt to make an adjustment and settle the damage claim. Now suppose Able had no orders between the order on which $500 was unpaid and the most recent order. The credit manager might be more concerned about the credit quality of Able, might want to push for collection immediately after the due date if the $2000 is not paid, and might want to limit credit sales in the meantime.

Baker Plumbing is an account that demands immediate attention. There is clear pattern of late payment for the last three months. Charlie Construction appears to be a good credit customer, with no outstandings that are not current.

Clearly, the individual account aging schedule could be expanded to include information on the number of orders, the size of each order, the credit limit, and any other information that would give the credit analyst insight into the activity and payment pattern of the customer. The level of detail may be a function of the number of products, the number of divisions, and the amount ordered by the customer. Depending upon credit terms, it may be desirable to break the aging schedule into finer increments than the 30 days we have used in this example.

Table 13-1. Aging Schedule for Individual Accounts

Customer	Total outstanding	Age of accounts receivable (days)			
		Current	31–60	61–90	91–120
Able Builders	$2500	$2000	—	—	$500
Baker Plumbing	$3000	$1500	$1000	$500	—
Charlie Construction	$1200	$1200	—	—	—

Average Collection Time. Another useful measure for monitoring individual accounts is to calculate the average collection time for the account. The collection time is found by tracking each order and determining the number of days between the invoice date and the date available funds are received. The number of days for the collection is multiplied by the dollar amount of the order. This calculation expresses the collection in dollar days, which is comparable to the float calculations that we did in the earlier chapters. The total number of dollar days is divided by the total amount of all the orders. The result is a weighted-average collection time. Examples of this calculation are given in Table 13-2. The use of a weighted average places more importance on large-dollar orders. Customers having an average collection time substantially beyond the credit terms are prospects for early collection action. In addition, by looking at the "Total Days" column it is easy to see if a pattern of later collection is developing.

Monitoring Total Accounts Receivable

It is also important to monitor the total collection time for the entire accounts receivable portfolio. Suppose individual accounts drift from a collection period of 28 days to 35 days. This shift in collection may not be sufficient to trigger collection activity for any one account. However, if all

Table 13-2. Calculating the Average Collection Time

Customer	Order date	Order size	× Total days	= Dollar days
Delta Partners	2/5	$ 4,000	31	124,000
	3/7	$ 5,000	35	175,000
	4/15	$ 2,000	30	60,000
	5/10	$ 3,500	37	129,500
		$14,500		488,500

$$\text{Average collection time} = \frac{488,500 \text{ dollar days}}{\$14,500} = 33.7 \text{ days}$$

Easy Cabinets	1/18	$ 7,000	42	294,000
	2/4	$ 5,500	38	209,000
	2/27	$ 2,000	35	70,000
	3/15	$ 3,500	40	140,000
	4/12	$ 6,000	45	270,000
		$24,000		983,000

$$\text{Average collection time} = \frac{983,000 \text{ dollar days}}{\$24,000} = 41.0 \text{ days}$$

behave in a similar fashion, funds invested in accounts receivable will increase by 25 percent. This large an increase is sufficient to cause funding problems for most companies. Thus, it is necessary to monitor the collection experience from the aggregate portfolio of accounts to identify shifts in payment experience that may require corrective action.

Days Sales Outstanding. A common measure of aggregate payment experience is the days sales outstanding. The DSO is calculated by dividing the total accounts receivable by the average daily sales. An example of a DSO calculation is given in Table 13-3. The DSO for June is calculated by dividing the accounts receivable at the end of June by the average day's credit sales. We have used the average daily sales over the quarter for the calculation. We see the DSO at the end of June is 52.8 days. Rather than try to determine if this particular DSO is acceptable, let's see if there is any shift over time. The DSO at the end of September is only 43.2 days. This reduction of approximately 9 days in the DSO appears to be an improvement in the collection of the accounts receivable.

Unfortunately, there are several problems with the use of DSO. First, the analyst must choose an averaging period for the sales. We have averaged the sales over the quarter for our example. The analyst has to decide what is the correct averaging period. There is no clear-cut answer to this. The

Table 13-3. Calculation of DSO for Total Accounts Receivable

Calculation for the end of June

Ending accounts receivable June 30	$220,000

Month	Credit sales
April	$100,000
May	$125,000
June	$150,000

$$\text{DSO} = \frac{\text{accounts receivable}}{\text{average daily sales}} = \frac{\$220,000}{\$375,000/90 \text{ days}} = 52.8 \text{ days}$$

Calculation for the end of September

Ending accounts receivable September 30	$180,000

Month	Credit sales
July	$150,000
August	$125,000
September	$100,000

$$\text{DSO} = \frac{\text{accounts receivable}}{\text{average daily sales}} = \frac{\$180,000}{\$375,000/90 \text{ days}} = 43.2 \text{ days}$$

reader is encouraged to try different averaging periods, say, 30 days and 60 days, to see the impact of changing the averaging period. Second, the DSO is affected by trends in sales. We will see when we look at the payment-pattern monitoring measure below exactly how changes in sales can affect DSO.

Aging Schedule. A second commonly used measure is the *aging schedule*. To see how an aging schedule is calculated let's look at Table 13-4. This table contains information on the composition of the outstandings in accounts receivable based on the month of the sale. The aging schedule lists the proportion of accounts receivable in each age category. At the end of June approximately 68 percent of the accounts receivable outstanding are current, 23 percent are one month past due, and 9 percent are two months past due. As we did with DSO, let's look for a trend in collection rather than trying to assess whether the absolute is acceptable. In September the current accounts have dropped to 56 percent of the total, the one month past due have increased to 28 percent, and the two months past due have increased to 17 percent. From this it appears the accounts receivable are older in September then they are in June. This would be interpreted as a decline in the average collection experience from June to September.

Table 13-4. Calculation of an Aging Schedule for Total Accounts Receivable

Month	Credit sales	Accounts receivable on June 30
April	$100,000	$ 20,000
May	$125,000	$ 50,000
June	$150,000	$150,000
	Total	$220,000

Aging schedule on June 30	
61–90 days	9.1%
31–60 days	22.7%
Current (0–30 days)	68.2%
	100.0%

Month	Credit sales	Accounts receivable on September 30
July	$150,000	$ 30,000
August	$125,000	$ 50,000
September	$100,000	$100,000
	Total	$180,000

Aging schedule on September 30	
61–90 days	16.7%
31–60 days	27.8%
Current (0–30 days)	55.6%
	100.0%

This is exactly the opposite of the indication from the DSO measure calculated above. What is the true picture? To answer this question, let's look at the payment fractions.

Payment Fractions. The *payment fraction* is the percentage of the sales that are collected at any time after the sale. At the end of June we can calculate the percentage of June's sales that are collected at the end of the month of the sale, the percentage of May's sales that are collected one month after the sale, and the percentage of April's sales that are collected two months after the sale. These values are shown in Table 13-5. At the end of June none of June's sales have been collected. Thus, 0 percent of June's sales are collected. At the end of June there is still $50,000 of May's sales in accounts receivable. The remainder, $75,000, has already been collected. Thus $75,000/$125,000, or 60 percent of May's sales, has been collected. Looking at April's sales and accounts receivable, we see that $20,000 is still outstanding. That means that $80,000, or 80 percent, has been collected.

Again, let's look at the trend in collection experience. The payment fractions at the end of September are as follows. None of September's sales are collected at the end of the month of the sale. From August's sales of $125,000 there is still $50,000 outstanding. Thus, 60 percent has been collected by one month after the sale. Finally, $120,000 of July's sales of $150,000, or 80 percent, has been collected by the second month after the sale.

The pattern of collections is identical for the end of June and for the end of September. In reality there has been no change in the collection experience from June to September. We may not be happy with the collection experience for either time period, but at least we know it has not deteriorated.

Table 13-5. Calculation of Payment Fractions for Total
Accounts Receivable

Month	Credit sales	Accounts receivable on June 30	Percent of sales Uncollected	Collected
April	$100,000	$ 20,000	20%	80%
May	$125,000	$ 50,000	40%	60%
June	$150,000	$150,000	100%	0%

Month	Credit sales	Accounts receivable on September 30	Percent of sales Uncollected	Collected
July	$150,000	$ 30,000	20%	80%
August	$125,000	$ 50,000	40%	60%
September	$100,000	$100,000	100%	0%

Comparison of Monitoring Measures. From the stable payment fractions for both quarters we are sure there has been no change in the payment experience. Why did the DSO and the aging schedule give incorrect and opposite indications about the trend in collections? The simple answer is that both are affected by the trend in sales as well as the collection experience. One problem with the DSO is that the accounts receivable outstanding at a point in time are not generated evenly by the months represented, whereas the calculation of the average sales per day spreads the sales evenly. Typically, the major portion of accounts receivable is from the most recent sales. Thus, for a given total amount of sales, accounts receivable will be higher if sales have been increasing than they will be if sales have been decreasing. In our example we can see accounts receivable are larger at the end of the June quarter than at the end of the September quarter, even though total sales were the same for both quarters. It might appear this problem would be alleviated by choosing a different time period for averaging the sales. It won't be. A different averaging period just introduces a different bias in the results.

The aging schedule can also give misleading results. The problem can be illustrated by making a slight change in the collection pattern and observing what happens to the aging schedule. What would happen if some of September's credit customers paid early and 20 percent of the sales were collected in September? This would clearly be better than the original conditions. But let's see what would happen to the aging schedule. Accounts receivable from September would now be $80,000, and total accounts receivable would be $160,000. Now 80,000/160,000, or 50 percent of the accounts receivable, would be current; 50,000/160,000, or 31.25 percent, would be 31 to 60 days old; and 30,000/160,000, or 18.75 percent, would be 61 to 90 days old. The conclusion would be the collection has deteriorated from the original situation for September. This is the opposite of what actually happened.

Why does the aging schedule give this misleading indication? The problem is the aging schedule relates the accounts receivables from a particular month's sales to the total accounts receivable outstanding at a point in time, not to the sales that generated the receivables.

If sales are constant over time, all three measures—DSO, aging schedule, and payment fractions—will give consistent measures of changes in collection experience. How much do sales have to change for the results from DSO and the aging schedule to be misleading? The only way we can tell is to compare these measures with the payment fractions, which we know are affected only by collection experience, not sales patterns. If we have to compare the DSO or aging schedule with the payment fractions to determine whether the signal is correct, why bother with them in the first place? Just use payment fractions as the measure of changes in collection experience.

It is more accurate and requires no more information than is required for the aging schedule. It just makes the proper comparison: comparing the accounts receivable outstanding with the sales that generated the receivables. Tracking the payment fractions over time allows the financial manager to monitor quickly and accurately any changes in collection experience and respond with appropriate changes in credit policies or procedures.

Accounts Receivable Monitoring and Cash Forecasting

Earlier we discussed the cash manager's role in providing information to the credit manager. The information flow should be both ways. As the accounts receivable monitoring process identifies changes in collection experience, this should be conveyed to the cash manager. The changes in payment patterns are critical to developing an accurate forecast of cash inflows. The quicker the cash manager knows about any changes in payment patterns, the quicker the cash forecast can be updated to reflect the best estimate of future cash inflows. As we saw in Chap. 11, historical patterns are an important source of information for cash forecasts. Payment fractions can do double duty: they provide the best monitoring system for accounts receivable, and they represent a valuable source of cash inflow information.

Collecting Accounts Receivable

Most cash managers have minimal direct involvement in the collection of delinquent accounts. The cash manager should, however, be aware of the practices used because they either interface with or bypass the normal collection system. For example, if a lockbox is used for normal collections but delinquent accounts are handled by personal visits to the customer, procedures must be established to deposit the payment into the company's banking system and to process the deposit information outside of the bank lockbox system.

Collection activities not only affect the current information systems, such as balance reporting, but also affect the cash forecast. The sequence of collection practices followed influences how quickly customers will pay. At the extreme, if an account is turned over to a collection agency, the forecast of the timing and the amount of the payment needs to be changed. It is important that this information is conveyed to the cash manager, particularly when large accounts are involved.

Collection Practices

The goal of collection practices is to make the customer want to pay your bill. It is interesting how astute some companies are in appealing to customers' emotions to make a sale and how unsophisticated they are when trying to induce them to pay the bill. Two factors are important in collecting accounts: motivating the customer to want to pay and applying the right amount of pressure to get them to pay.

An old adage says you can catch more flies with honey than you can with vinegar. This holds for collecting from many customers. Being understanding of the problems of the customer, convincing them paying their bill is mutually beneficial, making them aware you are willing to work with them, and convincing them you should be treated in the same manner they want their customers to treat them are all important steps in improving their desire to pay.

The second step is applying pressure to ensure they don't forget about the bill. Continuous and consistent pressure also convinces the customer you are serious about pursuing the payment and aren't likely to forget about it.

Some companies split their customers into several categories, with different collection practices for each. One such approach might be to categorize customers, before they have become delinquent, into good, fair, and marginal credit risks. Good credit risks would be those customers who are almost always on time and have a long and consistently good credit record, both with you and with other creditors. Delinquency is usually due to a simple oversight or an unusual circumstance. Collection effort should be low key and have a very understanding tone. These customers usually either respond quickly with a payment or attempt to work out a mutually agreeable payment plan.

Fair credit risks might be customers who have a record of occasionally being late with payments, either to you or to other creditors. Here understanding is necessary, but quick and consistent pressure is also necessary. If they must occasionally let a creditor slide, you want that to be some other creditor, not you.

Marginal credit risks might be customers with somewhat more shaky credit histories. They are less likely to respond to courteous reminders. They are used to receiving multiple reminders before they pay. Quick and significant pressure may be required before they will pay.

Systematic Collection Procedures

Regardless of whether credit customers are categorized for different collection approaches or whether all customers are treated alike, it is essential to follow a systematic set of collection procedures. Many companies use a variant of the following sequence of collection efforts.

1. *Sending the initial statement.* The first notification of payment due is the statement or invoice. The amount, due date, and payment location should be clearly stated. Also, the statement should be sent out in a timely manner. If your monthly bill with a statement date of the 5th of the month doesn't arrive until the 20th, the customer may not think your due date of the 30th is to be taken seriously.

2. *Sending an overdue notice.* This should be sent out as quickly as possible after the due date. In Chap. 12 we discussed the importance of quick cash application from the cash collection system to the accounts receivable system to know whether a bill had, in fact, been paid. An overdue notice is not likely to be sent if an on-time payment is still being processed internally. Some companies send out a second statement, duly noted, as a reminder. Others use a separate collection letter. One company sends out a computer-generated letter stating that at the present time no person knows the payment is late. If payment is received within seven days, no person need be contacted. If payment is not received, a person will be notified of the late payment and will be contacting the delinquent customer. Perhaps this is most effective with the good-credit-risk customers mentioned above. Many companies have a sequence of overdue notices, with each successive notice being more harsh and demanding in tone.

3. *Making a telephone call.* The telephone is a very effective collection tool. Many customers who don't respond to a letter do respond to this more personal touch. This also gives the delinquent customer the opportunity to explain any extenuating circumstances.

4. *Converting the open account to a note.* This elevates the priority of the claim, both legally and in the mind of the customer. Frequently an interest payment is attached to the amount owed to compensate for the delayed payment.

5. *Turning the account over to a collection agency.* This step is an admission that it is not likely the company will be able to collect using the normal procedures. The collection agent charges a substantial fee, frequently 50 percent or more of the account. Taking this step should be a recognition that normal relations with the customer are being severed. Sales after this point should be made only on a cash-in-advance or COD basis.

6. *Filing a suit for payment.* This step can be very expensive. It is usually pursued only if all other efforts have failed and the amount of the debt is fairly large. Some companies will occasionally file suit for small amounts as a warning to other potential delinquent accounts.

Adhering to Procedures

Perhaps the most critical factors are to have the procedures carefully spelled out and to have them followed in a systematic manner. This accomplishes several objectives. It lets the customers know you are serious about being paid and have given some thought to what you will do if they don't pay. It sends the message to your own collection department that you are serious about getting what is due to you. And it provides a better base for forecasting cash inflows from collection efforts.

In this section we have briefly covered some of the aspects of collecting from delinquent customers. Since this topic is tangentially related to most cash managers, we have not covered the topic in detail. The cash manager who has responsibility for these efforts is encouraged to consult one of the excellent books written on credit and collections. In addition, many industry associations have a section of their organization devoted to collection efforts and publish sample collection letters and other suggestions for effective collection.

Feedback to Credit Policy

The final step in managing the credit process is to complete the feedback loop shown in Fig. 13-1. If the credit policies and procedures adopted by the firm are not having the desired result, a change in the policies or procedures is in order. The monitoring system determines the efficacy of the policies and procedures. When the monitoring system indicates the results are less than desired, managers have to consider what changes might alter these results. If the policies are not being correctly implemented, then a change in procedures is in order. If the procedures are correctly carrying out the policies, then a change in policy is in order. This is part of the continual improvement process that is a key ingredient in most total quality management programs.

Summary

In this chapter we examined the role of monitoring accounts receivable and collection practices in carrying out an efficient and effective credit policy. The information processed by the cash collection system is the basis for updating accounts receivable. A good collection system design incorporates the needs of the accounts receivable manager. The focus of the credit department should be on the effectiveness of the credit policies in enhancing value, not on the absolute level of receivables. However, it is necessary to monitor accounts receivable to ensure the credit policies are achieving the desired results. Monitoring occurs on both an individual and an aggregate level. We saw that two metrics frequently used for aggregate monitoring—DSO and aging schedule—can give misleading signals about shifts in collections. A better measure is the payment fraction, the fraction of credit sales paid within a given time period. In addition to being a better measure of the trend in credit policy, the payment fraction measure provides the cash manager with information in a form that can be used directly to update the cash forecast.

Self-Test

1. The credit manager for Smart Electronics has gathered the information given below. She wants to determine if there is a trend in the collection experience from credit customers. To determine if there is any trend, calculate the DSO, the aging schedule, and the payment fractions for each month March through August. Use a 90-day period to determine average credit sales for the DSO measure.

Accounts Receivable at End of Month

Month of sale	Sales	March	April	May	June	July	August
January	10,000	1,000					
February	12,000	5,000	1,000				
March	15,000	13,500	6,000	1,500			
April	19,000		17,000	7,500	2,000		
May	23,000			21,000	9,000	2,500	
June	25,000				22,500	10,000	2,500
July	26,000					23,500	10,500
August	26,000						23,500
Total accounts receivable		19,500	24,000	30,000	33,500	36,000	36,500

14
International Issues

Introduction

In an effort to reduce its cost structure, Haley Manufacturing, a medium-sized toolmaker, is planning on purchasing and running a parts manufacturing plant in Ireland. The decision to go to Ireland was prompted in part by the Irish government's commitment to impose no property taxes on the facility for the next 10 years and to absorb the costs of improving the road and utilities into the plant. Purchase of the plant will be completed in 60 days, and Haley must pay the seller in British pounds. When the plant goes into operation, the work force and local suppliers will also be paid in pounds. The cash manager at Haley is wondering how to go about arranging for the purchase payment and then working with the banking system in Ireland to handle ongoing payments.

Today it is not uncommon for even small and medium-sized firms like Haley to expand sales, manufacturing, and supplier relationships into other countries. We live in a global economy, and you will need, more and more, to understand the complexities of cash flow management within and between other countries.

This chapter gives you an overview of some of the major international issues you will face. As it turns out, the tasks of international cash management are basically the same as those we face domestically, but time dimensions may be longer, banking practices and service products somewhat different, and risks potentially greater.

Important International Issues

When you are faced with managing cash flows across international borders or within other countries, a number of new cash management problems arise.

Exchange Rates

The Risk of Fluctuating Rates. When cash flows from one country to another, we may have to exchange one currency for another. We may use dollars, but the seller may require payment in British pounds. Therefore we have to exchange dollars for pounds. If the exchange is to occur some time in the future, we do not know what the future exchange rate will be. Hence, we face a risk called *exchange rate risk*. By the time we make the payment, the rate may have changed and so we end up paying more dollars than we had anticipated. Or the rate could have moved the other way and we end up paying fewer dollars than we expected. Cash managers dealing with international cash flows usually consider exchange rates to be a major risk factor.

The exchange rate between two currencies fluctuates constantly and is determined by market forces of supply and demand for the two currencies and the difference in interest rates between the two countries. As the exchange rate moves, the value received in a transaction fluctuates. Let's take an example. Suppose Haley Manufacturing has signed a contract to purchase the plant in Ireland for 4 million British pounds (£). The current exchange rate is, say, 1.82 U.S. dollars per pound. That means that Haley is expecting to pay £4,000,000 × 1.82 = $7,280,000 for the plant. The closing date on the plant, however, is in 60 days. Today we don't know exactly what the rate will be in 60 days. Suppose the rate has changed to $1.88/£ by the closing date. Since Haley has agreed to pay in pounds, Haley will have to come up with £4,000,000 × 1.88 = $7,520,000 in order to make the exchange to the £4,000,000. Unfortunately, this is $240,000 more than Haley planned to pay for the plant. Of course, the rate could have gone the other way and Haley could have ended up paying less than $7,280,000.

Transactions Costs. The other problem encountered in exchanging currency is the transactions cost incurred when the exchange is made. Any traveler knows that when you exchange U.S. dollars for another currency, the exchange agent often charges a fixed payment and a variable rate as well. The variable rate is included in the spread between the bid and asked prices for the currency. If you want to exchange U.S. dollars for German deutsche marks (DM), the agent will quote one rate. If you want to go the other way and exchange your deutsche marks for dollars, then the agent has another rate.

Suppose you want to exchange $1000 into deutsche marks and the bank's exchange window quotes a bid rate of DM 1.55/$ plus a commission of 4 percent. The "bid" rate means the rate at which the bank will buy dollars. You would receive

$$\$1000 \times DM1.55/\$ \times (1 - 0.04) = DM1488$$

Note that with the transactions cost, this is equivalent to receiving an effective exchange rate of 1.488. Now, suppose you decide to exchange your deutsche marks back into dollars. The same bank quotes an asked rate of DM 1.62/$ plus a 4 percent commission. For your DM1488, you would receive

$$(DM1488/DM1.62/\$) \times (1 - 0.04) = \$881.78$$

You can see why it is not very profitable to exchange money back and forth. The commission and the difference between the bid and ask rates eat up 11.8 percent of our original $1000.

For larger transactions, financial intermediaries like banks generally charge a smaller percentage than the 4 percent we illustrate here. However, 4 percent would not be unusual for consumer or small corporate transactions. In addition, for larger transactions, the bid-ask spread is also much smaller than we have illustrated here. Nevertheless, be aware that the cost of moving money across international borders is usually much higher than the cost of moving money from California to Utah.

Time Delays

Cash flow within other countries and across international borders may involve longer time delays than you experience domestically. Mail from rural Mexico to Mexico City may take ten days. Clearing for a check deposited in a large bank in Jakarta, Indonesia, may require eight days to clear at a distant island bank in the same country. A check drawn on a Japanese bank and deposited in Chicago will be treated as a collection item and take two to four weeks to become available. Wire transfers between Germany and Switzerland may be delayed two days because of "value dating." Letters of credit may take several days or weeks before good funds can be received even after all documents are in order.

On the other hand, time differences could be shorter than they are in the United States. In Canada, for example, all checks are available on the day they are deposited. There is no availability delay with Canada's nationwide clearing system. In Singapore, almost all payments are electronic; few checks are ever written. In Germany, most mail is delivered overnight. So time differences may be worse or they could be better, depending on the country and the technology involved.

Credit Risks

Buying and selling abroad bring new risk dimensions. First of all, credit information about potential customers may be more difficult to obtain. Even if a Japanese firm applying to you for credit sent you its financial statements, you might not be able to read them! Not only would you probably not understand the language, but even if the information were translated into English, the accounting conventions may be different. Furthermore, the credit rating agencies may not have any information on the firm, although more international information is becoming available.

Suppose you did decide to sell to a very creditworthy customer in Yugoslavia. In addition to the credit risks of that particular Yugoslavian firm, you would have to worry about political problems that could potentially affect cash flows from the customer. It is not unknown for governments to completely stop international currency flows during economic or other emergencies.

Enforcing credit terms is also potentially more difficult internationally. It's more expensive to follow up late payments, and if a customer doesn't pay at all, what action would you take? There are few legal remedies to bring against delinquent international customers.

Taxation

International tax agreements between the United States and other countries tend to be complex. This means that if you have operations in other countries, you must have tax accountants in those countries and a well-informed tax accountant in the United States to help you avoid running afoul of tax laws. Cash flows across international borders may trigger tax consequences even if the flows do not relate directly to profits.

High Cost of Moving
Information and Payments

Multiple Parties. International payments are typically more expensive than domestic payments simply because more parties are involved. An international wire, for example, may have to pass through five or six banks before it arrives at the target account. In addition, trade documents like customs clearing forms and bills of lading may have to pass through a chain of parties including customs brokers, the importing country's customs office, the exporting country's customs office, several freight forwarders, and multiple transportation carriers. Each party, of course, adds time delay to the process and charges for its services. You can begin to appreciate why electronic data interchange may be a good idea especially for international transactions.

Value Dating.   To add to the cost of making payments, many non-U.S. banks practice what is called *value dating*. For example, suppose on *Tuesday* you want to wire the equivalent of $100,000 from your bank account in Germany to your bank account in Sweden. The German bank will likely remove the $100,000 from your account on *Monday,* and the Swedish bank will add the $100,000 to your account on *Thursday.* Hence, for two business days, you have $100,000 in neither the German nor the Swedish bank and you lose two days' worth of interest. At 10 percent per annum, that two days' lost interest would cost you

$$\$100,000 \times 0.10 \times 2/365 = \$54.79$$

in addition to any transactions charges the banks would impose. The practice of value dating means that, unlike the case with U.S. banks, the transactions costs for international payments vary with the size of the transaction. In the United States most banks charge a fixed fee for a wire transfer regardless of the size of the transfer.

Value dating is practiced with checks, too. If a check clears your French disbursement account on Friday, the bank may subtract it from your available balance the previous day. In Italy, the check would be posted against your account according to the date the check is first presented to the banking system and not the date the check clears the drawee bank!

Dealing with International Cash Management Problems

Over the years cash managers and service providers like banks have developed approaches for dealing with all the issues defined above.

Foreign Exchange Risk

Measuring the Risk.   How much risk does your company face due to the potential shift in exchange rates? The magnitude of this risk is sometimes quantified in a measure called *foreign exchange exposure,* or simply *exposure.* The two most commonly used measures are transaction and translation exposure.

Transaction Exposure. Transaction exposure relates to how much you owe someone else in a foreign currency compared with how much someone else owes you in that same currency. If you owe a German supplier DM 10,000 and a German customer owes you DM 10,000 at about the same time, then you won't mind if the exchange rate for German marks shifts or not. Any gain you might realize on the inflow side would be exactly offset by a loss on the outflow side of the transaction. But what if you owed DM 20,000 and were owed only DM 5000. Then you would say that you have an exposure of DM 15,000. Fluctuation in the exchange rate could cause you an economic loss only on the DM 15,000 exposure.

Your actual dollar loss would, of course, depend not only on the difference (DM 15,000) but also on the likelihood that the deutsche mark/dollar exchange rate would move unfavorably to your position. Since this is an unknown factor, managers generally speak of exposure only in terms of the difference between receivables and payables in a particular currency.

In addition, transaction exposure is usually stated in dollars so you can sum across all foreign currency exposures. The DM 15,000 exposure could then be stated, at the current exchange rate of DM 1.50/$ as an exposure of $10,000. If all currency exposures were expressed in terms of dollars, you would sum them up and have a picture of how much foreign exchange risk you face in total.

Translation Exposure. This is another form of exposure that your accountant will worry about if you have a foreign subsidiary. Translation exposure refers to the risk that changes in the exchange rate will cause the firm's net worth to drop when the foreign subsidiary (or subsidiaries) is consolidated with the parent company's balance sheet. The magnitude of this exposure depends upon the book value of assets and liabilities to be translated from a foreign currency into dollars:

$$\text{Translation exposure} = \begin{array}{c} \$ \text{ value of} \\ \text{all assets} \\ \text{denominated in} \\ \text{foreign currency } j \end{array} - \begin{array}{c} \$ \text{ value of} \\ \text{all liabilities} \\ \text{denominated in} \\ \text{foreign currency } j \end{array}$$

The net worth of the foreign subsidiary is a residual value and is not translated. Current accounting principles require that all assets and liabilities be translated into U.S. dollars at the exchange rate prevailing at the date of the statement. Gains or losses on translation are posted to translation reserve accounts on the parent's balance sheet.

How Currencies Are Exchanged. We see that Haley Manufacturing has at least a transaction exposure: it owes £4 million in 60 days to purchase the plant and has no offsetting receivable. Before we discuss how Haley Manufacturing can protect itself from this exposure, we need to discuss how one currency is converted into another. The current exchange rate is, say, $1.82/£. Haley hopes the rate doesn't change over the next 60 days. As we saw above, if the rate goes up, Haley would have to pay more in dollars than it anticipated. There are several avenues open to Haley for exchanging dollars to pounds. Each possibility involves differences in timing, risk, and cost.

Option 1: The Spot Market. Haley could wait until the payment is due in 60 days and then convert dollars to pounds. If the exchange rate remains unchanged by then, Haley will pay £4,000,000 × 1.82 = $7,280,000. Haley must accept whatever the rate happens to be at that time since the firm agreed to pay in pounds. Haley could end up paying more than $7,280,000 or less than that.

To use the spot market (the "immediate" market), Haley would contact its bank at least one business day in advance of the payment due date. Most large banks participate directly in the spot foreign currency exchange market. Regional and local banks may also participate through larger correspondent banks. Haley would instruct its bank to buy pounds at the *spot rate*, i.e., at the current exchange rate. In this market, banks exchange drafts denominated in different currencies with each other. There are bid and asked prices quoted by participating banks and other parties. These prices change constantly. Settlement in the New York market is one day for North American currencies and two days for other currencies. Faster settlement is available at higher cost.

Option 2: A Forward Exchange Contract. Haley may not want to run the risk of waiting to find out what the exchange rate is in 60 days. As we saw above, Haley could lose hundreds of thousands of dollars with an unfavorable exchange rate. An alternative to using the spot market is entering into a *forward exchange contract.* Haley could agree to exchange dollars for pounds in 60 days at an exchange rate that is locked in today. Large banks are generally the other party to such a contract. Standard forward exchange contracts are usually available that extend over 1, 2, 3, 6, and 12 months. Some banks will tailor a contract to fit other circumstances. Haley could work out a contract with its bank to convert dollars to £4 million at a rate of, say, 1.85. This means that Haley is guaranteed that in 60 days it can buy the plant for £4,000,000 × 1.85 = $7,400,000—even if the actual exchange rate by that time is above 1.85. Haley's position is *hedged,* meaning that the price is locked in. Of course, with this hedged position, Haley has to spend more than the anticipated $7,280,000, but Haley would consider the extra $120,000 to be insurance against the possibility that the exchange rate in 60 days could have been worse than 1.85. Haley may be willing to trade off uncertainty for a known, hedged position.

Of course, the rate in 60 days might drop to 1.78. If Haley used the spot market instead of a forward exchange contract, the plant would only cost £4,000,000 × 1.78 = $7,120,000—or $280,000 less than it would pay with the contract. Unfortunately for Haley, forward exchange contracts are not options that can be walked away from if a better deal comes up. They must be fulfilled.

In practice, most firms do not hedge 100 percent of their transaction exposure. While hedging reduces potential losses from exchange rate fluctuations, it may be expensive. Many managers think that over the long run the benefits from hedging may not outweigh the costs. Most managers hedge only very large transactions or exposures in very volatile currencies.

Option 3: A Futures Contract.   A forward contract, discussed above, is an agreement between two parties and may be tailored to the common needs of each. A *futures contract,* on the other hand, is a standardized forward contract bought and sold only at certain clearinghouses such as the International Monetary Market (part of the Chicago Mercantile Exchange) and the New York Futures Exchange. A futures contract is not directly between the buyer and the seller but between the buyer or seller and the exchange. Futures contracts are offered only in standard denominations (e.g., in multiples of DM125,000) and mature at fixed dates throughout the year (generally a specified day in March, June, September, and December). Why bother with futures contracts? Because the standardization makes the transaction generally much cheaper than forward contracts. The exchange makes it possible for many parties to become involved in the market without worrying about the creditworthiness of the opposing party to the transaction. All dealings are with the exchange. In addition, it is easy to close out a contract position on short notice.

Futures contracts, however, accomplish the same objective as do forward contracts. They provide a hedge against potential losses due to unstable exchange rates. Because of standard sizes, futures contracts are only useful for relatively large transactions. To learn about how you might participate, contact your investment adviser or banker.

There are other more complex methods of dealing with foreign exchange exposure. Some banks offer "long-date forward contracts" that extend beyond the typical one-year horizon for forward and futures contracts. In some currencies, options are available that let you buy or sell a given amount of a currency at a predetermined rate. Unlike futures and forwards contracts, options allow the holder to decide not to exercise the option if the rate is unfavorable.

International Credit Risks

The additional credit risks imposed by international dealings require the use of credit arrangements that are different from domestic relationships. These arrangements are based on three key principles: (1) the use of a third party to keep goods from being released to the customer until the customer pays or makes satisfactory arrangements to pay for the goods, (2) the transfer of credit risk from the customer to a third party, and (3) where possible, the backing of a government (or better yet, both governments). It is often not possible to have the backing of governments, but this may be possible for some transactions. There are several standard ways to implement the first two principles, and so we will focus on these.

Documentary Collections. Documentary collections implement the first principle. The key to documentary collections is a document called a bill of lading which is issued to the seller by a common carrier (such as a transport company) when goods are accepted for shipment. Title to the goods, represented by the bill of lading, remains under control of the seller or the seller's agent until the seller agrees to release them. As illustrated in Fig.14-1, the seller sends the bill of lading through the banking system to a bank located in the buyer's country. Acting as the seller's agent, the bank releases the bill of lading to the buyer only when authorized to do so by the seller. After the buyer has made satisfactory payment or arrangements to pay, the bank releases the bill of lading which the buyer must present to the shipping company in order to receive the goods.

Letters of Credit. Coupling a letter of credit with documentary collections accomplishes both principles and provides fairly complete protection to the seller. With only documentary collections, there is still the risk that the seller may have to absorb shipping costs if the buyer doesn't pay and

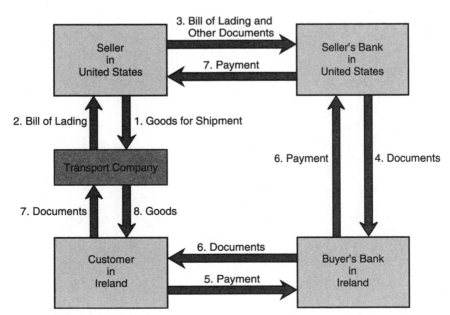

Figure 14-1. Documentary collections. Note that timing of payment depends on agreement with banks.

goods must be sent back. This may represent not only a loss of two-way shipping costs but perhaps spoiled product in addition. To solve this problem, it is possible for the seller to transfer all risk to the banking system by adding in the requirement of a letter of credit. An LC is prepared by the buyer's bank and states that the bank will honor a draft drawn on the buyer's account by the seller if the terms of the LC are honored. Such terms include when payment will be made, which currency is to be used, and which documents are to be presented to the bank. Documents required are usually the bill of lading, insurance documents showing the shipment has been insured against loss, invoice, bill of materials, freight bills, etc. Figure 14-2 outlines the steps followed in an import transaction. When the steps are completed and the documents comply exactly with terms in the LC (be aware that most banks are *very* picky about details here), then the bank stands behind the transaction unconditionally (we call this an *irrevocable LC*). Even if the buyer refuses shipment or doesn't pay for the goods, the seller gets paid and the bank and the buyer have to argue about who absorbs the loss—usually the buyer. The LC may be sent from the buyer's bank to a bank the seller uses in the United States. This second bank might also *confirm* the LC and offer to stand behind it, providing further assurance to the seller. If the seller's bank doesn't choose to confirm the LC, it would only *advise* the seller that an LC had been received.

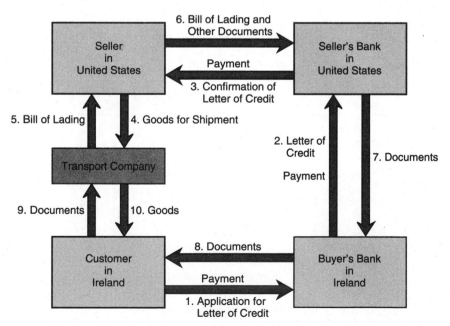

Figure 14-2. Letter of credit transaction. Note that timing of payment depends on letter of credit specifications.

An LC is arranged for in a procedure similar to that of applying for a loan or credit line. The potential buyer has to demonstrate its financial soundness to the bank. Some banks, after initial credit analysis, offer electronic LCs that can be approved very quickly. LCs may be valid for one transaction or could be issued for multiple transactions. The bank may back the buyer for open account purchases up to a specified amount.

International Bank Service Products for Cash Management

A number of service products are available to help cash managers effectively manage international cash flows.

Wire Transfers.   Most banks offer wire transfer services. Smaller banks use larger correspondent banks to assist them. Since there is no Federal Reserve at the international level, settlement must occur through correspondent balances. When Haley Manufacturing sends cash to meet its payroll in Ireland, for example, Haley's domestic bank could send a cable message to a correspondent bank in Ireland. Assuming the two banks have a correspondent relationship with each other, Haley's U.S. bank would debit Haley's account and credit the Irish bank's correspondent account. The Irish bank would then credit Haley's payroll account in Ireland. If Haley's U.S. bank does not have a correspondent relationship with the Irish bank, then the information would have to be routed through a third bank which has a correspondent relationship with both the U.S. bank and the Irish bank. As we discussed in Chap. 4, SWIFT is a bank-operated communications network that connects thousands of banks internationally and facilitates such transfers. In most cases, your local banker will be able to help you make international wire transfers.

Lockbox Systems.   While lockbox collection systems are common in the United States, they are unnecessary within many countries such as Great Britain, Japan, or Germany, where postal systems are highly efficient and there are relatively few banks with national scope. Nevertheless, for checks mailed between countries you may find benefit in using the international lockbox services offered by some branches of U.S. banks. For example, if you have customers in Germany who mail checks to you, you could have these checks intercepted by a lockbox in Frankfurt. The checks would be deposited into an account in Germany and receive fast availability and then be concentrated into your account in the United States within a few days. This is a faster process than waiting for the checks to arrive in the United States and then depositing them as collection items that receive two- to four-week availability.

In countries where the postal system is not so well-developed, some banks offer lockbox or other collection services. In Mexico City, for example, it is common to have a courier physically pick up customer checks and bring them to the bank.

Bank Deposit and Balance Information Services. Compared with domestic banking, it is more difficult to obtain timely deposit and balance information from banks located outside the United States. Nevertheless, a number of banks and third parties do provide limited levels of balance reporting. SWIFT, for example, handles such information. If you do maintain bank accounts in other countries, check with your current bank to see if timely information can be accessed through the bank's communication network.

Bank Deposit Conventions in Other Countries. While U.S. banks are prohibited from paying interest on demand deposits, such restrictions are rare in other countries. Banks, in fact, pay interest on positive balances and then charge interest for negative balances. In many countries, if you overdraw your checking account, the bank automatically covers it with an overdraft loan (up to certain limits, of course). In addition, in many foreign countries, firms have deposit accounts for several different currencies. Only recently were U.S. banks permitted to offer accounts denominated in currencies other than U.S. dollars. The banking systems in various countries differ significantly. Before you set up bank accounts and engage in other bank activities in another country, it would be wise to investigate banking conventions in that country. It is not safe to assume that another country's banking practices resemble those in the United States.

Summary

Even if you are not doing business outside the United States today, if current trends continue, there is a very good chance that before long a significant part of your cash flow will cross international borders. When that day arrives, you will face new and different kinds of risk, unfamiliar banking practices, complex taxation issues, difficult timing differences, increased transaction costs, and more complex information flows.

While cash management tasks are basically the same in the international arena, exchange rates add a new dimension to the cash management problem. Fortunately, financial instruments and procedures have been developed to help reduce this element of risk—at a price. Similarly, for all the added challenges presented by international cash management, strategies and products are available to help cash managers deal with them.

Self-Test

1. Haley Manufacturing will pay £4 million for its plant in 60 days.
    a. If the current exchange rate is $1.80/£ and remains at that level for 60 days, how much will Haley pay for the plant in U.S. dollars?
    b. If the rate falls to $1.75/£ in 60 days and Haley uses the spot market, how much would the firm gain or lose in U.S. dollars (compared with the anticipated price at 1.80)?
    c. If the rate rises to $1.85/£ in 60 days and Haley uses the spot market, how much would the firm gain or lose in U.S. dollars (compared with the anticipated price at 1.80)?
    d. If a forward contract were available today at 1.82, how much would Halcy pay in 60 days in U.S. dollars?
    e. Discuss the pros and cons of hedging using forward contracts.

2. Haley Manufacturing must pay a German supplier DM 100,000 in 30 days. A German customer owes Haley DM 65,000 due in about 30 days. Today's exchange rate is DM 1.50/$.
    a. What is Haley's transaction exposure in deutsche marks? in U.S. dollars?
    b. How much would Haley gain or lose if the exchange rate went to DM 1.55/$?
    c. How much would Haley gain or lose if the exchange rate went to DM 1.45/$?

3. A wire transfer for the equivalent of $250,000 from a bank in France to a German bank involves a total value dating delay of two calendar days. Each bank charges the equivalent of $15. With an opportunity cost of 9 percent, what is the total cost of this transfer?

Solutions to Chapter Self-Test Questions

Chapter 2

1.

	Mon.	Tues.	Wed.	Thurs.	Fri.	Sat.	Sun.
Company Books							
Beginning	$10,000	$16,000	$ 3,000	$ 2,000	$ 2,000	$ 4,000	$ 4,000
+ Deposits	16,000	2,000	6,000	8,000	20,000	—	—
− Withdrawals	−10,000	−15,000	−7,000	−8,000	−18,000	—	—
Ending	$16,000	$ 3,000	$ 2,000	$ 2,000	$ 4,000	$ 4,000	$ 4,000
				Average balance =	$ 5,000		
Bank Ledger							
Beginning	$10,000	$10,000	$26,000	$28,000	$24,000	$17,000	$17,000
+ Deposits	—	16,000	2,000	6,000	8,000	—	—
− Withdrawals	—	—	—	−10,000	−15,000	—	—
Ending	$10,000	$26,000	$28,000	$24,000	$17,000	$17,000	$17,000
				Average balance =	$19,857		
Book Available							
Beginning	$10,000	$10,000	$10,000	$18,000	$17,000	$ 6,000	$ 6,000
+ Deposits	—	—	8,000	9,000	4,000	—	—
− Withdrawals	—	—	—	−10,000	−15,000	—	—
Ending	$10,000	$10,000	$18,000	$17,000	$ 6,000	$ 6,000	$ 6,000
				Average balance =	$10,429		

Explanation: The one-day delay in the deposit means Monday's receipts at the company receive ledger balance credit on Tuesday. With the availability delay, one-half of Tuesday's deposit is credited on Wednesday, the other half on Thursday. From Wednesday's deposit of $2000, $1000 is credited to the available balance Thursday and the other $1000 on Friday. Thus, Wednesday's available balance credit is $8000. Thursday's is $8000 + $1000 = $9000.

Bank float is the difference between the average ledger balance and the average available balance, or $9428.

Deposit float is most easily identified by examining the deposits in isolation of the other activities and comparing book and available activities.

	Mon.	Tues.	Wed.	Thurs.	Fri.	Sat.	Sun.
Book deposit	16,000	2,000	6,000	8,000	20,000	—	—
Book sum	16,000	18,000	24,000	32,000	52,000	52,000	52,000
Avail. deposit	—	—	8,000	9,000	4,000	—	—
Avail. sum	0	0	8,000	17,000	21,000	21,000	21,000
Difference	16,000	18,000	16,000	15,000	31,000	31,000	31,000
			Average = $22,571				

Disbursement float is calculated the same way.

	Mon.	Tues.	Wed.	Thurs.	Fri.	Sat.	Sun.
Book withdrawal	10,000	15,000	7,000	8,000	18,000	—	—
Book sum	10,000	25,000	32,000	40,000	58,000	58,000	58,000
Avail. withdrawal	—	—	—	10,000	15,000	—	—
Avail. sum	0	0	0	10,000	25,000	25,000	25,000
Difference	10,000	25,000	32,000	30,000	33,000	33,000	33,000
			Average = 28,000				

We can see that net float = disbursement float − deposit float = 28,000 − 22,571 = \$5429 is also equal to the difference between the average available balance, \$10,429, and the average book balance, \$5000, or \$5429.

2. Net float = available balance − book balance: \$55,000 = \$20,000 − book balance; book balance = −\$35,000. He would carry an excess \$55,000. This is worth \$55,000 × (0.09/360) = \$13.75/day, or \$412.50/month, or \$4950/year.

3. Kores needs earnings credits of \$500. Assuming a 10 percent reserve requirement, we have (avail. balance) (1-0.10) (0.06/10) = 500, or available balance = \$111,111. With a bank float of \$10,000 the ledger balance would be \$121,111.

Chapter 3

1. *a.* Available on Monday.
   b. Available on Tuesday (assuming it was counted before 4 p.m. Tuesday).
   c. Available Tuesday, made the deadline.
   d. Available Wednesday, missed the deadline
   e. Available Monday, missed the one-day deadline, and so it has two business days' availability.

f. Available Tuesday.

g. Available Monday, missed the two-day deadline, and so it has three-day availability.

2. Acme saves three days, two internal and one available. For an average of $3 million/month, the average daily cash flow is $100,000. For each day's activity the opportunity cost is ($100,000) (0.1/360) = $27.78/day, or $10,000/year. The cost is ($200) (12) = $2400. The net benefit is $7600/year.

Chapter 4

1. *a.* Checks: Security is good; each check is small, so default risk is small on any one account; transactions costs are low.

b. ACH: Low cost, can initiate payment in advance with a delayed value date.

c. Check: Easiest to include a statement of invoices being paid and discounts taken. (Could be ACH if both using ANSI X12 format.)

d. ACH direct deposit: Lowest cost, best security.

e. Wire: Size of payment, timing, security.

f. ACH: Cost, security.

g. ACH debit: Low cost; certain payment; fixed amount should not present acceptance problem.

h. ACH or wire: ACH lowest cost when you know amount in advance. Tradition may dictate wire.

2. Payment	Transaction cost	Opportunity cost	Total cost
Check	$ 0.25	(3) ($20,000) (0.1/360) = $16.67	$16.92
ACH	0.10	(1) ($20,000) (0.1/300) = $ 5.55	$ 5.65
Wire	$35.00	0	$35.00

3. ACH cost: (2) ($60,000) (0.07/360) + $1.50 = 23.33 + 1.50 = $24.83

Wire cost   0 + $11.50   = $11.50

The wire is the cheapest.

Chapter 5

1. The benefit is $3 \times \$1,200,000 \times 0.1/360 = \$1000$/day, or $360,000/year.

2. The inventory would be reduced by 1/12, or $4,166,667. This reduces financing and holding costs by $(0.1 + 0.15) \times \$4,166,667 = \$1,041,667$.

3. The CCD format only accommodates limited payment information. Complex corporate-to-corporate payments involve multiple invoices, adjustments, and discounts which exceed the information capabilities of

the CCD format. One alternative is the CTP format. Advantages: A large number of addenda can be included. Disadvantages: The fixed-field nature of the format limits its automated application, few banks are capable of processing this format, and it is decreasing in acceptability. A second alternative is the CTX format. Advantages: A large number of addenda can be included, it uses the ANSI X12 format with variable-record-length fields which is more easily automated, and it is gaining in acceptance. Disadvantages: Few banks are capable of processing this format at the present time. A third alternative is to use an ACH debit after you receive an ANSI X12 820 from your customer authorizing the debit either through direct communication or through a VAN. Advantages: The debit uses the CCD format which most banks can process, and you have advance notice of the amount and timing of the payment. Disadvantages: Many companies are concerned about letting others debit their accounts electronically.

Chapter 6

1. Funds are delayed for an average of six days: four days in the mail and two days in internal processing. The average float is $20,000 \times 6$ days delay = $120,000. At an opportunity cost of 12 percent the daily cost of the float is $120,000 \times 0.12/360 = $40. For a 30-day month this cost is $1200.

2. Float savings would be approximately one day on average. Average daily receipts are $500 \times 3000/30 = $50,000 (ignoring the difference between calendar and business days for simplicity). The value of the float savings from the lockbox for a month would be $50,000 per day $\times$ 1 day's savings $\times$ (0.12/360) $\times$ 30 days per month = $500. Currently Alpha spends $800 per month on employee costs and $3000 \times $0.08 = $240 on check deposit charges, for a total of $1040. With the lockbox the charges will be $200 plus $3000 \times $0.30 = $900, or a total of $1100. The total savings from using the lockbox would be the sum of the float savings, $500, and the extra operating cost of $60, or $440 per month. Additional factors to consider include the administrative time involved with resolving problems with the bank lockbox operation, differences in accuracy between company and bank procedures, the effect of the day's delay in receiving the return documents, and the amount of time it will take for the information on the deposit to be received.

Chapter 7

1. The effective annual interest from paying on day 45 instead of day 15 is $(300/14,700) \times 365/(45 - 15) \times 100\% = 24.83$ percent. He should pay on day 15 and take the discount. If Barelli borrows $14,700 from the

bank for 30 days, he will owe the bank $14,700 + ($14,700 × 0.15 × 30/365) = $14,700 + $181.23 = $14,881.23. He saves $118.77 by borrowing from the bank to pay on day 15 and take the discount. Both calculations indicate it is better to pay on day 15 with the discount rather than pay on day 45 and pay the net price.

If Barelli can delay payment until day 60, the effective rate of missing the discount is 16.55 percent. Using the dollar-cost calculation, the payment to the bank on day 60 is $14,700 + $271.85 = $14,971.85. Both calculations indicate a slight advantage to paying on day 15 and taking the discount. If Barelli is nearing the credit limit from the bank, it may be better to pay the slightly higher cost of missing the discount to obtain the extended financing from the supplier. However, he should question whether his assumption that there would be no cost to supplier relations is valid.

2. There are two components to the cost savings: float savings and opportunity cost savings on the reduced balances. Monthly float savings will be $5,000,000 × 1 day × 0.12/360 = $1667. Opportunity cost savings on the reduced balances will be $40,000 × 0.12 × 30/360 = $400. Total savings are $2067 versus a cost of $1500, for a net savings of $567. The largest portion of these savings is from float savings. If suppliers shift collection to a different collection site after the switch in disbursement banks, some of these savings will not be realized.

Chapter 8

1. The price would be $500,000 × (1 − 0.0525 × 91/360) = $493,364.58. If held to maturity, the holding-period yield would be ($500,000 − $493,364,58)/$493,364.58 × 100 percent = 1.34 percent. The annualized yield would be 1.34 percent × 365/91 = 5.37 percent.

2. The selling price would be $500,000 × (1 − 0.051 × 31/360) = $497,804.17. The holding-period yield would be ($497,804.17 − $493,364.58)/$493,364.58 = 0.90 percent. The annualized yield would be 0.90 percent × 365/60 = 5.47 percent.

3. The cash flow at maturity would be the principal plus 90 days interest at 5.75 percent, or $500,000 (1 + 0.0575 × 90/360) = $507,187.50. The selling price will be the discounted value 30 days before maturity, or $507,187.5/(1 + 0.056 × 30/360) = $504,831.62. The holding-period yield will be $504,831.62 − $500,000)/$500,000 × 100% = 0.97 percent. The annualized yield will be 0.97 percent × 365/60 = 5.90 percent.

Chapter 9

1. Monthly compounding for the first month pays interest at a rate of 0.09/12 = 0.0075; at the end of month 1, Mr. Wilson owes $100,750. The

compounding occurs by borrowing the $750 in the second month to "pay" the interest from the first month. Continuing through the third month, we have

100,000 $(1+0.0075)$ $(1+0.0075)$ $(1+0.00833) = \$102{,}351.50$. If we use daily compounding, each day's interest is registered to the account, and must be borrowed. At the end of month 1 we would have 1.00025, the daily rate, multiplied by itself 30 times, or $(1.00025)^{30}$. Now we would have

$$100{,}000 \ (1.00025)^{30} \ (1.00025)^{30} \ (1.000278)^{30} = 102{,}360.46$$

Daily compounding is more expensive than monthly compounding because more interest is paid than with monthly compounding. The difference in this instance is small.

2. Collateral:

Raw materials	(0.5) ($200,000)	$100,000
Work in process	(0.05) (100,000)	5,000
Finished goods	(0.70) (100,000)	70,000
Accounts receivable	(0.8) (470,000)	$376,000
	Total	$551,000

3. *a.* Crafton has to provide $15,000 as a compensating balance. It either has to liquidate securities earning 12 percent or borrow the money from the bank at a cost of 12 percent. This would be $1800 for the year.

Month	Loan amount	Unused line	Interest
Jan.	0	300,000	0
Feb.	0	300,000	0
Mar.	50,000	250,000	500
Apr.	70,000	230,000	700
May	70,000	230,000	700
June	100,000	200,000	1,000
July	150,000	150,000	1,500
Aug.	150,000	150,000	1,500
Sept.	250,000	50,000	2,500
Oct.	250,000	50,000	2,500
Nov.	150,000	150,000	1,500
Dec.	50,000	250,000	500
	Average $107,500	Average $192,500	Total $12,900

Total commitment fee = $481.25. (*Note:* The $481.25 could be obtained by multiplying the average unused line by ½ percent or multiplying the unused line for each month by 0.02083 percent and adding up the monthly payments.) The effective interest rate is ($1800 + 12,900 + 481.25)/$107,500 = 14.12 percent.

 b. If there is no compensating balance and no commitment fee, Crafton is charged only for the actual use of the line. The effective rate would be the stated rate of 14 percent. (We encourage you to calculate the monthly interest payments, find the total payments, and calculate the effective rate to verify it is 14 percent.) It would be better for Crafton to accept this credit line since it has a lower effective annual rate.

1. *a.* Effective rate: $\dfrac{2}{98} \times \dfrac{365}{20} \times 100\% = 37.24\%$; take discount.

 b. Effective rate: $\dfrac{1}{99} \times \dfrac{365}{20} \times 100\% + 18.43\%$; take discount.

 c. Effective rate: $\dfrac{0.5}{99.5} \times \dfrac{365}{20} \times 100\% + 9.17\%$; pay on day 30.

 d. Effective rate: $\dfrac{2}{98} \times \dfrac{365}{50} \times 100\% = 14.90\%$; take discount.

2. Discount lost is 2 percent of $2 million, or $40,000. The firm's gain is the interest it could earn for 20 days on $1,960,000 (the amount net of the discount) at 12 percent. This will generate interest of $13,067 (using a 360-day year). Thus, the firm has a net loss of $26,933.

3. *a.* Factor fee $0.015 \times \$1,000,000 \times 12$ months = $180,000. If funds are advanced, the average funds advanced are $2 million (two months' sales), at a cost of $240,000. Total charges are $420,000 for an average advance of $2 million, or 21 percent.

 b. Cost of doing its own financing and its own credit department: $100,000 costs plus 11 percent of $2,000,000 = $220,000, or a total of $320,000. Cost of factor is $420,000. Thus, don't go with the factor.

Chapter 11

1. *a.* Projected Income Statement

	First estimate	Revision*	Comments
Sales	1650	1650	
Cost of Goods Sold	1100	1100	Same % of sales
Gross Margin	550	550	
General Administrative			
Expense	370	370	Given
Interest Expense	20†	16‡	See below
Depreciation	60	60	Given
Pretax Profit	100	104	
Taxes (40%)	40	42	Given rate
Net Income	60	62	

 *After adjusting interest from loan below.

 †10% of 200 outstanding at beginning of year.

 ‡10% of average beginning and ending first estimate loan.

b. Projected Balance Sheet

	First estimate	Revision	Comments
Cash	70	70	Given
Accounts Receivable	183	183	40 days of sales
Inventory	220	220	Same % of sales
Net Fixed Assets	<u>455</u>	<u>455</u>	Old + new – depreciation
Total	928	928	
Accounts Payable	107	107	35 days of cost of goods sold
Short-Term Bank Loan	111	109	Plug figure
Paid-in Capital	370	370	Old + 50
Retained Earnings	340	342	Old + net income
Total	928	928	

c. Approximately $109,000 loan needed.

d. Based on the projection after revision for loan and interest amount.

Net income after tax	62
+ Depreciation	+60
+ Decrease in Accounts Receivable	+67
− Increase in Inventory	−20
− Fixed asset purchase	−40
− Decrease in Accounts Payable	−43
+ Increase in Capital	+50
+ Increase in Cash	<u>−45</u>
Net decrease in loan	91

e. Reduction in assets would free up cash; perhaps reduce cash or inventory. She also could increase borrowing to obtain funds. If extra cash is available, it could be put in marketable securities.

2. *a.* Projected Income Statements

	Jan.	Feb.	Mar.	Apr.	May	June
Sales	50.0	80.0	120.0	125.0	130.0	200.0
Cost of Goods Sold	33.3	53.3	80.0	83.3	86.7	133.3
Gross Margin	16.7	26.7	40.0	41.7	43.3	66.7
General Administrative Expenses	30.8	30.8	30.8	30.8	30.8	30.8
Interest Expense*	1.7	0.8	1.4	2.4	2.5	2.6
Depreciation	5.0	5.0	5.0	5.0	5.0	5.0
Pretax Profit	−20.8	−9.9	2.8	3.5	5.0	28.3
Taxes	−8.3	−4.0	1.1	1.4	2.0	11.3
Net Income after Tax	−12.5	−5.9	1.7	2.1	3.0	17.0

	July	Aug.	Sept.	Oct.	Nov.	Dec.
Sales	220.0	220.0	200.0	130.0	95.0	80.0
Cost of Goods Sold	146.7	146.7	133.3	86.7	63.3	53.3
Gross Margin	73.3	73.3	66.7	43.3	31.7	26.7
General Administrative Expenses	30.8	30.8	30.8	30.8	30.8	30.8
Interest Expense*	4.5	4.5	4.4	3.7	2.0	1.0
Depreciation	5.0	5.0	5.0	5.0	5.0	5.0
Pretax Profit	33.0	33.0	26.5	3.8	−6.1	−10.1
Taxes	13.2	13.2	10.6	1.5	−2.4	−4.0
Net Income after Tax	19.8	19.8	15.9	2.3	−3.7	−6.1

b. Projected Balance Sheets

	Jan.	Feb.	Mar.	Apr.	May	June
Cash	50.0	50.0	50.0	50.0	50.0	70.0
Accounts Receivable†	74.0	96.7	146.7	165.0	171.7	243.3
Inventory	125.0	200.0	300.0	312.5	325.0	500.0
Net Fixed Assets	470.0	465.0	460.0	455.0	450.0	485.0
Total	719.0	811.7	956.7	982.5	996.7	298.3
Accounts Payable‡	41.3	58.9	88.9	96.7	100.6	147.8
Short-Term Loan	90.1	171.2	284.5	300.5	307.7	545.2
Paid-in Capital	320.0	320.0	320.0	320.0	320.0	320.0
Retained Earnings	267.5	261.6	263.3	265.4	268.4	285.3
Total	719.0	811.7	956.7	982.5	996.7	1298.3

	July	Aug.	Sept.	Oct.	Nov.	Dec.
Cash	70.0	70.0	70.0	70.0	70.0	70.0
Accounts Receivable†	286.7	293.3	273.3	196.7	138.3	111.7
Inventory	550.0	550.0	500.0	325.0	237.5	200.0
Net Fixed Assets	480.0	475.0	470.0	465.0	460.0	455.0
Total	1386.7	1388.3	1313.3	1056.7	905.8	836.7
Accounts Payable‡	168.9	171.1	157.8	108.9	77.8	63.9
Short-Term Loan	542.6	522.3	444.7	234.6	118.6	69.3
Paid-in Capital	370.0	370.0	370.0	370.0	370.0	370.0
Retained Earnings	305.1	325.0	340.9	343.2	339.5	333.4
Total	1386.7	1388.3	1313.3	1056.7	905.8	836.7

*Assume interest is ½ of 10% of last month's loan.

†Assume December sales from last year are 90% of this year's projection, or 72.

‡Assume cost of goods sold for last December was two-thirds of sales.

c. The peak bank loan needed is $545,200 in June. This is substantially above the $109,000 estimated in Prob. 1. The amount is larger because Problem 1 only looked at end-of-year values. The peak needs are seasonal, in the middle of the year. The cash inflows are positive during the latter half of the year, allowing the company to pay off part of the bank loan.

3. *a.* Computation of percentages collected:

Total of 3 invoices	1605					
Days after invoice	21	22	23	24	25	26
Amount collected	32	74	93	146	105	239
Percentage of invoices	2.0%	4.6%	5.8%	9.1%	6.5%	14.9%
Days after invoice	27	28	29	30	31	
Amount collected	348	429	62	55	22	
Percentage of invoices	21.7%	26.7%	3.9%	3.4%	1.4%	

b. Forecast of collections:

Date	1	2	3	4	5	8	9	10	11	12
Day of week	Mon.	Tues.	Wed.	Thurs.	Fri.	Mon.	Tues.	Wed.	Thurs.	Fri.
From Oct. 4		8.5	19.6	24.6	38.7	27.8	63.3	92.1	113.6	16.4
From Oct. 11							13.8	32.0	40.2	63.0
From Oct. 18										
Total		8.5	19.6	24.6	38.7	27.8	77.1	124.1	153.8	79.5

Date	15	16	17	18	19	22	23	24	25	26
Day of week	Mon.	Tues.	Wed.	Thurs.	Fri.	Mon.	Tues.	Wed.	Thurs.	Fri.
From Oct. 4	14.6	5.8								
From Oct. 11	45.3	103.2	150.3	185.2	26.8	23.7	9.5			
From Oct. 18		9.7	22.5	28.2	44.3	31.9	72.5	105.6	130.2	18.8
Total	59.9	118.7	172.7	213.5	71.1	55.6	82.0	105.6	130.2	18.8

Date	29	30
Day of week	Mon.	Tues.
From Oct. 4		
From Oct. 11		
From Oct. 18	16.7	6.7
Total	16.7	6.7

Chapter 12

1. An analysis of incremental after-tax profits would proceed as follows: (*Note:* All estimates are in thousands.)

Incremental sales: $0.10 \times \$500$ million =	$50,000	
Out-of-pocket costs: $0.6 \times \$50$ million =	30,000	
Incremental operating profit =		20,000
Bad debts: Current: $0.01 \times \$500$ million	5,000	
New: $0.02 \times \$550$ million	11,000	
Change:		6,000
Incremental taxable profits:		14,000

Incremental after-tax profits:		9,240	
Change in investment:			
Inventory:	−25,000		
Accounts receivable:			
Current: $ 50 million			
New: $150 million			
Change: $100 million			
Out-of-pocket investment:			
0.6 × $100 million	60,000		
Net investment:	35,000		
Opportunity cost: 0.15 × 35,000		5,250	
Net after-tax incremental profit:			$3,990

On the basis of this analysis, the proposed seasonal dating should be accepted. The after-tax incremental profits are more than sufficient to cover the opportunity cost of the additional investment.

Chapter 13

1.

	Mar.	Apr.	May	June	July	Aug.
DSO	47.4	47.0	47.4	45.0	43.8	42.7

It appears the collection experience is improving.

Aging schedule

61–90	5.1%	4.2%	5.0%	6.0%	6.9%	6.8%
31–60	25.6%	25.0%	25.0%	26.9%	27.8%	28.8%
0–30	69.2%	70.8%	70.0%	67.2%	65.3%	64.4%

It appears that collections have gotten worse since April.

Payment amount from month	Mar.	Apr.	May	June	July	Aug.
Jan. 10		—	1.0			
Feb. 12		—	4.0	1.0		
Mar. 15	1.5	7.5	4.5	1.5		
Apr. 19		2.0	9.5	5.5	2.0	
May 23			2.0	12.0	6.5	2.5
June 25				2.5	12.5	7.5
July 26					2.5	13.0
Aug. 26						2.5
Percent of sales	Mar.	Apr.	May	June	July	Aug.
Jan.		—	10%			
Feb.		—	33%	8%		

Payment amount from month	Mar.	Apr.	May	June	July	Aug.
Mar.	10%	50%	30%	10%		
Apr.		11%	50%	29%	10%	
May			9%	52%	28%	11%
June				10%	50%	30%
July					10%	50%
Aug.						10%

Some variability, but no basic change.

Chapter 14

1. *a.* £4,000,000 × $1.80/£ = $7,200,000
   b. New price = £4,000,000 × $1.75/£ = $7,000,000; Haley would lose $200,000.
   c. New price = £4,000,000 × $1.85/£ = $7,400,000; Haley would gain $200,000.
   d. It would pay £4,000,000 × $1.82/£ = $7,280,000.
   e. Pro: A company would lock in the dollar amount in the future. This avoids uncertainty. Con: It would give up the possibility of gain. It would also pay transactions costs.

2. *a.* Transaction exposure is the net of the two amounts: DM 35,000, or = DM 35,000/DM 1.5/$ = $23,333
   b. New value = DM 35,000/DM 1.55/$ = $22,581, or it would gain (since it is paying) $752.
   c. New value = DM 35,000/DM 1.45/$ = $24,138, or it would lose $805.

3. Value dating loss = $250,000 × 09/360 × 2 days = $125, plus additional fee of $15 each; total = $155.

Glossary

810: An ANSI X12 standard format for an invoice.

820: An ANSI X12 standard format for a payment order/remittance advice.

823: An ANSI X12 standard format for lockbox remittance information.

850: An ANSI X12 standard format for a purchase order.

Actual Availability: The granting of availability to checks based on the bank's actual processing delays. If a check is given one-day availability but it actually takes two days to clear, the bank adjusts the firm's availability balance to reflect the delay.

American National Standards Institute Accredited Standards Committee X12 (ANSI ASC X12): Often just called ANSI X12 or X12. A committee that defines format standards for EDI messages.

Anticipation: A practice used in cash concentration. Refers to the initiation of a transfer at a concentration bank before cash becomes available at the deposit bank.

Asset-Based Loan: A commercial loan for which the value of the asset is the primary security for the lender.

Automated Clearing House (ACH): A computer network that processes electronic debits and credits for member financial institutions. Also refers to a specific transfer of cash value using the ACH. A public ACH is operated primarily by the Federal Reserve system and administered by the National Automated Clearing House Association, which is, in turn, owned by member financial institutions.

Automated DTC: A centrally initiated depository transfer check.

Available Balance: The monetary amount in an account; it represents the amount on which credits can be earned or the amount that can be withdrawn.

Availability Schedule: A table arranged by transit routing number showing when checks of a specified transit routing number must pass through the deposit bank's sorting station in order to be considered an available deposit in a specified number of business days.

Backup Line: A credit line used to support a commercial paper issue.

Balance Averaging: Compensating a bank by providing account balances that move above the required balance and below it but, on average, equal the required compensating balance over a specified period.

Banker's Acceptance: A draft drawn upon a buyer by a seller for future payment. The bank, usually backed by a letter of credit, accepts the draft as its obligation. Accepted drafts are sold at a discount in the money markets.

Bearer Instruments: Securities or payment devices in which the value is conveyed to the holder of the instrument. They are negotiable without any endorsement.

Bill of Lading: A document issued to a shipper by a carrier evidencing the receipt of goods for transport. It describes the freight, the terms of the transportation contract, and the identity of the consignor, and it specifies the party to receive the goods. It serves as the receipt for the goods, the contract for their transport, and documentary evidence of title to the goods.

Captive Finance Company: A wholly owned subsidiary that may provide financing for inventory and accounts receivable for the parent firm, distributors, dealers, and/or customers. It may also provide financing to other entities not connected with the parent. The subsidiary raises funds by selling commercial paper, borrowing from banks, and/or selling stocks and bonds.

Cash Concentration: The task of moving cash from banks of initial deposit to one or more centralized cash pools.

Cash Concentration and Disbursement (CCD): An ACH payment message consisting of 94 characters. Used primarily in cash concentration and corporate-to-corporate payments.

CCD plus Addenda (CCD+): An ACH payment format that uses the basic CCD message format for payment information and adds a second 94-character addenda record to record remittance information for the receiver. Used primarily by the U.S. government's Vendor Express program.

Certificate of Deposit: An interest-bearing deposit held in a bank for a specified period of time.

Check: An order or draft upon a financial institution drawn on a deposit of funds for payment on demand of a certain sum of money to a certain person named therein or to that person's order.

Check Clearing: The process of physically moving a check from the point of deposit to the drawee bank account. In the process, appropriate accounts are debited and credited so that value moves between financial institutions and/or between accounts.

Check Presentment: Physical delivery of a check to a drawee institution or other institution in the delivery chain to the drawee bank.

Clean-up Period: A specified period during the time a credit line is in force when the borrower must pay down the credit line to zero.

Clearinghouse: A physical location at which checks or other payments are transferred between banks. Value transfer is also arranged through either the Federal Reserve or correspondent balances.

Clearing House Interbank Payment System (CHIPS): An electronic payment system involving major New York City banks and their correspondents. Transfers during the day are netted out at the end of the day. Settlement is through the New York Fed or through correspondent accounts.

Clearinghouse Item: A check or other draft deposited in one bank and cleared through a local clearinghouse.

Collection Float: The time lag between the date that a buyer's check is mailed (or payment otherwise initiated) and the date that availability is granted in the seller's deposit bank.

Commercial Bank: A financial institution that takes commercial deposits and makes commercial loans.

Commercial Finance Company: A corporation that makes business loans in usually more risky situations than would be typical for commercial banks. Often these loans are tied to assets like inventory or accounts payable.

Commercial Paper: An unsecured promissory note issued by a corporation for a short-term loan.

Commitment Fee: A fee paid to a lender in compensation for a credit line or credit agreement. Usually based on a percentage of the credit line itself or on a percentage of the amount not used.

Company Book Balance: The accounting record on a company's books of the amount of money in the cash account.

Compensating Balance: Demand deposits used to compensate a bank for its services, either tangible services or credit arrangements. The average compensating balance is usually computed by taking the average ledger balance and subtracting bank float and reserve requirements.

Competitive Equality in Banking Act (1987): A federal act that creates "bridge banks" to absorb troubled banks and recapitalizes the troubled FSLIC.

Confirmed Letter of Credit: A letter of credit backed by two banks in two different countries. It works this way: a letter of credit is issued by a foreign bank and a bank in the beneficiary's country is used to *confirm* the letter of credit. The confirming bank as well as the initiating bank stands behind the letter of credit.

Controlled Disbursement: A bank service where the bank receives only an early morning presentment of checks from the Federal Reserve and notifies the treasurer by late morning of all checks that will be paid out of the account during that day.

Correspondent Balances: Demand deposits that banks keep with each other for purposes of clearing payments and compensating for services.

Correspondent Bank: A bank with which another bank has a business relationship. Usually the banks have correspondent balances with each other and are able to provide check clearing and other services through the use of these balances.

Credit Agreement: A credit line formalized by a legally binding document.

Credit Card: A plastic card that authorizes the assignee to make credit purchases. The credit card voucher created is sold without recourse by the merchant to its bank where it is then processed back to the credit card–issuing bank. The purchaser makes payment according to terms specified by the issuing bank.

Credit Line: A more or less formal agreement by a lender to provide up to a specified loan amount to a borrower provided certain conditions are met and compensation paid. The borrower may borrow up to the stated amount, pay the loan down, and borrow up to the stated amount again any number of times during the time the credit line is in force.

Credit Union: A not-for-profit, member-owned financial institution that takes member deposits and makes loans to individual members.

Corporate Trade Exchange (CTX): An ACH format similar to the CTP (see below), but the addenda records contain data that enable the receiver to form a standardized ANSI X12 820 remittance advice.

Corporate Trade Payments (CTP): An ACH format used for making corporate payments. The basic 94-character ACH record may be supplemented with up to 4990 addenda records containing supporting remittance information.

Cutoff Time: Ledger cutoff time refers to the time of day after which a bank considers a ledger deposit to be made the following business day. Availability cutoff time refers to the time after which a check receives an added business day's availability.

Dealer Paper: Commercial paper issued through a dealer such as an investment bank.

Debit Card: A plastic card that allows the assignee to make a purchase against a bank account. The seller discounts the debit card voucher at a bank, which then sends the voucher through to the purchaser's bank. The purchase amount is debited soon after purchase. No credit delays are possible with a debit purchase. Some debit cards are tied into real-time processing systems that debit accounts on a same-day basis.

Demand Deposit: A monetary value held in a bank account subject to immediate withdrawal upon presentment of a check, other draft, wire transfer, or other transfer procedure; a checking account balance.

Deposit Float: The delay in value being added to an account from a receipt of funds.

Depository Transfer Check (DTC): A preprinted check that usually needs no signature and that is valid only for transfer of funds between specified accounts, usually within the same firm. Often used for cash concentration.

Direct Paper: Commercial paper issued by the organization receiving the funds rather than by a dealer.

Direct Send: A procedure for clearing a transit check whereby the deposit bank bypasses the local Federal Reserve clearing system and sends the check directly to the drawee bank, to a correspondent bank near the drawee bank, or in some cases to the Federal Reserve district of the drawee bank. The intention is to receive faster availability than that provided by local Federal Reserve clearing schedules.

Disbursement Float: The time delay between the preparation of a check and the check clearing at a disbursement bank. May also refer to this time delay times the average dollar flow per day.

Discount Loan: A loan that subtracts the interest payment from the amount loaned.

Documentary Collections: A procedure for controlling the release of an international goods shipment to the buyer until the seller makes or arranges payment. The banking system is generally the vehicle for controlling the flow of documents.

Driving Variable: In projecting cash flows, the variable upon which almost all others are based (such as sales).

Electronic Data Interchange (EDI): The electronic movement of business data in a structured format between computer applications.

Electronic Data Interchange for Administration, Commerce, and Transport (EDIFACT): The international EDI standards effort under the auspices of the UN.

Effective Interest Rate: An interest computation that considers all cash outflows, including opportunity cost of compensating balances, and loan proceeds, including only that cash available for the firm to use in its operations.

Electronic Funds Transfer (EFT): The electronic movement of information in a structured format between the computer applications of two financial institutions. The result is a value transfer.

Escheat Laws: State laws that say uncashed checks become the property of the state after a defined time period.

Eurodollar Deposit: A bank account denominated in U.S. dollars but controlled by an individual or corporation outside the United States. Such deposits may be either time deposits or negotiable certificates of deposit. The latter are traded primarily in London.

Excess Balance: A compensating balance at a bank that exceeds that required for fair or required compensation for the bank's services.

Exchange Rate: The rate at which one currency is exchanged for another.

Factoring: Selling accounts receivable to a third party, usually without recourse. The factor, in addition to purchasing receivables, usually performs a credit screening function as well.

Federal Deposit Insurance Corporation (FDIC): An independent federal agency created in 1933 to restore depositor confidence in the banking system by providing insurance for deposits up to a specified limit (currently $100,000 per depositor per financial institution). Also charged with determining which financial institutions are in poor financial condition and liquidating or otherwise disposing of failed institutions.

Federal Reserve Float: The extra monetary value that is created in the money supply when the Federal Reserve grants a depositing bank available credit for a check one or more days before it presents that check to the drawee bank.

Federal Reserve: The government organization created by the Federal Reserve Act of 1913 and empowered to provide liquidity in the financial markets, manage the nation's money supply, foster full employment, and help regulate financial institutions.

Federal Reserve District Bank: One of twelve semiautonomous banks composing the Federal Reserve System. These banks take Federal Reserve deposits, process checks, lend money, and otherwise service member banks and other financial institutions in their district boundaries.

FedWire: A communication system linking Federal Reserve district banks and branches. The most common use is to transfer reserve balances from one bank's reserve account to another bank's reserve account.

Financial EDI (FEDI): The electronic movement of business data in a structured format between a bank's computer application and a firm's computer application.

Financial Statement Lending: Lending to an organization on the strength of its income statement and balance sheet rather than on the basis of collateral.

Float: A delay in transfer of value caused by impediments in the payment system, including mail time, processing time, availability delay, and clearing time. Float can be measured either in days or in dollar days where both the amount of funds being delayed and the length of the delay are included.

Foreign Exchange Exposure: The degree of risk that fluctuating exchange rates will adversely affect the organization.

Forward (Exchange) Contract: An agreement between two parties to exchange a specified quantity of a commodity (e.g., currency) at a specified time at a specified price. Such contracts may be tailored between the two parties. In contrast with an option, a forward contract must be fulfilled.

Fractional Availability: Availability based on using nonwhole days to reflect the average clearing experience of the deposit bank. For example, 1.05-day availability means that 95 percent of the check is given one-day availability while 5 percent is given two-day availability. Adjustments then are not made to reflect actual clearing of a given check.

Functional Acknowledgment: A short message returned to a sender who has just sent an EDI message. The functional acknowledgment tells whether or not the receiver was able to read the message and notes any possible problems. It is the equivalent to certified mail for paper transactions.

Futures Contract: An agreement between a party and an exchange to deliver or receive delivery of a specified quantity of a defined commodity (e.g., currency) at a specified time and specified price. Such contracts are standardized and not subject to individual negotiation with the exchange. In contrast with an option, a futures contract must be fulfilled or closed out.

Generic EDI: EDI formats defined by industry, nationwide, or worldwide standards organizations.

Government Warrant: A draft on a government agency that can be honored after a specified time and/or with accompanying documentation showing performance of specified actions.

Hedge: A financial arrangement that locks in the price of something (often a commodity such as a currency) regardless of what happens to the price over some future time period.

Industry Conventional EDI: Generic EDI formats tailored for use by a specific industry or group of industries.

Ledger Balance: The accounting record on a bank's books of the amount of money in the cash account.

Letter of Credit (LC): A document issued on behalf of a buyer by a bank stating that under specified conditions the bank will honor drafts drawn on the buyer against the letter of credit.

Line of Credit: See *Credit Line*.

Liquid Resources: Sources of funds that are readily available in time to meet obligations.

Liquidity: The liquidity of a firm is the ability of the firm to pay its obligations as they are due. The liquidity of an asset is the ability of an asset to be converted into cash at a minimal loss of principal and at minimal transactions costs.

Lockbox: A check collection service provided to customers by a bank that receives checks from the post office (often via a unique ZIP code), processes the checks, and returns copies of the checks and accompanying information to the customers. A *wholesale lockbox* processes primarily large-dollar checks, while a *retail lockbox* processes primarily small-dollar checks. The latter uses more automated processing and attempts to reduce handling costs.

Lockbox Network: A lockbox service provided by a bank that collects checks in multiple collection sites in states other than the bank's headquarters state. The service is made possible by the bank having multiple lockbox processing sites, multiple mail intercept points, or arrangements with correspondent banks in other states.

Long-Date Forward Contract: A forward contract with a longer than usual maturity date—sometimes as long as 10 years.

Magnetic Ink Character Recognition (MICR): A system of printing numbers on the lower portion of a check or checklike document in magnetically readable characters. Magnetic read heads can capture a check's MICR line quickly and efficiently, thereby reducing manual processing. The MICR line contains the transit routing number, sequence number, account number, and amount.

Mail Intercept: A service provided by some banks in which checks from a specified geographic area are directed to a post office box in that area where they are picked up and sent by courier to the bank's primary check processing facility.

Master Note Agreement: An agreement between a bank's trust department and a borrower that the trust department will buy up to a specified amount of the borrower's short-term notes over some time period. Essentially, privately placed commercial paper.

Maturity Factoring: Factoring with no advance of cash to the firm selling the receivables. The factor performs primarily a credit screening function and not a financing function.

MICR: See *Magnetic Ink Character Recognition.*

Money Center Bank: A large bank that serves a nationwide client base.

Money Market: A market consisting of institutions that trade short-term securities. It is a telephone market, centered in major cities, but active throughout the world.

Money-Market Deposit Account (MMDA): A time deposit account that receives interest but can also permit a limited number of withdrawals per month via check. Permitted for corporations as well as consumers. Created by the Garn–St. Germain Act of 1982.

Money Order: A check in an amount paid for in advance by the payor to a third party of high creditworthiness. The check is drawn against the third party's account and sent to the payee.

Negotiable Certificate of Deposit: A bank time deposit that can be transferred to another party. Negotiable CDs are issued by large banks and traded in the money market. They usually pay interest at maturity.

Negotiable Order of Withdrawal (NOW): A draft that functions exactly like a check but is written against a time deposit instead of a demand deposit. Banking regulations permitted NOW accounts at some thrift institutions in the late 1970s in the northeast. The Depository Institution Deregulation and Monetary Control Act of 1980 permitted all depository institutions to offer NOW accounts, but only for consumers, nonprofit organizations, and partnerships.

Net Float: Disbursement float minus deposit float. If measured as the average dollars of float over a time period, it is also the difference between the company book balance and the bank available balance.

On-Us Item: A check or other payment that is deposited in a bank and drawn on an account in that bank.

Option: A financial instrument that gives the holder the option of buying (call option) or selling (put option) an asset at a specified price by a specified time. The option does not have to be exercised.

Originating Financial Institution (OFI): The depository institution that originates an ACH transaction and sends it to an ACH.

Overdraft: The attempt to withdraw more funds than are in an account.

Overdraft Banking: A banking practice common in some European countries by which negative available balances are charged interest and positive available balances are paid interest.

Payable through Draft (PTD): A checklike draft drawn on a payee rather than the payee's bank account. The payee has 24 hours to deny the draft or it will be paid by the bank from the payee's account.

Payee: The party receiving payment from a payor.

Payment Float: The time delay between the receipt of an invoice and the check clearing against a disbursement account.

Payor: The party making payment to a payee.

Preauthorized Check (PAC): A check prepared by the payee (rather than the payor) and drawn against the payor's account with the payor's permission.

Preauthorized Debit (PAD): An ACH debit transfer initiated by the payee and drawn against the payor's account with the payor's permission.

Primary Liquidity: Cash that will be in the available balance when a payment is due.

Prime Rate: A reference borrowing rate set by a bank, upon which other borrowing rates are based. Although each bank could, in theory, have a different prime rate, competitive pressures force most banks to change their prime rates simultaneously.

Proprietary EDI: EDI formats defined by one major organization for use by only its trading partners.

Public Warehouse: A facility used in secured lending where inventory serves as collateral for a loan. The warehouse stores inventory and issues a warehouse receipt to a lender. Items cannot be removed from the warehouse until the lender is satisfied that the borrower has repaid or made arrangements to repay the loan.

Receiving Financial Institution (RFI): The financial institution that receives an ACH transaction from the ACH.

Regional Check Processing Center (RCPC): Any one of the 11 Federal Reserve facilities that engage exclusively in check processing and offer no other Fed branch or district office services. Sometimes RCPC also refers to any of the Fed's check processing facilities at the 12 district banks or 25 branches.

Remote Disbursement: Disbursing funds from an account at a bank that is geographically remote to the payees with the primary intent of increasing disbursement float.

Reserve Balances: Monetary value held by a bank in a Federal Reserve account. Currently the Fed requires banks to hold 10 percent of demand deposits and does not pay interest on the balances.

Return Item: A debit instrument like a check or ACH debit that is returned to the original deposit bank because of nonsufficient funds, closed account, nonexistent account, or other condition encountered when the payment was presented at the drawee bank.

Reverse Repurchase Agreement: An agreement whereby an investor sells a security to a third party and agrees to repurchase it in the future with interest.

Revolving Credit Line (or Agreement): A credit line (or credit agreement) that extends over a time period of more than one year.

Savings and Loan (S&L): A financial institution whose primary purpose is to lend money to home buyers. May be owned by depositors or shareholders. Recent changes have permitted S&Ls to engage in wide-ranging loan activities outside residential mortgage lending.

Secondary Liquidity: Funds invested in marketable securities or an unused credit line that can be quickly accessed to provide cash for payment.

Secured Loan: A loan backed by legal documents identifying assets that become the property of the lender in the event the loan cannot be repaid.

Settlement Date: For ACH transactions, the day the payor's account is debited and the payee's account is credited.

Sight Draft: An instrument payable on presentment.

Society for Worldwide Interbank Financial Telecommunications (SWIFT): A communication system owned by member banks and used for transmission of information such as payment instructions, bank information, and security transactions.

Spot Market: The market in which commodities, including currencies, are sold for cash for immediate (or one- or two-day delay) delivery and payment.

Spreadsheet or Spreadsheet Program: A software program (like Lotus 1-2-3 or Excel) that permits the user to easily enter and manipulate large quantities of numbers in a two-dimensional array. Series of numbers can be generated and mathematical functions performed on the numbers with a minimum of effort. An important application of spreadsheets is the generation of pro forma financial statements.

Statewide Branching: A regulation in many states that permits a commercial bank to branch throughout the state.

Stretching: Paying an invoice after the stated terms.

Term Loan: A single payout loan (usually) that is repaid over multiple years often in annual or semiannual installments. Often such loans are backed by collateral such as capital equipment.

Time Deposit (TD): A monetary value held in a bank account for a minimum number of days defined by law and or by bank policy. Examples are savings deposits and certificates of deposit.

Time Draft: An instrument that contains a specified or determinable date for payment.

Trading Partners: Suppliers and customers that are involved in an ongoing relationship and view that relationship as mutually beneficial, rather than as adversarial where one gains at the loss of the other.

Transaction Balance: An amount kept in a demand deposit to support the depositor's transaction activity.

Transaction Exposure: The risk that known, future business transactions in foreign currencies will cause economic loss to the firm. Measured in part by the difference between accounts payable in a foreign currency and accounts receivable in that same currency.

Transit Item: A check or other draft that is deposited in one bank but must be sent to another bank for clearing.

Transit Routing Number: An eight-digit number that identifies the bank on which a payment is drawn. The first two digits indicate the Federal

Reserve district, the second two indicate the branch or other clearing route within that district, and the last four specify the specific bank within that district. A ninth digit is often added as a check digit.

Translation Exposure: The risk that restating a foreign subsidiary's balance sheet and income statement in another currency (e.g., U.S. dollars) will result in a drop in net worth.

Translation Software: Computer programs that enable the user to send and receive standardized EDI messages.

Transportation Data Coordinating Committee (TDCC): A voluntary group consisting of representatives from rail, trucking, ocean, and air carriers that developed the first intercompany EDI standards in the early 1970s. The organization is now known as the Electronic Data Interchange Association, or EDIA.

TXP: An ACH format specific for making ACH tax payments.

Uniform Commercial Code (UCC): A model code adopted and adapted on a state-by-state basis that defines commercial business relationships and transactions.

UCC 4A: Article 4A of the UCC specifies the responsibilities of banks and their customers in relation to electronic credit transactions such as wires and ACH credits.

Unit Banking: A regulation in some states that, in its strictest form, limits a commercial bank to one physical location with no branches.

Value-Added Network (VAN): A wide-area computer network offered by a third party that enables two parties with different computer systems, different technical communications protocols, and different time availabilities to easily communicate through an electronic mailbox.

Value Date: The date, usually in the future, on which a previously initiated transaction settles.

Value Dating: A procedure used in some foreign banks by which a cash transfer (such as a wire) is initiated on one day but may result in a debit to the sender's account *before* the initiation date ("back value") and a credit to the receiver's account *after* the initiation date ("forward value").

Zero Balance Account (ZBA): A system of accounts where all balances are held in the main account and transfers are automatically made to subsidiary accounts at the end of the day for all checks that have been presented against the account.

Index

About the Authors

WILLIAM L. SARTORIS and NED C. HILL are both Certified Cash Managers who have conducted numerous executive education seminars for banks and other organizations. They are coauthors of *Essentials in Cash Management,* the study guide for the National Corporate Cash Management Association exam, and *Short-Term Financial Management.* William L. Sartoris is a professor of finance at Indiana University. Ned C. Hill is a professor of business administration at Brigham Young University in Utah.

Final Examination

The McGraw-Hill 36-Hour Cash Management Course

Name _____

Address _____

City _____ State ____ Zip ____

Below is the 100-question final examination which tests your knowledge of the information presented in *The McGraw-Hill 36-Hour Cash Management Course*. The rules for taking this exam are:

1. The textbook may be used to prepare the answers for this exam. Greater satisfaction will be obtained by taking and passing the exam without the use of the textbook.

2. Answer each of the test questions directly on the test sheets by circling the letter that corresponds to the correct answer.

3. Each correct answer is worth one point. A passing grade of 70 entitles you to receive a Certificate of Achievement, suitable for framing, attesting to your proven knowledge.

4. Fill out your name and address in the spaces provided and send your completed exam to:

Certification Examiner c/o A. Ruiz
36-Hour Cash Management Course
Professional & Reference Division
McGraw-Hill Book Company
11 West 19 Street
New York, NY 10011

1. Money serves all of the following functions except:
   a. a medium of exchange
   b. a measure of value
   c. a store of value
   d. none of these

2. Cash flow differs from accounting income only because depreciation is a noncash expense recognized by accountants.
   a. true
   b. false

3. The importance of cash management is a direct function of interest rates. Cash management is only a significant issue when the interest rates are high.
   a. true
   b. false

4. When dealing with internal cash flows, the cash manager:
   a. can ignore opportunity costs because the firm has already received value for the funds
   b. does not have to deal with outside parties
   c. is concerned with the impact on liquidity
   d. none of these

5. The available balance is increased when:
   a. a check is received
   b. a deposit is made at the bank
   c. value is transferred into the account
   d. a check is presented for payment

6. The average company book balance for January is $100,000. The average bank ledger balance is $250,000, and the average bank available balance is $190,000. The amount of bank float is:
   a. $150,000
   b. $60,000
   c. $90,000
   d. none of these

7. What is the net float for the company in Question 6?
   a. $100,000
   b. −$90,000
   c. $90,000
   d. none of these

The following information applies to Questions 8–10. A bank availability schedule indicates a ledger cutoff of 4 p.m. A check with a transit routing number of 0703-xxxx has a cutoff of 10 a.m. for immediate availability. The bank uses fractional availability, and this check has a 95 percent availability. A company deposits a check for $50,000 at 11 a.m. on Tuesday.

8. The increase in the ledger balance will be:
   a. $50,000 on Tuesday
   b. $17,500 on Tuesday, $2500 on Wednesday
   c. $50,000 on Wednesday
   d. none of these

9. The increase in the available balance will be:
   a. $47,500 on Tuesday, $2500 on Wednesday
   b. $50,000 on Wednesday
   c. $47,500 on Wednesday, $2500 on Thursday
   d. none of these

10. If the bank granted whole-day availability instead of fractional availability, the increase in the available balance would be:
    a. $50,000 on Tuesday
    b. $50,000 on Wednesday
    c. only $47,500 on Wednesday
    d. none of these

11. A company ends Friday with an ending ledger balance of $150,000, an ending available balance of $125,000, and $25,000 in one-day availability float. On Monday $40,000 in checks are deposited, with one-half of the checks receiving immediate availability and the other half receiving one-day availability. A total of $30,000 in checks is also presented for payment on Monday. Monday's ending ledger and available balances will be:
    a. $160,000 ledger, $140,000 available
    b. $140,000 ledger, $135,000 available
    c. $185,000 ledger, $115,000 available
    d. none of these

12. A company has an annual (assume a 360-day year) opportunity cost rate of 10%. The company receives a check for $500,000 one time per month. The treasurer can speed up the receipt of this monthly check by five days. What is the annual value of this action?
    a. $50,000
    b. $20,833
    c. $8333
    d. none of these

13. Anderson Company has an average available balance of $250,000 during February. The bank applies a reserve requirement of 10% and grants an earnings credit rate of 5% per annum. The earnings credits generated on the account for February are:

  a. $11,250
  b. $1042
  c. $937
  d. none of these

14. If a firm has excess earnings credits at the end of a quarter, the treasurer has the choice of carrying the credits over to the next quarter or having the bank write out a check in the amount of the excess.
  a. true
  b. false

15. Corporations generally do not earn interest on their checking account balances because:
  a. interest-bearing accounts that corporations can own have too many restrictions
  b. banks are not allowed to pay interest on any transactions accounts
  c. they use the balances to compensate for short-term loans
  d. none of these

16. The Federal Reserve provides all of the following services except:
  a. clearing checks for banks not in the same city
  b. managing the money supply to control interest rates
  c. providing an emergency source of funds for large corporations
  d. none of these

17. Firms using coin and currency for transactions are faced with security problems because:
  a. the value is in the instrument and belongs to the bearer
  b. it is too time-consuming to record all the serial numbers
  c. it is not possible to create an audit trail for coin and currency
  d. none of these

18. A check is an order for the bank to allow the payee to debit your account for the amount written on the check.
  a. true
  b. false

19. Checks may have a delayed availability because:
  a. it takes time for banks to check the signature cards
  b. banks generally delay crediting value to an account until the check has time to be presented for payment at the drawee bank
  c. the use of float is how banks make most of their money
  d. none of these

20. Banks are required to use the Federal Reserve to clear checks drawn on banks in other Federal Reserve districts.
  a. true
  b. false

21. All electronic funds transfers result in immediate transfer of value from the sender to the receiver.
    a. true
    b. false

22. ACH transfers are cheaper than wires because:
    a. the Federal Reserve won't let banks charge full costs for ACH
    b. many banks are not capable of carrying out wire transfers
    c. ACH payments are batch transactions, whereas wires are done one at a time
    d. none of these

23. An ACH transfer costs $1 and has a one-day settlement delay, while a wire costs $10 and has zero delay. A customer of Johnson Supply has agreed to use a wire transfer instead of an ACH if Johnson pays for the incremental cost of the wire. Johnson has an opportunity cost rate of 10% per annum. What is the minimum size payment that Johnson should accept to cover the cost of the wire?
    a. $32,400
    b. $36,000
    c. $10,000
    d. none of these

24. As long as a company maintains tight internal security and follows the security procedures suggested by the bank, the bank retains all liability for errors in wire transfers.
    a. true
    b. false

25. Most international wire transfers:
    a. are same-day transfers, just like domestic wires
    b. transfer value through correspondent balances
    c. are done over CHIPS if SWIFT is too busy
    d. none of these

26. Many companies do not want to use ACH debits for corporate payments because:
    a. they are unsure of the security issues involved
    b. they fear losing control if another party can debit their demand deposit account
    c. ACH credits are significantly cheaper than ACH debits
    d. none of these

27. EDI transactions are superior to paper-based transactions for all of the following reasons except:
    a. EDI transmission costs are cheaper than paper mailing costs
    b. EDI transactions have fewer opportunities for errors

    c. EDI transactions are faster than paper-based transactions
    d. none of these

28. A fax is not usually considered an EDI message because:
    a. it uses the telephone lines for communication
    b. only alphanumeric characters can be sent by fax
    c. it cannot go directly into a computer application
    d. none of these

29. Which of the following services can a VAN perform?
    a. mailboxing, holding the message until it is picked up later
    b. conversion from an old to a new version of communication standards
    c. protocol conversion
    d. all of the above

30. If a firm pays a supplier with an EDI transmission and electronic transfer of funds:
    a. remittance information can be transmitted either with the payment or separately
    b. it must use an ACH debit
    c. wire transfers must be used since it is illegal to use the ACH system to transmit payment information
    d. none of these

31. Compared to ACH credits, which of these is an advantage of using ACH debits for making payments?
    a. Security requirements are less severe than for ACH credits.
    b. The liability for missed payments is shifted to the payee.
    c. The banks charge less for ACH debits.
    d. none of these

32. Nationwide branch banking, such as exists in Canada, eliminates the need for lockboxes.
    a. true
    b. false

The following information applies to Questions 33–35. Evan's Enterprise's current collection system results in the following average delays: mail 4 days, processing 1 day, and availability 2.5 days. The company's bank has proposed the company use a lockbox to collect its receipts. The lockbox would have a 3-day mail time and a 1.5-day availability delay. There would be no processing delay. The company receives an average of 500 checks per month, with an average size of $2000 each. Evan's has an opportunity cost rate of 12% per annum. The bank will charge a processing fee of $0.25 per item plus a $250 per month maintenance fee. The company currently pays

$0.07 per check deposited. (For simplicity assume a 30-day month and a 360-day year.)

33. The annual dollar benefit from float savings by using the lockbox will be:
    a. $360,000
    b. $1000
    c. $12,000
    d. none of these

34. The additional cost (or cost savings) from using the lockbox will be:
    a. $340
    b. $125
    c. $375
    d. none of these

35. Joseph's has the same characteristics as Evan's except it receives 5000 in checks per month of an average size of $200 each. Since the average check size is smaller, Joseph's will have smaller float savings from going to a lockbox.
    a. true
    b. false

36. Float savings are generally more important than operating costs for wholesale lockboxes, whereas the opposite is true for retail lockboxes.
    a. true
    b. false

37. The payment form accepted (currency, checks, credit cards, etc.) is a marketing decision, and the cash manager should not be involved.
    a. true
    b. false

38. An over-the-counter collection system generally has more banks than a mailed payment collection system because:
    a. regulations limit the geographic area in which banks can branch
    b. for security reasons cash managers want to use a bank close to the field office
    c. checks will have better availability if deposited in local banks
    d. all of these

39. The sole objective of a good collection system is to get the funds in the deposit bank as fast as possible.
    a. true
    b. false

40. Friday deposits are more important than other deposits during the week because:

a. Friday's ending balance is also the ending balance for Saturday and Sunday
b. most theft of funds occurs over the weekend
c. banks do most of their coin counting over the weekend
d. none of these

41. The credit manager should be consulted when designing a cash collection system because:
    a. credit policy decisions are usually made at a high level in the firm
    b. credit managers usually know more about time value of money than do cash managers
    c. cash managers process the information that credit managers need to update accounts receivable
    d. none of these

42. Firms concentrate funds for all of the following reasons except:
    a. to maintain better control of cash
    b. to reduce transactions costs for investing excess cash
    c. to get higher returns by investing in larger quantities
    d. none of these

43. Concentration systems for over-the-counter collections are usually more complex than those for mailed payment collections because:
    a. lockbox banks usually have poorer information systems than local deposit banks
    b. small banks can't wire funds, and so other procedures have to be used
    c. there are usually more deposit banks in an over-the-counter collection system
    d. none of these

44. Electronic payment systems, such as POS, EDI, or ACH, reduce the need for a concentration system because:
    a. geography is not important in an electronic system, and thus fewer collection locations are needed
    b. few deposit banks can initiate ACH payments
    c. most electronic payments are debits, which can't be concentrated
    d. none of these

45. Aaron Associates has $25,000 in a deposit bank. An ACH transfer costs $1, and a wire costs $15. Aaron receives earnings credits at a rate of 4% at the deposit bank but could earn 7.5% if the funds were moved to the concentration bank. What are the net savings (cost) of concentrating the funds by wire instead of ACH? (For simplicity use a 360-day year.)
    a. $2.43
    b. −$14.00
    c. −$11.57
    d. none of these

46. Disbursement systems can be analyzed in the same way as collection systems, except the float is a benefit in disbursement systems, whereas it is a cost in collection systems.
    a. true
    b. false

47. A carpet store receives terms of 5% 10 days, 4% 30 days, net 31 days on a $20,000 order. The store borrows under a credit line at a rate of 15%. When should it pay the bill?
    a. on day 10
    b. on day 30
    c. on day 31
    d. none of these

48. In Question 47, the effective annual cost of not paying on day 30 and instead paying on day 31 is approximately:
    a. 37%
    b. 48%
    c. 1500%
    d. none of these

49. Controlled disbursing allows the firm:
    a. to determine the amount of presentments against the account early in the day
    b. to have 24 hours to decide whether to authorize payment on a draft
    c. to delay payment because of significantly greater clearing time
    d. none of these

50. The advantage of using a system of zero balance accounts for disbursements is:
    a. the firm can carry lower balances than if separate accounts are used
    b. accounting information is separated by account type
    c. account funding is done automatically at the end of the day
    d. all of these

51. A firm is considered to be liquid if:
    a. it has a current ratio above 2.0 and a quick ratio above 1.0
    b. it has very little work-in-process inventory
    c. it can pay its bills on time
    d. none of these

52. One of the shortcomings of current ratio or quick ratio as a liquidity measure is:
    a. it ignores operating cash flows
    b. it may be calculated from unaudited financial statements
    c. not all marketable securities have a good secondary market
    d. none of these

53. In establishing its short-term investment policy, a firm should have maximization of yield as its highest priority.
    a. true
    b. false

54. A $100,000 T-bill is issued with a 91-day maturity at a quote of 4.50%. The purchase price is:
    a. $955,000
    b. $988,625
    c. $100,000
    d. none of these

55. A T-bill with a face value of $1,000,000 and 30 days remaining to maturity is purchased at a price of $995,250. What is the annualized yield if the security is held to maturity?
    a. 4.77%
    b. 5.73%
    c. 5.81%
    d. none of these

56. A bank CD with a face value of $100,000 was issued with a coupon rate of 6.5% and an initial maturity of 180 days. Currently 60 days remain until maturity, and the CD is quoted at a rate of 6.20%. The total amount of money required to purchase the security is:
    a. $102,194
    b. $102,143
    c. $100,000
    d. none of these

57. A firm has a 40% effective federal tax rate. It can earn a 3.5% return on a municipal security which is exempt from federal taxes. What return would a fully taxable security have to offer to result in the same after-tax return?
    a. 8.75%
    b. 5.83%
    c. 2.1%
    d. none of these

58. Banks charge variable interest rates on many short-term loans because:
    a. that is the only way they can adjust for changing credit risks
    b. they can lower the rate if the company runs into trouble paying the loan
    c. their liabilities have variable rates and they match interest rate risk
    d. none of these

59. A credit line is generally issued:
    a. to cover seasonal or other variable needs for funds
    b. only if the company does not plan to use it

    c. for a term covering two to five years
    d. none of these

60. To keep a credit line available upon demand a bank usually requires:
    a. compensating balances or commitment fees
    b. accounts receivable as collateral
    c. quarterly audited financial statements
    d. none of these

61. A bank makes a loan for $100,000 for three months at a rate of 9% per annum. If the bank compounds monthly, how much interest will be due at the end of the third month?
    a. $2250.00
    b. $2266.92
    c. $9000.00
    d. none of these

The following information applies to Questions 62 and 63. Wilson Company has the funds needs shown below by quarter. The bank requires a commitment fee of ½% per annum of the unused portion of the line. Interest is charged at a rate of 8% per annum. The credit line is for $250,000. (*Note:* Use simple interest; do not compound.)

Quarter	Total funds needed
1	$ 0
2	50,000
3	200,000
4	75,000

62. The effective annualized rate for borrowing under this loan arrangement is:
    a. 8.00%
    b. 8.50%
    c. 9.04%
    d. none of these

63. A second bank offers a credit line with the same conditions except it wants a compensating balance of 5% of the total amount of the line instead of the commitment fee. Wilson has some securities that are generating a 7% return. They could be sold and the funds put into the cash balance. What is the dollar cost of the compensating balance requirement?
    a. $12,500
    b. $591

c. $875
d. none of these

64. Unsecured loans usually carry a lower interest rate than secured loans because banks only make unsecured loans to the most creditworthy customers.
    a. true
    b. false

65. Once you have missed the discount on a payable, you may as well take a long time to pay since you have already incurred all the cost of stretching your accounts payable.
    a. true
    b. false

66. Jackson, Inc., has a lending arrangement that uses accounts receivable and inventory as a borrowing base. It can borrow 80% of the accounts receivable, 50% of raw materials inventory, 10% of work-in-process inventory, and 40% of finished goods inventory. If it has the following level of receivables and inventory, what is the maximum it can borrow?

Accounts Receivable	$150,000
Inventories: Raw Material	$ 25,000
Work in Process	$ 50,000
Finished Goods	$100,000

    a. $325,000
    b. $177,500
    c. $146,250
    d. none of these

67. Which of the following is true about asset-based loans?
    a. The rate tends to be lower than on unsecured loans because of the collateral.
    b. They are only available to large companies with good credit ratings.
    c. They are made on asset value, not on the credit rating of the company.
    d. none of these

68. Maturity factoring is:
    a. used to replace the credit department, not to advance funds
    b. cheaper than a loan with receivables as collateral
    c. only used by firms in financial difficulty
    d. none of these

69. Ashley's is considering using a factor to handle its accounts receivables. It has sales of $12 million per year, with an average collection period of 30 days. It currently has credit department expenses of approximately $200,000 per year. The factor would charge a fee of 1.5% of the amount sold and would advance funds at a rate of 12% per annum. The effective annualized interest cost of using the factor is:
    a. 10.0%
    b. 12.0%
    c. 13.5%
    d. none of these

70. Which of the following statements is true about commercial paper?
    a. It can only be used by large companies.
    b. It is more expensive than bank lending.
    c. It bypasses financial intermediaries.
    d. none of these

71. Commercial paper with a maturity of 30 days, a face value of $100,000, and a dealer spread of 12 basis points is sold at a rate of 5.50%. What proceeds will the issuer realize from the sale of the paper?
    a. $100,000.00
    b. $99,531.67
    c. $99,421.67
    d. none of these

72. Medium-term forecasting is most useful for:
    a. funding disbursement accounts
    b. managing money-market investments
    c. planning credit line usage
    d. none of these

73. Daily cash forecasting allows a treasurer to:
    a. substitute commercial paper for bank borrowing
    b. extend the investment horizon and increase returns
    c. use zero balance accounts for disbursements
    d. none of these

74. Net cash flow needs can be determined by forecasting the income statement, forecasting the balance sheet, and using the short-term financing as a "plug" figure.
    a. true
    b. false

75. A percent-of-sales method is more likely to be an accurate forecast of cash flows in the short term than in the medium term.
    a. true
    b. false

The following data are to be used for Questions 76–78. The Disan Company is trying to forecast its financing needs at the end of the next quarter. December sales were $100,000, and sales are expected to be $100,000 in January, $150,000 in February, and $250,000 in March. Cost of goods sold (consisting only of purchased goods) averages 75% of sales. Operating expenses are constant at $20,000 per month. Depreciation is $5000 per month. There are no plans to purchase any new fixed assets, pay any dividends, or sell any stock during the quarter. The long-term debt consists of a mortgage on the fixed assets. Interest payments at the rate of 12% per annum on the unpaid balance are made quarterly. Taxes are 40% of income before taxes and are paid in the quarter incurred. The current balance sheet is given below. The treasurer feels the company should maintain a cash balance of at least $25,000. The average receivables collection period is 45 days. Inventory, at cost of sales, is carried equal to the current month's sales. To take advantage of discounts, payments for purchases are made in 10 days on average.

Cash	20,000	Accounts Payable	25,000
Accounts Receivable	150,000	Bank Loan	0
Inventory	75,000	Long-Term Debt	300,000
Net Fixed Assets	375,000	Common Stock	150,000
Total	620,000	Retained Earnings	145,000
		Total	620,000

76. The forecasted net income after tax for the quarter is:
    a. $24,600
    b. $41,000
    c. $50,000
    d. none of these

77. The total assets to be financed by the end of the quarter are:
    a. $897,500
    b. $698,500
    c. $661,000
    d. none of these

78. The short-term loan needed at the end of the quarter is:
    a. $215,400
    b. $171,000
    c. $50,000
    d. none of these

79. Which of the following is not true about a scheduling approach to daily cash forecasting?
    a. Data requirements are large even after the system is set up.
    b. It is more useful for numerous relatively small items.

c. It is easier to use for large items such as taxes or leases.

d. none of these

80. Brown Company has identified the following patterns for the checks clearing its biweekly and monthly payroll. Friday the 30th both the biweekly payroll of $150,000 and the monthly payroll of $100,000 will be paid. How much should the treasurer plan to deposit into the payroll disbursement account on Monday?

Business days	Biweekly % cleared	Monthly % cleared
Payday	20%	30%
Plus 1 day	50%	60%
Plus 2 days	10%	5%
Plus 3 days	10%	3%
Plus 4 days	5%	2%
Plus 5 days	5%	—

a. $50,000

b. $75,000

c. $135,000

d. none of these

81. Credit policies are offered to customers as a convenience whether or not there is any anticipated difference in sales with different policies.

a. true

b. false

82. A credit policy change that has an impact on total market demand is more likely to be worthwhile than one that affects only market share, because one affecting total market demand is less likely to be undone by competitors' actions.

a. true

b. false

83. Credit standards should be established to minimize the amount of bad debts.

a. true

b. false

84. Which of the following statements is true about the use of judgmental, qualitative approaches to evaluating credit applicants?

a. A qualitative approach is easier to defend against discrimination complaints.

b. A qualitative approach is easy to pass on to others in the firm.

c. A qualitative approach can more easily incorporate nonquantifiable factors.

d. none of these

85. Which of the following is not a function of credit limits?
    a. to reduce the amount of loss if payment does not occur
    b. to gain experience with a new customer
    c. to force credit personnel to monitor accounts more closely
    d. none of these

86. TKD, Inc., is considering selling to a new class of companies that are not current customers. It is estimated that total sales would be $500,000 per year. Out-of-pocket costs would be 80% of sales. Allocated fixed costs would be an additional 15% of sales. Accounts receivable would average $100,000. There would be no increase in inventory. Bad debts are estimated to be 10% of sales. The tax rate is 40%, and the opportunity cost rate is 15% after taxes. What action should TKD take on the proposal?
    a. Accept it; the net after-tax profit would increase by $18,000 more than needed to cover opportunity costs.
    b. Reject it; the net loss would be $15,600 before considering opportunity costs.
    c. Reject it; a 10% bad debt loss is too large, regardless of the profit changes.
    d. none of these

87. The five C's of credit analysis are an attempt to assess the applicant's ability to repay and willingness to repay, neither of which can be measured directly.
    a. true
    b. false

88. Which of the following is an advantage of receiving bank lockbox information in an ANSI X12 format?
    a. Information from several banks all appear in the same form.
    b. It is the standard format used by most banks.
    c. It is automatically encrypted, and so data are secure.
    d. none of these

89. Firms should monitor individual accounts:
    a. only for their large customers
    b. whenever they exceed the credit limit
    c. to determine when to initiate collection practices
    d. none of these

90. The payment fractions measurement of accounts receivable is a better measure than DSO because:
    a. DSO uses average annual sales
    b. DSO is sensitive to changes in sales as well as changes in payments
    c. the payment fractions are easier to calculate
    d. none of these

91. The receivables payment fraction approach to monitoring accounts receivable is OK theoretically, but most firms just don't have the information necessary for its application.
    a. true
    b. false

92. A firm has credit sales of $100,000 in January. From those sales, accounts receivable are $85,000 at the end of January and $40,000 at the end of February. Total accounts receivable at the end of February are $150,000. The payment fractions for January's sales are:
    a. January 85%, February 27%
    b. January 85%, February 40%
    c. January 15%, February 45%
    d. none of these

93. A firm has credit sales of $200,000 in June, $300,000 in July, and $400,000 in August. At the end of August the total accounts receivable are $450,000. The firm uses a 90-day period to average sales. The DSO for the end of August is:
    a. 35 days
    b. 33.8 days
    c. 45 days
    d. none of these

94. Accounts receivable aging schedules are not a good means of monitoring accounts receivable because:
    a. they usually consist of three or four categories, which are too difficult to understand
    b. the typical breakdown is a month, which is too long a time period for meaningful analysis
    c. most firms do not have the information systems capabilities to report the necessary data to calculate aging schedules
    d. none of these

95. International business presents a number of risks not present in domestic transactions. The most significant for the cash manager is translation risk.
    a. true
    b. false

96. Credit risk is different when a company sells to customers in different countries. Which of the following is a way to deal with international credit risk?
    a. Take out credit insurance.
    b. Use documentary credits.
    c. Denominate all transactions in U.S. dollars.
    d. none of these

97. The exchange rate between dollars and deutsche marks is DM 1.65/$.
    A purchaser of machine tools from Germany has a bill for DM 500,000
    due in 60 days. Assuming no change in the relative value of the dollar
    and the deutsche mark, what is the expected cost to the purchaser in
    dollars?
    a. $303,030
    b. $825,000
    c. $500,000
    d. none of these

98. The treasurer for the company in Question 97 expects the exchange
    rate to be DM 1.55/$ in 60 days. The action she should take is to:
    a. enter a forward contract to convert dollars to deutsche marks at
        DM 1.65/$
    b. enter a forward contract to convert deutsche marks to dollars at
        DM 1.65/$
    c. wait and use the spot market
    d. none of these

99. A local Ford dealer was recently overheard to say, "Since I don't sell
    import cars, I don't need to worry about currency exchange rates." Is
    his statement true or false?
    a. true
    b. false

100. A French bank back-value-dates international transactions. Webster's
    transfers 5 million French francs into sterling. The French bank back-
    value-dates the account by two days. If the opportunity cost is 12%, the
    cost of the transaction in francs (using a 360-day year) is:
    a. 1667
    b. 3288
    c. 3333
    d. none of these